# The Archaeology of Ocmulgee Old Fields

## CLASSICS IN SOUTHEASTERN ARCHAEOLOGY
Stephen Williams, Series Editor

# THE ARCHAEOLOGY OF OCMULGEE OLD FIELDS, MACON, GEORGIA

Carol I. Mason

With a New Foreword by Marvin T. Smith

THE UNIVERSITY OF ALABAMA PRESS
*Tuscaloosa*

Copyright © 2005
The University of Alabama Press
Tuscaloosa, Alabama 35487-0380
All rights reserved
Manufactured in the United States of America

Typeface: Bembo

∞
The paper on which this book is printed meets the minimum requirements of American National Standard for Information Sciences—Permanence of Paper for Printed Library Materials, ANSI Z39.48-1984.

Library of Congress Cataloging-in-Publication Data

Mason, Carol I.
  The archaeology of Ocmulgee Old Fields, Macon, Georgia / Carol I. Mason ; with a new foreword by Marvin T. Smith.
    p. cm. — (Classics in southeastern archaeology)
  Includes bibliographical references and index.
  ISBN 0-8173-1446-6 (alk. paper) — ISBN 0-8173-5167-1 (pbk. : alk. paper)
  1. Indians of North America—Georgia—Ocmulgee National Monument—Antiquities. 2. Creek Indians—Georgia—Ocmulgee National Monument—Antiquities. 3. Excavations (Archaeology)—Georgia—Ocmulgee National Monument. 4. Ocmulgee National Monument (Ga.)—Antiquities. I. Title. II. Series.
  E78.G3M373 2005
  975.8′552—dc22

                                                2004020134

# Contents

List of Plates, Tables, and Figures   vii

Foreword by Marvin T. Smith   ix

Preface   xix

Original 1963 Preface   xxi

Introduction   1

1. The Historical Setting   5

PART I. ARCHAEOLOGICAL EVIDENCE

2. Excavations at Ocmulgee   25

3. The Trading House   31

4. The Lower Creek Town Site   47

5. Artifacts   82

Plates   125

PART II. ARCHAEOLOGICAL AND HISTORICAL IMPLICATIONS

6. Identification of the Creek Town   151

7. The Lower Creeks and Their Neighbors   160

8. The Origins of Lower Creek Ceramics   178

9. Conclusions   194

Appendix I. Catalogue Numbers of Illustrated Artifacts   197

Appendix II. Pottery Types   199

References Cited   203

Index   213

# Plates, Tables, and Figures

PLATES

I. The Trading House    125

II. The Trading House Ditch and Refuse Pits    125

III. Trading House Ditch and Cleared Stockade    126

IV. Burial 1    126

V. Figure 1, Burial 5; Figure 2, Burial 6    127

VI. Profile of Lower Creek Trading Path and Burial 8    128

VII. Burial 10    128

VIII. Burial 51    129

IX. Lock Plates with Mechanisms    129

X. Figure 1, Gun Parts; Figure 2, Gun Parts    130

XI. Figure 1, Gun Parts; Figure 2, Hardware    131

XII. Figure 1, English Ceramics; Figure 2, Spanish Ceramics    132

XIII. Figure 1, Trade Beads; Figure 2, Bells, Buttons, and Buckles    133

XIV. Figure 1, Pipes and Scrapers; Figure 2, Clay Pipes    134

XV. Figure 1, Iron Objects; Figure 2, Axes    135

XVI. Figure 1, Hoes; Figure 2, Knives    136

XVII. Figure 1, Artifacts of Brass and Clay; Figure 2, Miscellaneous Ornaments    137

XVIII. Figure 1, Miscellaneous European Artifacts; Figure 2, Shell Gorget and Beads    138

XIX. *Ocmulgee Fields Incised* Cazuela    139

XX. *Ocmulgee Fields Incised* Cazuela   139

XXI. Figure 1, *Ocmulgee Fields Incised* Cazuela; Figure 2, *Ocmulgee Fields Incised* Cazuela   140

XXII. *Ocmulgee Fields Incised* Jar; Figure 2, Base of Historic Vessel   141

XXIII. *Ocmulgee Fields Incised* Jar   142

XXIV. Figure 1, Plain Historic Vessel; Figure 2, *Ocmulgee Fields Incised* Bowl   143

XXV. *Walnut Roughened* Bowl   144

XXVI. *Walnut Roughened* Bowl   144

XXVII. Historic Vessel of Unknown Type   145

XXVIII. Inverted Bowl from House Site III   145

XXIX. *Ocmulgee Fields Incised* Scrolls   146

XXX. *Ocmulgee Fields Incised* Scrolls   146

XXXI. *Ocmulgee Fields Incised* Linked Lines   147

XXXII. *Ocmulgee Fields Incised* Nested Geometric Figures   147

XXXIII. Figure 1, *Walnut Roughened* Designs; Figure 2, Miscellaneous Designs   148

## TABLES

1. Percentages and Totals of Trade Artifacts   103
2. Cazuela Design Elements   111
3. Sherd Totals   122

## FIGURES

1. Map of Georgia Territory   8
2. Map of Ocmulgee National Monument   28
3. Map of the Middle Plateau   29
4. The Trading House   35
5. Houses I, II, and V   52

# Foreword
*Marvin T. Smith*

When I was asked to write the introduction to Carol Mason's "The Archaeology of Ocmulgee Old Fields, Macon, Georgia," I jumped at the chance. In my opinion, this volume is one of the most outstanding works to come out of the 1960s. In many ways, it was way ahead of contemporary archaeological studies of contact period archaeological sites, and it still provides useful data forty years later. By any measure, it is a classic study.

## THE AUTHOR

Rochelle Marrinan (1999) provides a biographical sketch of Carol Irwin Mason that I have liberally utilized for this brief overview. Carol Mason (then Carol Irwin) began her career as an archaeologist as an undergraduate student at Florida State University. Here she studied under Charles Fairbanks, who was to become her mentor, and Hale G. Smith. She received a National Science Foundation fellowship to attend graduate school at the University of Michigan, where she studied under Fairbanks's teacher, James B. Griffin. Yet Fairbanks would still influence her career. He arranged for Irwin to study the Ocmulgee collections for two summers. The results of that study are presented in this volume, which was originally her doctoral dissertation at Michigan, completed in 1963.

After completing her degree, Carol Mason, now married, worked in the University of Wisconsin system in association with her husband, archaeologist Ronald J. Mason of Lawrence University. She retired from the University of Wisconsin–Fox Valley in 1998 and is currently adjunct professor of anthropology at Lawrence University.

## CREEK OR CONTACT STUDIES IN THE EARLY 1960s

While "The Archaeology of Ocmulgee Old Fields" was not the first treatment of either the historic Creek occupation of Ocmulgee or Creek studies in general, it was easily one of the most exhaustive treatments of a contact period society in the Southeast at the time it was written. Unfortunately, with few exceptions, this statement is still true today.

Arthur Kelly had already written articles on the Macon Trading Post (Kelly 1938, 1939; Kelly and Friedlander 1939), but these descriptions provided little analytical detail of the discoveries. Pottery type descriptions for historic Creek wares were provided by Jennings and Fairbanks (1939, 1940) based on excavations at Ocmulgee. With limited changes, these types are still in use today. Charles Fairbanks (1952, 1956a) further described the Ocmulgee Fields period, with trait lists and ceramic counts and general descriptions.

Further afield, Willey and Sears (1952) published an article on the Lower Creek town of Kasihta on the Chattahoochee River. They briefly described the European trade goods and provided sherd counts. To the west in Alabama, DeJarnette and Hansen (1960) reported results of excavations at the Childersburg site, the location of the eighteenth-century Upper Creek town of Coosa. They provided descriptions of features, burials, European trade goods, and Upper Creek ceramics and made a few comparisons with the Ocmulgee collections. Caldwell (1948) briefly described the site of Palachicolas Town on the lower Savannah River, a Historic Creek site contemporary with the Macon Plateau site. During the 1920s and 1930s, members of the Alabama Anthropological Society had been "researching" Creek sites in the Montgomery, Alabama, area and publishing some of their finds in their journal, *Arrowpoints*. In essence, these reports constitute most of the accumulated knowledge of historic Creek archaeology at the time Mason undertook her study.

Mason's work significantly advanced Creek archaeology in particular and the archaeology of European-Indian contact studies in general. She was writing in an era when there was little interest in studying the effects of European contact on Native Americans. Although, as Mason notes, some progress had been made in New York and Florida, intensive studies of the contact period in the interior Southeast were relatively new (see Williams 1962, Webb 1962 for examples). Mason saw the Contact Period as an exciting time of "special interest." She combined excellent historical research with archaeological analysis, yielding a historical archaeological synthesis that was groundbreaking for the emerging discipline of historical archaeology. Here I suspect her influence from pioneering historical archaeologists Charles Fairbanks and Hale Smith at Florida State University were overshadowing her later Michigan training.

Her analysis of material culture went far beyond the usual descriptions of the day. For example, her ceramic descriptions went well past classifying sherds into types. She also very carefully described and quantified the various incised motifs—an analysis that would not be duplicated in this region until Hally (1994) looked at motifs of protohistoric Lamar ceramics across Georgia. She further described vessel forms. Comparisons were made with "Creek" ceramics from central and northern Alabama to the west to the Savannah River to the east—essentially all of the known Creek-related wares at the time.

Her exhaustive treatment of European trade goods (including both basic descriptions, comparisons with other known archaeological specimens, consultation with other experts, and historical documentation) was well above the usual treatment of such artifacts in the 1960s. Typologies for European goods had not been developed when Mason began her study. Pioneering typologies for such items as beads (Kidd and Kidd 1970), bells (Brown 1975), and gun parts (Hamilton 1968) were developed later, but Mason's descriptions are still useful today.

Mason also attempted to describe Creek architecture for the first time. Unfortunately, questions about the field notes leave some doubt as to the size of the structures she described (Mason, personal communication). It has been suggested that the large structures she discussed near the trading post were actually rebuilt council houses (Smith 1992:71–72). Her description of the European trading post and analysis of aboriginal features intruding this European feature are extremely detailed. She also was able to document Native use of the trading post area by the Creeks after the post was abandoned.

One of the most interesting sections of Mason's work deals with the identification of the Creek town represented by the Ocmulgee site. First she reviewed earlier interpretations; then after consulting historical documents and early maps, she identified the town as Ocmulgee. Ocmulgee town does not appear on any maps of the area, and she based her identification primarily on a statement by Benjamin Hawkins that Ocmulgee was formerly located at Ocmulgee Fields on Ocmulgee River (Hawkins 1916:173). She was also influenced by the apparent continuity of the name Ocmulgee Old Fields. James Adair (Williams 1930:39) tied in Okmulge with the Lower Creek Trading Path, which crosses the Macon Plateau at the site.

In my own research (Smith 1992:42), relying on the Herbert-Hunter map of 1744, which I believe is actually the Herbert Map of 1725 with some updates by Hunter in 1744, I suggested a different identification. The Herbert-Hunter map places Cusitees (Kasihta) near the mouth of a major stream coming from the northeast, which I believe is Walnut Creek. Thus the Macon Plateau site would be Kasihta. Further reinforcing this interpretation is the fact that the Herbert map shows the Colomies on the western bank of the river opposite the town of Kasihta. There is a cluster of historic Creek archaeological sites in this area that would fit that interpretation, some of the few identified historic Creek sites located on the western bank of the Ocmulgee River. It made sense to me that the major, impressive archaeological Macon Plateau site with its fortified English trading house would be a major town such as Kasihta, not a barely mentioned minor town such as Ocmulgee.

In his report on the excavations of the nearby Tarver sites, Pluckhahn (1997) reconsidered the evidence for the identification of archaeological sites with historically named Creek towns and suggested that the Tarver sites represent Kasihta, with the creek shown on the Herbert-Hunter maps being Town Creek instead of "Walnut Creek" as I have suggested. Pluckhahn thus believes that "Macon Plateau, Lamar, and other sites on the eastern side of the river could then represent the town of Ocmulgee, as Mason [this volume] suggested" (Pluckhahn 1997:358). Pluckhahn does point out several weaknesses of his identification, including the apparent small size of the Tarver sites when Kasihta should be a major town and the lack of known Creek sites opposite the Tarver sites on the western side of the Ocmulgee River that could be the Colomies. Clearly more research is needed before we can confidently identify archaeological sites with historically named towns. We need additional survey data and site size data. There is always hope that additional historical documentation will be located.

## CREEK STUDIES AFTER MASON

For all practical purposes, Carol Mason has had the last word in the archaeology of the Ocmulgee site. She did continue to publish additional articles based on her dissertation research (Mason 1963, 1971, 1973). Nelson et al. (1974) analyzed material from excavations in the Ocmulgee Bottoms below the Macon Plateau and were able to demonstrate that the historic Creek occupation continues down into the river bottoms. I have summarized much of what was known about the Ocmulgee region in *Historic Period Indian Archaeology of Northern Georgia* (Smith 1992).

Recent excavations at the Tarver and Little Tarver sites, a few miles north of Ocmulgee National Monument, have revealed evidence of another early eighteenth-century Creek town (Pluckhahn 1997). This work now supplants Mason's Ocmulgee study as the most detailed analysis of a Creek town of the 1690–1715 period on the Ocmulgee River, but unfortunately this report has not been widely distributed. Several large block excavations revealed houses, burials, and pit features. Analysis included the usual descriptions of ceramics and historic artifacts but also included a demographic study of the sixteen historic Creek burials recovered, faunal analysis showing lack of introduced European domesticates, and a detailed floral analysis showing continued reliance on corn, cultivated Chenopod, hickory, walnut, and peach. The best-preserved structure at Tarver indicates a house size of approximately 7 by 3 meters and is comparable to Creek summer houses excavated in Alabama (Waselkov et al. 1990).

Further west, Lower Creek sites continued to be excavated and reported in the Chattahoochee Valley of Georgia and Alabama. DeJarnette (1975) reports on survey and excavations in the Walter F. George Reservoir. This report contains brief descriptions of work at several Creek sites. In recent years, more detailed reports have been prepared on historic sites in this region. Knight and Mistovich (1984) provide a much more detailed phase breakdown for Historic Creek occupations in this region. Excavations at Yuchi Town (Braley 1998; Hargrove et al. 1998), Kasihta (New South Associates 1997; ongoing work by Panamerican Consultants under the direction of Thomas Foster), and other Creek sites in the area (Elliott et al. 1996; Espenshade and Roberts 1992) provide a more modern analysis of Creek occupations in this region. Much information is summarized in Chad Braley's *Historic Indian Period Archaeology of the Georgia Coastal Plain* (1995) and a major synthesis of Lower Creek archaeology by John Worth (2000). Farther upstream, excavations at the late-eighteenth-century town of Okfuskenena were conducted by Harold Huscher, but only a preliminary report was ever published on this important site (Huscher 1972; see also Smith 1992).

Archaeology of the Upper Creeks in central Alabama also continues to be the focus of much research. Major projects have been completed for the Tallapoosa towns of Tukabatchee (Knight 1985) and Fusihatchee (Waselkov et al. 1990). With the final analysis of the extensive work at Fusihatchee still ongoing, we have much to anticipate for the future of Creek studies. Farther up the Tallapoosa, Roy Dickens (1979) conducted excavations at Horseshoe Bend and the Nuyaka town site.

Work on eighteenth-century occupation of the Coosa River has also continued since Mason's study of Ocmulgee. The contemporary late-seventeenth-century to early-eighteenth-century Woods Island site has been reported (Morrell 1965; Smith 1995), and Smith (2000) has traced the development of the Upper Creeks of the Upper and Middle Coosa Valley from the protohistoric period to the late eighteenth century. Near the southern end of the valley, Mueller (1992) reports work at the late-eighteenth-century town of Hickory Ground. Upper Creek archaeology has recently been synthesized by Gregory Waselkov and Marvin Smith (2000).

## TRADING HOUSES

Mason's study includes a detailed look at the fortified English trading house at Ocmulgee. It remains the most complete description of a trading establishment available at this time. Waselkov (1994:193) updated Mason's interpretation of the trading post by suggesting, based on historical records, that the fortifications would have been begun in 1702 when the English feared reprisals for their attacks on Spanish Florida but would have been unnecessary by 1704 when the English destroyed the Spanish Mission system. This relatively brief interval when fortifications were necessary perhaps explains, in Waselkov's view, why the fortifications were never completed. Waselkov also points out that the trading establishment was constructed with Native building techniques but built in an English style and with English dimensions, suggesting that the construction was done by Creeks under English supervision.

Other examples of English trading houses in the deep Southeast are rare. Although archeological research was conducted at Fort Moore where a fortified trading house was excavated, the site remains largely unreported (Polhemus 1971). Another early-eighteenth-century trading post in South Carolina, the Congaree Fort (Michie n.d.), has been located but not excavated in more than a testing phase. Recently, the Musgrove trading establishment near Savannah, Georgia, has been thoroughly excavated by Southeastern Archaeological Services under the direction of Chad Braley, but it dates to a slightly later period and is not typical of the early trading forts. Analysis of this important site is currently ongoing.

Mason's pioneering study of the historical Native American occupation and associated English trading post at Macon Plateau will be an important reference for years to come. Out of this work, Mason (1963) published an important article of Creek culture change. Waselkov (1994:193) points out that this article was an early example of studies of the adaptations of Native Americans to European contact and competition with European colonial societies. Now that The University of Alabama Press has published the complete dissertation, the basis of this article can be fully appreciated and utilized by other scholars.

## SUPPLEMENTAL REFERENCES

Braley, Chad
- 1995 *Historic Indian Period Archaeology of the Georgia Coastal Plain.* Laboratory of Archaeology Series, Report No. 34. University of Georgia, Athens.
- 1998 Yuchi Town (1RU63) Revisited: Analysis of the 1958–1962 Excavations. Manuscript on file at the National Park Service Southeast Archaeological Center, Tallahassee, Florida. Contract No. 1443CX509096001.

Brown, Ian W.
  1975  Historic Trade Bells. *Conference on Historic Site Archaeology Papers 1975* 10:69–82.

DeJarnette, David
  1975  *Archaeological Salvage in the Walter F. George Basin of the Chattahoochee River in Alabama.* University of Alabama Press, Tuscaloosa.

Dickens, Roy S.
  1979  *Archaeological Investigations at Horseshoe Bend National Military Park, Alabama.* Special Publications of the Alabama Archaeological Society No. 3.

Elliott, Daniel T., Karen Wood, Rita Folse Elliott, and W. Dean Wood
  1996  Up on the Upatoi: Cultural Resources Survey and Testing of Compartments K-6 and K-7, Fort Benning Military Reservation, Georgia. Manuscript report prepared for Environmental Management Division, U.S. Army Infantry Center, Fort Benning. Contract No. DABT10-95-R-0018.

Espenshade, Chris, and Marian Roberts
  1992  Archaeological Assessment of 1RU135, a Nineteenth Century Creek Site, Uchee Creek Recreation Area, Fort Benning, Alabama. Manuscript Report submitted to the N.A.F. Procurement Office, Fort Benning, Georgia. Contract No. NAFTB1-91-M-4791.

Hally, David J.
  1994  An Overview of Lamar Culture. In *Ocmulgee Archaeology, 1936–1986,* edited by David J. Hally, pp. 144–174. University of Georgia Press, Athens.

Hamilton, T. M.
  1968  *Early Indian Trade Guns: 1625–1775.* Contributions of the Museum of the Great Plains No. 3, Lawton, Oklahoma.

Hargrove, Michael, Charles McGimsey, Mark Wagner, Lee Newsom, Laura Ruggiero, Emanuel Breitburg, and Lynette Norr
  1998  The Yuchi Town Site (1RU63), Russell County, Alabama: An Assessment of the Impacts of Looting. Manuscript on file, Environmental Management Division, Department of the Army, Ft. Benning, Georgia.

Huscher, Harold
  1972  Archaeological Investigations in the West Point Dam Area: A Preliminary Report. Manuscript report to the National Park Service. Laboratory of Archaeology, University of Georgia, Manuscript No. 166.

Kidd, Kenneth, and Martha Kidd
  1970  A classification system for glass beads for the use of field archaeologists. In *Canadian Historic Sites: Occasional Papers in Archaeology and History,* no. 1, pp. 45–89.

Knight, Vernon J.
  1985　*Tukabatchee: Archaeological Investigations at an Historic Creek Town, Elmore County, Alabama, 1984.* Office of Archaeological Research, Alabama State Museum of Natural History, Report of Investigations 45.

Knight, Vernon J., and Tim Mistovich
  1984　*Walter F. George Lake: Archaeological Survey of Fee Owned Lands, Alabama and Georgia.* Office of Archaeological Research, Report of Investigations 42, University of Alabama, Tuscaloosa.

Marrinan, Rochelle
  1999　Carol Ann Irwin Mason: A Biographical Sketch. In *Grit-Tempered: Early Women Archaeologists in the Southeastern United States,* edited by Nancy Marie White, Lynne Sullivan, and Rochelle Marrinan, pp. 198–204. University Press of Florida, Gainesville.

Mason, Carol Irwin
  1963　Eighteenth Century Culture Change among the Lower Creeks. *Florida Anthropologist* 16(3):65–80.
  1971　Gunflints and Chronology at Ocmulgee National Monument. *Historical Archaeology* 5:106–109.
  1973　Historical Archaeology at Ocmulgee National Monument. Manuscript on file, National Park Service, Southeast Archaeological Center, Tallahassee, Florida.

Michie, James L.
  ca. 1989.　*The Discovery of Old Fort Congaree.* Institute of Archaeology and Anthropology, University of South Carolina Research Manuscript Series 208.

Morrell, L. Ross
  1965　*The Woods Island Site in Southeastern Acculturation 1625–1800.* Notes in Anthropology Vol. 11. Florida State University, Tallahassee.

Mueller, Dianne Sylvia
  1992　Report on the Archaeological Investigations at the Hickory Ground (1EE89), Elmore County, Alabama (1990–1991). Manuscript report submitted to the Poarch Band of Creek Indians.

Nelson, Ben A., David Swindell III, and Mark Williams
  1974　Analysis of Ocmulgee Bottoms Materials at the Southeast Archaeological Center. Manuscript on file, National Park Service, Southeast Archaeological Center, Tallahassee, Florida.

New South Associates
  1997　Cultural Resources Survey Lawson Army Airfield. Manuscript on file, National Park Service, Southeast Archaeological Center, Tallahassee, Florida.

Pluckhahn, Tom
   1997    *Archaeological Investigations of the Tarver (9JO6) and Little Tarver (9JO198) Sites, Jones County, Georgia.* Southeastern Archaeological Services, Inc. Prepared for the Federal Emergency Management Agency, Region IV, Atlanta. Contract No. EMW-95-C-4685.

Polhemus, Richard
   1971    Excavation at Fort Moore–Savano Town (38AK4&5). *The Institute of Archaeology and Anthropology Notebook* 3(6):132–133.

Smith, Marvin T.
   1992    *Historic Period Indian Archaeology of Northern Georgia.* Laboratory of Archaeology Series Report No. 30. University of Georgia, Athens.
   1995    Woods Island Revisited. *Journal of Alabama Archaeology* 41:93–106.
   2000    *Coosa: The Rise and Fall of a Southeastern Mississippian Chiefdom.* University Press of Florida, Gainesville.

Waselkov, Gregory
   1994    Macon Trading House and Early European–Indian Contact in the Colonial Southeast. In *Ocmulgee Archaeology 1936–1986,* edited by David J. Hally, pp. 190–196. University of Georgia Press, Athens.

Waselkov, Gregory, and Marvin T. Smith
   2000    Upper Creek Archaeology. In *Indians of the Greater Southeast: Historical Archaeology and Ethnohistory,* edited by Bonnie G. McEwan, pp. 242–264. University Press of Florida, Gainesville.

Waselkov, Gregory, John Cottier, and Craig Sheldon
   1990    Archaeological Excavations at the Early Historic Creek Indian Town of Fusihatchee (Phase 1, 1988–1989). A report to the National Science Foundation Grant No. BNS-8718934.

Webb, Clarence H.
   1962    Early 19th Century Trade Material from the Colfax Ferry Site, Natchitoches Parish, Louisiana. *Southeastern Archaeological Conference Newsletter* 9(1):30–33.

Williams, Stephen
   1962    Historic Archaeology in the Lower Mississippi Valley. *Southeastern Archaeological Conference Newsletter* 9(1):53–63.

Worth, John
   2000    Lower Creeks: Origins and Early History. In *Indians of the Greater Southeast: Historical Archaeology and Ethnohistory,* edited by Bonnie G. McEwan, pp. 265–298. University Press of Florida, Gainesville.

# Preface

Ocmulgee Old Fields near Macon, Georgia, is part of the multi-component, major Mississippian site of Macon Plateau. This great temple mound site early attracted archaeological attention, and the Lower Creek village and associated English trading house were but small parts of the large-scale excavations that took place there as part of public works following the Great Depression. Analysis of the late-seventeenth- and early-eighteenth-century materials from the trading house and village did not take place until nearly 30 years after initial excavation. Part of the significance of this site lies in its secure identification with a known group of people and the linkage of those people with recognizable archaeological remains. It was among the very first for which this kind of identification was possible and thus stands at the head of a continuing tradition of historic sites archaeology in the Southeast. The report itself includes a discussion of the historic setting and an analysis of the archaeological materials with an identification of the Lower Creek town and possibly of the English trader who lived there.

When I began work at Ocmulgee, I was a newly minted anthropology major from Florida State University, not yet enrolled in graduate school but eager to understand what archaeology could tell of that fascinating period when Europeans and native peoples came into intimate and life-changing contact. What I did not know then about trade materials amounted to almost everything, and the site at Ocmulgee was my teacher. I can look back on my labors and wish I had known more at the time. I might have understood the differences between copper and brass, for example, and been able to negotiate more surely the pitfalls in European ceramic analysis. Since then I have learned about trading establishments through excavating them and about artifacts through leaning even more heavily on the expertise of others. The site at Ocmulgee was a continuing discovery as the unfamiliar became familiar, and the world of the contact period came alive.

This second edition owes much to the kindness of people who helped me in the preparation of this edition, and I gratefully acknowledge their assistance: Richard I. Ford, Geoffrey Gajewski, Peter Peregrine, Marvin Smith, Stephen Williams, Corinne Wocelka, and, as always, Ronald J. Mason.

Page numbers in brackets in the text refer to the original pagination of the dissertation.

I would like to dedicate this re-publication to all those archaeologists, past and present, who have worked at the Ocmulgee site and in its collections and learned from its many archaeological splendors.

Carol I. Mason

# Original 1963 Preface

During the years immediately following the depression of 1929, a number of large archaeological sites were excavated with labor provided by government agencies. Some of these sites have yet to be written up and their data made generally available; others have provided much of the backbone for archaeological interpretation in the Southeastern United States. The present paper is a report on part of one of the former sites, Ocmulgee National Monument, Macon, Georgia. This site, although not yet analyzed in its entirety, has functioned as one of the latter, with rich amounts of archaeological information available in a series of general and specific reports (Kelly 1938; Fairbanks 1956a).

I spent the summer of 1957 and the summer and fall of 1958 at Ocmulgee National Monument working with the archaeological collections and preparing the descriptive sections of this report. Dealing with material twenty-five years after its excavation involves some special problems in addition to the expectable ones of loss and misplacement during storage. For one thing, the unusually cumbersome field nomenclature has had to be retained for the benefit of those who may wish to use the site materials in the future; this is because the nomenclature is tied into the Ocmulgee National Monument catalogue system and is the only way of locating specific materials in the large collections. In addition, certain of the field records, photographic negatives in particular, have not aged very gracefully and have thus hindered the analysis.

I am grateful to a number of scholars who generously made their special knowledge available to me and in so doing contributed substantially to my understanding of the Ocmulgee material: John M. Goggin, University of Florida, who identified and dated the majolica; Ivor Noel Hume, Colonial Williamsburg, who identified and dated other European ceramics; Harold L. Peterson, National Park Service, who provided dates and identifications for the gun parts; J. C. Harrington, who examined some of the pipes; and

David L. DeJarnette, University of Alabama, who kindly permitted me to examine trade materials from the Childersburg site.

The superintendent, Louis R. Caywood, and staff of Ocmulgee National Monument made my stay in Macon most enjoyable, and I thank them all for their many kindnesses during the course of my research. Other National Park Service personnel, Wilfred D. Logan and John M. Corbett, have provided aid in many ways, and their assistance is gratefully acknowledged. I would like to express my special thanks to Richard A. Marshall, University of Missouri, for providing the sherd drawings of *Ocmulgee Fields Incised* designs.

My husband, Ronald J. Mason, deserves my thanks for his moral support during the writing of this report and for his substantial contributions in the form of photographing speciments, preparing illustrations, and criticizing the manuscript.

I also would like to express here my appreciation to Charles H. Fairbanks, Florida State University, who provided the impetus for this study and aided it materially through his encouragement, criticism, and always valuable counsel.

Two institutions deserve special mention for their direct and indirect contributions. The staff and director, Donald Pieters, of the St. Norbert College Library, West DePere, Wisconsin, have been most helpful in obtaining for me many special books. Much of the following report was written while I was a fellow of the National Science Foundation. The generous financial support of that agency is deeply appreciated.

Carol I. Mason

# Introduction

[1]In recent years, research in the early colonial history of the eastern United States has been receiving information from purely archaeological sources. Excavations at Jamestown (Cotter 1958), Williamsburg (Hume 1958), Hopewell Iron Furnace (Mason 1958), and other early white settlements are contributing significantly to a more realistic and detailed picture of how colonial America functioned from day to day and to a more detailed knowledge of specific events cited heretofore only by documentary sources. Strictly aboriginal archaeology is also profiting from the expansion of interest and the extension of funds to historical research of this kind. As more and more data are made available, a more precise treatment of historic site material and a more hopeful approach to historic Indian archaeology are made possible.

Historic archaeology in all of its many varieties has been for a long time the step-child of North American archaeology as a whole. The work of Quimby, Kidd, Cotter, and others notwithstanding, there has been a far less adequate treatment of this particular phase of American culture history than of any other comparable unit. A long tradition of interest in historic archaeology has [2]persisted since a comparatively early date (Swanton 1922; Strong 1940; Stirling 1940), but in practice archaeologists have much preferred working with pristine American Indian culture. Of the large numbers of different Indian groups present in eastern North America at contact, comparatively few have been successfully identified as archaeological complexes and have sufficient historical source material to make these identifications convincing.

The nature of the "historic period" itself restricts the kinds of research that may be undertaken since comparative work over broad areas for other than very limited purposes is almost impossible. The historic label in America is simply a time marker placing sites and Indian cultures in relation to each other on the basis of white contact alone. It is usable only in describing the temporal relationships of all such complexes, and it has comparable implications for similarity in culture type only insofar as preceding pre-contact cultures and contact situations are similar. In every region, then, depending upon many external factors, the term "historic period" has a different meaning and the historic culture type a different setting and structure.

Some of the external factors influencing the direction and speed of culture change into a "historic period" have very far-reaching effects. These factors include not only basic differences between European nations setting up spheres of influence among the native peoples but also their attitudes toward colonization and purposes [3]for establishing colonies. In addition, such things as differences in levels of cultural complexity among groups contacted by the same Europeans affect significantly the results of such contact. Even the distances of culturally similar peoples from points of immediate European influence may result in areal separation according to their nearness to the sources of acculturation. These and many other variables combine to make the "historic period" a confused hiatus in the ideally conceived continuum from the prehistoric into the historic. This never-never land of thankless historical and archaeological research is nonetheless one of special interest. Traumatic culture change notwithstanding, pursuing Indians from their archaeological identities to their ethnographic ones provides useful information for reconstructing the social organization and political structure of archaeological complexes and provides a tool for more accurately filling out some of the barer bones of prehistory.

One of the most important problems to be solved in this type of research is that of treating historic material in more precise chronological terms. Culture change within the historic period of any one area is a progressive phenomenon which cannot be handled successfully solely under the blanket term "historic." A much more sensitive time scale must be devised in order to follow the rapid changes that did occur and place historic archaeological sites accurately with relation to each other. Small time units representing periods of real culture change [4]have been worked out in several areas of the eastern United States. In New York a division of the Seneca sequence into fifteen-year time periods (Wray and Schoft 1953) seems to reflect meaningful changes in the type of European contact and acculturation occurring during these periods. Rouse (1951) handled the historic period on the Malabar coast in Florida in terms of less strictly delimited subsections—exploration, hostility, friendship, decline—which are defined in specific Indian sites largely on the basis of the types of European goods made available to the people during these periods. Smith (1956) has extended somewhat analogous period divisions to the rest of Florida; and if sufficient information were available, similar divisions would presumably work in areas of

Spanish influence on the Guale coast in Georgia. In this sort of splitting, there is always the danger of cutting the cake too thin, but this is much to be preferred to treating "historic"—whatever its time level—as an all-or-nothing horizon style.

In Georgia and Alabama, the Lower Creeks and related groups were subject to European influence during a "historic period" extending from the sixteenth century into the nineteenth (Nunez 1958). During this long period, Creek town sites were occupied, abandoned, and reoccupied, particularly in the valley of the Chattahoochee River and its branches. There Creek settlements were made and remade for literally hundreds of years.

[5] Tracing developments during this three-century period involves not only locating, identifying, and excavating town sites but also building a chronology from historic records that can be firmly tied to specific Creek towns. As far as the earliest stages of this chronology are concerned, three short time periods cover the emergence of the Lower Creeks as an identifiable body and pinpoint them as a definite archaeological complex. The first of these is that of early English contact between 1670 and 1685. These were the years when Carolina was being founded and the native peoples wooed by the newcomers. While actual contacts with the English during this period were few, some Spanish influence was present in the form of trinkets and beads in at least some of the back country towns. The next period covers the years between 1685 and 1715, which represent the opening of the deerskin trade. Trade with the English started in earnest during these thirty years, and the first real influx of trade goods began. The last of the early stages includes the years between 1715 and 1717 when Carolina trade was dramatically shut off, and French and Spanish sources were sought by the Creeks for trade.

During the period of early English trade, the Lower Creek town site at Ocmulgee National Monument at Macon, Georgia, was one of a number of towns located outside the Chattahoochee River Valley, the major locus of Lower Creek settlement for most of known Creek history. Archaeological evidence from this site is evidence from an [6]area where there was no previous nor any subsequent Creek settlement, and for this reason there is no chance of mixing of different period Creek materials. This fact assumes importance when contrasted with the multiple Creek occupations in the Chattahoochee Valley; there any one town site is likely to represent years of successive occupations by several different towns. As far as Lower Creek archaeology is concerned, then, the Ocmulgee town is a "pure" site of the 1685–1715 period and an important temporal anchor for the whole sequence.

Coupled with the Lower Creek town site at Macon was an English built and operated trading house, apparently a familiar fixture in the native towns of that period. The presence of the trading house adds another dimension to any study of the Creek town itself. Set within the larger matrix of European political intrigue and power politics, the English trade in Carolina was of crucial significance in controlling the Indians of the back country and insuring English dominance in the competition with Spain. Seen solely against the background of Lower Creek culture, the trading house was also important as a direct instrument of acculturation and the precursor of certain kinds of social change. The trading house and the Indian town surrounding it together form a unit which is representative of the 1685–1715 period in Lower Creek history and archaeology. Together they are a starting place for tracing sequences either backward into the prehistoric past or forward into the development of the historic Creek Indians.

# I
# The Historical Setting

[7]The brief thirty-year interval during which the Creek Indians and the Carolinian trading house shared the site at Macon is but one short scene in a long and complex series of events that moved inevitably toward the eventual displacement of the Indians. The principal actors in this scene were the Carolinian settlers and traders, whose dreams for commercial empire and political control in the hinterlands reflected the beginnings of industrialization and economic expansion in the Europe of 1700. Alternately helping and hindering them, the original Indian inhabitants served as both villains and victims in a long series of military forays and exploitative commercial adventures.

English settlement in Carolina was first organized as a result of a royal grant of New World territory to eight proprietors, who were empowered to develop and govern the area much as they saw fit. The vast tract of land granted in 1663 by Charles II originally extended north and south between latitude 36 degrees to 31 degrees and east and west from the Atlantic Ocean to the Pacific (Salley 1953: 33). Within this province, which included the bulk of the United States between the lines formed by [8]what is now the northern boundary of North Carolina and the southern boundary of Georgia, the Lords Proprietors were responsible for government. They appointed executive officers, established the form of governmental machinery, and attempted to create an ideal social order. Their main interest in the settlement of the province, however, was frankly commercial; profit from colonial trade, from crops, and from traffic in land was their objective (Cheves 1897). Government under the Lords Proprietors continued in Carolina until 1719 when growing discontent with the governmental system produced political agitation that eventually placed the colony under the immediate control of the British crown (McCrady 1897).

By 1670, the earliest permanent settlers in Carolina at the site of Charles Town had a small palisaded city with a precarious foothold on the Atlantic seaboard. Charles Town was unprotected by natural features such as mountains, but it was nevertheless very well situated as far as geography is concerned. The protecting mountains that formed an effective barrier to colonial expansion in the northern part of eastern North America dropped away near Carolina, and the early settlers had an open road into the west and an almost unlimited potential for spread once the way had been made clear through the Indian nations. The Mississippi River was well within their sights as they pushed their trading empire ever westward.

Economically, the Indian trade was the most important factor in the development of the colony although plantations [9]and ranches provided a number of valuable exports. In addition to mixed farming and cattle raising, the colonists attempted to produce other than agricultural products—tar, turpentine, and even raw silk (Carroll 1836: 1: 267). Rice, introduced about 1700, provided an important crop and was for a long time a profitable export (McCrady 1897: 346). Sources on early Carolina history (Carroll 1836; Lawson 1860) seem to indicate that generally the agricultural projects carried on in the early years of settlement and so earnestly encouraged by government officials in London lacked good management. The Lords Proprietors themselves (Salley 1928: 83, 84) and many of the early writers complain that the Carolinians simply did not know the proper arts of farming and raising domestic animals in the Carolina country. Not enough attention was paid to using crops adapted to the climate or in caring properly for the animals that could be successfully raised there (see Klingberg 1956 for examples). Such crops that did prove productive in the climate were not exploited to their fullest extent. In direct contrast, similar complaints cannot in any way be leveled at the Indian trade, which was pursued by many of the colonists with a vigor and determination conspicuous by their absence in other areas of colonial life.

When the first settlements were made in Carolina (see Figure 1), the vast bulk of the southeastern territory was part of extensive Spanish claims in the New World. Both by right of discovery and by right of settlement, the Spanish were [10]able to lay irrefutable legal claim to it (Bolton and Ross 1925; Serrano y Sanz 1912: 81) although they soon discovered that the Carolinians recognized no rights other than those of actual possession and even then were not above disputing them. The coast of Carolina itself had been the site of early Spanish missions and military posts, but by the time the English arrived, actual Spanish occupation was well south of the Savannah River. Ready fuel for the resulting Anglo-Spanish conflict was supplied in Carolina by planters who had emigrated from Barbadoes. These people carried an active hostility toward the Spanish to the North American mainland and provided much of the grass roots anti-Spanish sentiment in Carolina

(Cheves 1897: 183). Religious antagonisms also provided yet another source of conflict or, at least, a ready excuse for it. Competition between Spain and England for control of the southeastern territory in North America was simply another fragment of the contest being waged between these two nations on a broad international scale.

Specifically, Carolina's nearest Spanish neighbors in the first years of settlement were the mission and garrison in the territory of Guale, at that time on St. Catherine's Island (Swanton 1922: 90). Other missions were located in peninsular Florida in areas inhabited by the Timucua and Apalachee Indians. The main Spanish stronghold was the presidio at St. Augustine, where the Spanish government maintained a strong garrison. For many years this Spanish fortress remained a threat, sometimes in fact only a psychological one, to the safety of the colony in Carolina.

The differences between the Spanish and English settlement systems in North America are very instructive for understanding the eventual outcome of their competition as well as appreciating the effects of these two separate systems on the Indians. Primarily, the Spanish system was based on the mission, which operated as a center for the permanent settlement and pacification of the Indians. Spanish subjects did not colonize old Florida to any great extent, and principal contact with the Indians was through priest and soldier. The major aim of the Spanish in the settlement of the Indians was to facilitate religious conversion and instruction in agriculture through the creation of permanent villages. Besides attempting to develop a truly sedentary population, the mission system was exploitative in that labor and produce were frequently required of certain groups in order to support St. Augustine.

The English system was solely exploitative in that the Indians functioned only as a means to an end, the obtaining and maintaining of a profitable trade. Attempts at conversion, pacification, and settlement of the Indians were foreign to this system, which in certain instances required unrest and warfare to keep it functioning at optimum. The market for slaves in the West Indies and in Carolina provided still another dimension to the English trade, particularly in the post-1690 period, by regarding the Indians themselves as actual and potential commodities. The English also used the various Indian nations as buffers to protect a colony unprotected by virtue of geographical position and as military allies in playing out the local version of competitive European power politics.

The first gambits in the long and sometimes dangerous game of profitably manipulating the Indian tribes were made by Henry Woodward, "first settler in Carolina" and its "first interpreter and Indian agent" (Crane 1956: 6). Woodward established peaceful relations with several important Indian

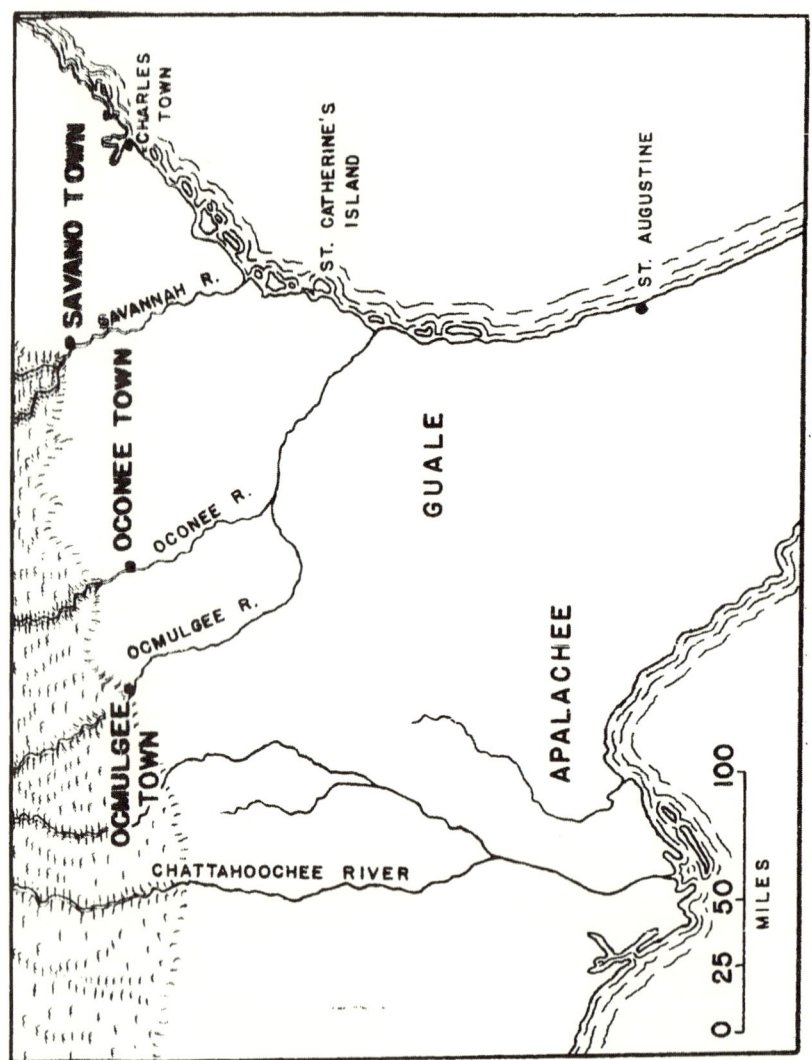

Figure 1. Georgia Territory.

groups and opened the lucrative inland trade with the Westo in 1674 (Cheves 1897). The relationship of the colony with this tribe was the main concern of the Indian policy of Charles Town during the first years of colonization, and Woodward's establishment of trade agreements with them was a major coup as far as the safety of the entire colony was concerned. Even during early Spanish efforts to missionize peoples of the coast, the Westo had been infamous among other Indians as a fierce and powerful tribe which raided them with impunity and terrorized most of the groups living along the Atlantic seaboard. Trade relationships assured immediate protection from this menace, but the presence of such a potentially hostile group on the very flanks of Charles Town was a deterrent to expansion and had the effect of preventing any serious westward movement of either settlers or traders.

The alliance with the Westo continued from 1674 to [13]1680 and proved to be of primary importance to the young colony in permitting a period of peaceful growth unhindered by any major Indian wars. The main troubles between the Carolinians and their neighbors occurred in minor skirmishes along the frontiers of the settlement where the Indians and the English colonists were both competing for the same land (Salley 1928: 55). Crane (1956: 17) credits this minor border warfare with the origins of the important and profitable Carolina slave trade, which had the doubtful virtue of clearing away the competition and producing a profit at the same time. Throughout the early period of settlement, impetus was given the slave trade by Carolinian encouragement of raids for slaves into nearby Guale. All of their various Indian allies—Westo, Lower Creeks, Cherokee—participated consecutively in these raids on the luckless peoples of Spanish territory to the south.

In the beginning, trade with the inland tribes was a proprietary monopoly; and the ordinary citizen, merchant, and planter could not trade with any Indians outside those in the immediate vicinity of Charles Town (McCrady 1897: 177; Salley 1928: 60). These individuals, denied the lucrative trade in the interior, seem to have been instrumental in causing a war with the Westo, the first really serious Indian threat to the Charles Town settlement. "Wars brought slaves, and slaves commanded profits in the West Indies" (Crane 1956: 19), and even the proprietors themselves blamed the eagerness [14]for Indian slaves as the principal reason for the opening of war with the Westo (Salley 1928: 258). After the defeat of the Westo, the Savannah Indians replaced them as a buffer tribe, but the Savannah—unlike the Westo—did not hinder the westward expansion of the Indian trade. The inception of the Westo War broke the Lords Proprietors' grip on the inland trade, and they never again were able to monopolize it.

With the Westo out of the way, English trade began to spread westward, seeking first to re-establish trade relationships with the Lower Creeks. These people had been first reached by the Carolinians at about the same time that they opened negotiations with the Westo, and apparently the Westo War had interrupted any contact that had been taking place (see Chapter 7). After the war, the Lower Creek towns can be definitely located in the middle valley of the Chattahoochee River. Here they had been approached by the Spanish, whose mission towns and garrisons in the Apalachee country were within reach of the Creek towns by following the banks of the Chattahoochee River into Florida. The Spanish were making plans for establishing at least one small mission among the towns up the river, but these plans were disrupted by the interference of English trade. In 1685 Henry Woodward had reached the Chattahoochee River towns with promises of plentiful English trade goods and was wooing the Indians again into the circle of Carolina influenced tribes (Bolton 1925; Bolton and Ross 1925).

[15]Understandably, the Spanish garrison in Apalachee reacted to Woodward's invasion as a hostile act by the English in what was unquestionably Spanish territory. From Florida the Spanish soldiers marched up to stop his activities and punish the towns that had welcomed him. In September of 1685, the Spanish commander Matheos burned Woodward's stockade but failed to capture any of the elusive Englishmen. In December of the same year, Matheos returned to find the English once again entrenched among the Lower Creeks and carrying on an active trade in deerskins. Again he was unable to catch the traders, but he secured the submission of eight of the Lower Creek towns and burned those of Coweta, Kasita, Taskigi, and Kolomi. By 1689 a small Spanish fort was built and garrisoned near Coweta to prevent the return of the English and keep the Indians subdued. Apparently these disciplinary actions plus the lure of the trade that Woodward promised them were enough to uproot the Creeks from their Chattahoochee Valley towns and draw them closer to Carolina (Bolton 1925). By 1690 a group of them had left the Chattahoochee Valley and built new towns eastward on the upper Ocmulgee River, known then as Ochese Creek. The evidence for this movement from the Chattahoochee to the Ocmulgee is documented in Spanish sources and provides the earliest permissible date for the construction of the town and trading house near Macon.

For many years the Ochese Creek center was the [16]most important of the Carolinian commercial outposts. Primarily, of course, it served as a trade station for the Creek towns in the immediate area. Secondarily, it was the jumping off place for the expansion of the trade ever westward until the Carolinian traders were knocking at the very gates of the French claim in

Louisiana. The Ochese Creek settlements also functioned as the base for campaigns against the failing might of Spain, once such a formidable threat to Carolina (Boyd 1953: 469). In 1702, a Spanish punitive force was sent from Apalachee against the English and was met and decisively defeated by a force of Lower Creeks led by the traders stationed in the Creek towns (Bolton and Ross 1925: 58). The Indians from the Macon site and their trader may have been part of this expedition along with the traders from Coweta and elsewhere along the river. In 1704, Moore's famous raid into the Apalachee country departed from the Ocmulgee area with many of the Ochese Creek Indians in his following. Even though St. Augustine remained as a potential threat, the decimation of the Florida tribes and the eventual withdrawal of the mission chains spelled the end of real Spanish competition from Florida. The Carolina trade empire was permitted an unopposed spread westward.

The focus of Carolinian expansion switched toward Louisiana, and the first decade of the eighteenth century is filled with the intrigue and the counter intrigue directed at the winning over of French allied Indian tribes [17]and the eventual conquest of Louisiana. The Carolinians managed to re-open an old feud between the Choctaw and the Chickasaw, and in 1711 made an expedition to destroy the Choctaw nation, "the bulwark of Louisiana" (Crane 1956: 95). The Lower Creeks were enlisted in this enterprise and marched with their English allies to scatter the Choctaw (Salley 1941: 48). Peace in Europe after Queen Anne's War stopped open military action and left the Carolinians to encroach upon the French in subtler ways. The center of frontier intrigue had moved beyond the old Ochese Creek settlements and was focused upon the borders of the French claims in the west. Concentration upon Louisiana apparently made the Carolinians neglect their own backyard; and consumed with dreams of empire, they did not see the enemy at the door until he was almost in and upon them.

Among the nearby Lower Creeks and particularly among the neighboring Yamassee, the expansion of the English settlers into Indian lands, the accumulation of huge debts owed the English by the Indians, and the many abuses of the Indians by the traders (see below) formed an insupportable burden to the native peoples, whose demands for redress of grievances went for the most part unanswered. Finally, conditions became such that a general uprising occurred in several parts of the frontier. In April of 1715, on Good Friday, the Yamassees rose and attacked the Carolinians, killing the traders in their midst and looting the storehouses (Carroll 1836: 2: 145). [18]At the same time, the Lower Creeks did likewise, burning and looting the trading houses in their towns (Klingberg 1956: 159). The following Yamassee War, generally credited as being the result of Lower Creek intrigue, wiped out the Indian trade for the time being and ruined the vast network of alliances and trade relationships established by the Carolinians during the years since their arrival. Unfortunately for the Indians, the Yamassee War failed of its objectives, and within two years an uneasy peace fell over the frontier. By the end of two years, the Creeks sought peace, re-established themselves as an important segment of the English trade, and were drawn once again within the Carolina sphere of influence. The most important event of the Yamassee War as far as the Ochese Creek settlements are concerned is that it removed the Creeks from the Ocmulgee River area and caused them to retreat westward away from possible Carolinian reprisals. By the end of 1716, they had returned to their old lands along the Chattahoochee River and left the Ocmulgee River entirely empty of Indian settlements. Never after this movement was the upper Ocmulgee River area inhabited by Indians. Thus two historically documented events, the movement to the Ocmulgee by 1690 and the Yamassee War of 1715, serve to bracket in time the Creek town and trading house at Ocmulgee National Monument and provide this segment of the Creek archaeological sequence with absolute dates.

## [19] THE INDIAN TRADE

In the history of the Charles Town community, the Indian trade occupies a position of real economic importance. All during the first decades of the colony's existence, the Indian trade produced almost the sole exports that could be relied on for reasonable returns. From 1699 to 1715, the average yearly export per year of skins from the colony stood at around 54,000 and was often considerably more. The peak year of 1706–1707 saw 121,355 skins leave the Charles Town port for Europe while the ruin of the trade is echoed in the meagre 5,000 skins exported in the tragic year of 1715 (Crane 1956: 111). Well into the middle of the eighteenth century, the trade in skins represented the important source of income for the Carolina colony. After this period a decline set in, probably owing to the decimation of the deer, once so plentiful as to be described enthusiastically as "infinite herds" (Carroll 1836: 2: 72). The Charles Town trade must also have represented an important source of income for the mother country in terms of goods sold for the Indian market. The value of these goods annually ranged between 10,000 and 50,000 pounds sterling (Carroll 1836: 2: 145; Klingberg 1956: 159).

While its sheer economic importance was not lost sight of, even those engaged in the trade at the lowest levels were able to see clearly that the plentiful, cheap English trade goods represented a wonderfully effective means of controlling the Indian nations of the back [20]country and bringing them easily and permanently under English influence (Salley 1947: 196). It was the existence of this plentiful supply of trade goods that brought about the ruin of the Spanish and won most of the Southeast for the English. Spain, never an important manufacturer herself, could not at this time afford to spend the funds necessary to keep Indian allies supplied with goods in this obscure corner of her vast New World empire. Had not the Yamassee War brought a premature end to the work of Carolina traders in Louisiana, the lure of intensive trade might well have deprived the French settlements of even their most loyal Indian allies (Williams 1930: x). The small quantity of French goods available to the southeastern Indians through Louisiana could not begin to compete with the endless supplies that poured into the area through Charles Town. The French government, preoccupied with Canada, devoted much less attention to the winning over of the southeastern territory even though individual French officials in Louisiana labored skillfully toward that end with the limited means at their disposal.

It is hardly possible to overstate the lengths that the Indians would go to be placed within reach of European trade once European goods had acquired the status of necessities of life. "The first bond of union and affection between Europeans and Americans was conveniency. At this early period to the Indian, a knife, a hatchet, or a hoe, was a useful and valuable acquisition.... he would rather give them the profits of a year's hunting [21]than want such instruments. Having obtained these in process of time, he found the tomahawk and musket equally useful; these also he coveted, and he could not rest til he obtained them. What was at first only convenient, as his wants increased, became absolutely necessary..." (Carroll 1836: 2: 63, 64). Possession of firearms revolutionized the relationships between Indian groups on the frontier and placed the Indians in contact with English traders at an incredible advantage over those allied with Spain, who were seldom permitted the use of guns (Fairbanks 1956c: 19).

Once a town or nation of Indians became used to the trade and accustomed to English weapons and tools as well as English clothing, it was in turn placed at a disadvantage in future dealings with the Carolinians. Any disobedient or rebellious group could be quickly brought to terms simply by threatening to cut off the trade and withdraw the traders from the towns. Throughout the literature covering the relationships of the Carolinians with the Indians, there is a standard lecture delivered through the years over and over again to the Indians in order to keep them generally obedient. One of the most polished versions of this lecture is the "talk" of Governor Glen to the Cherokees in 1750. At this time the Cherokees were giving the Carolinians some cause for alarm, and the governor, after recounting the sins of the natives, concluded his admonition with the usual warning that unless they mended their ways, the Cherokees were [22]liable to find themselves without the benefits of trade:

> I shall conclude with an advice to such of your Warriours as are too young to remember when you first had a Trade with the English, Let them consult your old Men, what was the Condition of your Country at that Time, and compare it with your Circumstances now. Instead of the admirable Fire Arms that you are now plentifully supplied with, your best Arms were bad Bows, and wretched Arrows headed with Bills of Birds, Bones of Fishes, or at best with sharp Stones. Instead of being decently or comfortable dressed in English Cloaths, you were forced to cover yourselves with the Skins of wild Beasts. Your Knives were split Canes, and your Hatchets were of Stone. . . . (McDowell 1958: 45)

Reminders such as these and threats to halt the trade were a powerful persuasive weapon in maintaining Indian alliances since the Indians themselves were well aware of the fact that they had "been brougt up after another Manner then their forefathers and that they must consider that they could not live without the English" (Mereness 1916: 112–113).

Coupled with the trade in skins, trade in Indian slaves was an important factor in the commercial picture of the day as well as being a decisive element in the disintegration of the Indian nations of the interior (Fairbanks 1956c). From the earliest contacts of the Carolinians with the Indians, slaves were among the items of trade mentioned. Woodward in his early Westo journey remarked that the articles he expected from the Westo were "deare skins, furrs, and younge slaves" (Salley 1953: 134). As time went on, slaves became more and more important until by 1715 it seemed to at least one observer (Francis LeJau) that traffic in slaves was replacing traffic in [23]skins (Klingberg 1956: 134). Many of the slaves that found their way into Charles Town to be sold at auction were destined for the West Indies and labor on the plantations there. Indian slaves were not easy to keep in the Charles Town area since they were too apt to escape into the forests.

In the early years of the settlement at Charles Town, there were attempts to suppress the slave trade because of the unrest it caused, but it proved too profitable a business to eliminate. Slave taking among the Indians remained a perfectly legal and acceptable part of the trade. The problem was to restrict it to those groups definitely classified as enemies of the English and to prevent the illegal enslaving of neighboring friendly peoples and of English political allies. The best that was eventually managed was to include the surrounding tribes in a general amnesty that would prevent their enslavement and insure stability among the Indians around Charles Town. In 1685 the proprietors ordered Governor West to take all Indians within four hundred miles of Charles Town under his protection and to prevent their being transported as slaves (Salley 1929: 20). Such instructions, however, were very difficult to enforce since even members of the governing council were involved in the Indian slave trade, and the four hundred mile limit would seriously affect the availability of slaves. Enslaving Indians illegally within the limits set by the government remained throughout the early part of the eighteenth century a source of serious friction between [24]Europeans and the native peoples.

In order to feed the slave trade from sources outside the legal limit, the Carolinians encouraged raiding and warfare between the towns and nations of the far interior (Carroll 1836; Klingberg 1956: 41). This set in motion a destructive machine that not only rid the Europeans of competitors and Indian enemies but also permitted them to make a profit in the process. The slave trade quite effectively syphoned off a large part of the Indian population in the towns and villages of the lower Southeast and at the same time scattered the remainder in disorganized bands. Particularly hard hit were the tribes of Spanish Florida, the objects of many slave raiding expeditions by the Indians and their European allies (Fairbanks 1956c; Salley 1934). Many of these early slave raids were organized in and set out from the trading settlements along Ochese Creek. In large part, they were instigated by the traders in residence there and included Carolinians in their train.

In addition to skins and slaves, several other products were traded from the Indians. These items, labeled most often as "sundries" in the trade lists of the day (McDowell 1955), included herbs, furs, baskets, medicinal plants (Williams 1930: 446), bear fat, and wild honey. Fur bearing animals such as beaver, otter, wildcat, fox, bison, and bear provided most of the furs exported from the colony (Courtenay 1907: 175; Carroll 1836: 2: 93; Salley 1947: 204). Later, horses became an important item [25]in the trade (McDowell 1955: 310), and horse stealing developed into a favorite sport among the Indians (Hawkins 1916).

The Indian trade changed character as far as its organization and control from Carolina were concerned several times in the years preceding the Yamassee War in 1715. At the very first, the trade was operated as a monopoly for the benefit of the Lords Proprietors in London. Private traders were permitted to trade with the groups in the immediate vicinity of Charles Town, but the lucrative back country trade was denied them. The weak tribes in the vicinity of the settlement must have suffered at their hands since it was to protect them from slave taking and consequent unrest that the government began its policy of protecting Indians within a certain distance of

Charles Town. The Lords Proprietors, in the early years so careful of Indian relationships, instituted a special court to judge disputes between these nearby Indians and the private traders among them (Salley 1928: 98). A contemporary observer noted that "care is taken by the Lords Proprietors that no injustice shall be done them [the Indians]; in order to which they have established a particular court of Judicature, (composed of the soberest and most disinterested inhabitants), to determine all deficiencies that should happen between the English and any of the Indians; this they do upon Christian and moral consideration . . . " (Carroll 1836: 2: 31). This court, established in 1680, was to attempt some regulation of the [26]Indian trade within a 200 mile radius of Charles Town (Salley 1928: 99). Unfortunately, the "sober" and "disinterested" members of this early commission included a number of active slave traders, and little effective management of the trade was accomplished. The proprietors were very much interested in the control of illegal slave taking since it did cause enough disruption among the Indians as to interfere with the peaceful operation of the skin trade, but they never managed to suppress it. Even after the Westo War, when the illegal slave trade was at an unprecedented height, the proprietors—perhaps indicative of their waning powers—were unable to regulate it (Salley 1928: 290).

After the Westo War eliminated the only major obstacle to westward expansion, the Carolina trade began as a whole to move into the interior and at the same time to lose the character of a private monopoly of the Lords Proprietors. Planters of the Carolina area started to participate in the back country Indian trade and sent factors among more remote peoples to trade with them for the planters' benefit. Apparently during this rather brief period of planter dominance, there were attempts by them to create individual monopolies much in the same manner as did the Lords Proprietors. In 1691 the governor of Carolina himself was reputedly seeking a personal monopoly on the back country trade through legislation ostensibly for its regulation (Rivers 1856: 154). By the beginning of the eighteenth century and the real opening of trade with the [27]Lower Creeks, the planter dominated trade began to fail, and a number of Charles Town merchants and citizens were also allowed to trade in the back country. Eventually, the Indian trade became everywhere a free-for-all situation involving uninhibited individual competition among the traders in place of the neat trade territories maintained in the days of government monopoly on a lion's share of the trade. Governmental control of the trade and regulation of it to prevent abuses were resisted strenuously by the large numbers of influential Charles Town citizens engaged in it (see Salley 1914; 1932; 1939). Finally, though, an act was passed in 1707 by the General Assembly (Salley 1940) which provided for a board of nine commissioners to regulate the Indian trade. This board of commissioners attempted to curtail the many abuses of the Indians in the course of the trade, but the board as a law enforcement agency lacked the teeth to make its bites effective. The Yamassee War was a splendid example of how ineffective the operations of this board proved to be since by that time it had been operating eight years to prevent the conditions that were directly responsible for the war.

The numbers of persons engaged in the trade and the huge territory over which the trade was scattered made any attempts at regulation extremely difficult even granting the existence of governmental machinery capable of handling actual trade reform. The Board of Commissioners of the Indian Trade took on the formidable task of enforcing [28]the existing laws and instituting reforms; they attempted to right some of the wrongs suffered by the Indians as well as to establish some kind of control over the actions of individual traders. For the most part, the commissioners seem to have been fairly disinterested men who were honestly attempting to bring justice and order to the Indian trade. That they were not totally disinterested can be witnessed by the fact that one of the later members of the commission was also a notorious trader and was himself once a defendant before the board (McDowell 1955: 6).

The principal on-the-scene instrument of the Board of Commissioners of the Indian Trade was the Indian Agent, who lived and traveled among the Indian nations for at least ten months of each year. The Indian Agent was in all respects a remarkable man, functioning as a caretaker along the entire Indian frontier. He not only served as a judge and sheriff but also acted as a supervisor, political adviser, and peacemaker to all his charges. He was empowered to send traders up to Charles Town for examination before the board, to arrest evildoers, and, if necessary, to confiscate goods. The agent traveled ceaselessly in these tasks, but apparently he could never move fast enough to keep abreast of, much less ahead of, the injustices and economic exploitation perpetrated against the Indians on the frontier. When the Yamassee War broke out, the then agent, the very able Thomas Nairne, was among the first to be killed by the Indians (Swanton 1922: 98).

[29]Licensing the traders was the unfulfilled objective of the Board of Commissioners and the problem whose solution the reform acts failed to accomplish. Licensing of the traders was the only practical way of ensuring responsible people in the trade and weeding out those who persisted in breaking the laws designed to regulate dealings with the Indians. The board lacked the means to force compliance with its plan for licensing, and by the time the Yamassee War began the whole scheme for issuing licenses and requiring traders to have them was a recognized failure. The traders them-

selves were never overly impressed by the authority of the commission as long as many miles lay between them and Charles Town. There is at least one recorded example of certain unlicensed traders being so unimpressed by the authorized warrants issued by the board as to tear them up before the very eyes of the messenger sent to serve them (McDowell 1955: 6). The commission attempted to put force into its pronouncements by empowering traders to seize the slaves or goods of anyone trading without a license (p. 12), but it is doubtful if this did anything but encourage the traders to prey upon each other with the government's blessing. The Yamassee War interrupted the labors of the board and served to demonstrate as no amount of verbiage could have that the means employed by the board to regulate the trade were ineffectual and that good regulation must be instituted if the colony were to survive at all.

After the Yamassee War when peace returned to the [30]frontier, the Indian trade was re-established as a government monopoly in order to insure its regulation. Eventually, however, the trade returned to private hands and to many of the abuses that the government had briefly managed to eliminate.

The abuses suffered by the Indians under the Carolina trade were legion. They ranged all the way from actual physical violence to simply cheating the Indians during the course of the trade. The 1710–1715 Journals of the Commissioners of the Indian Trade (McDowell 1955) are filled with examples of the grievances caused among the Indians by the traders. "Extortion, forced payment of debts, abduction of women and children, beatings, and murder" (McDowell 1955: viii) were among the more common complaints brought before the Board of Commissioners for judgment. Particularly prominent in addition were instances of Indians being taken illegally as slaves by the traders and sold in Charles Town. Obtaining proof that any one Indian was outside the legal bounds of enslaving was often difficult, and many Indians found themselves transported as slaves before they could establish their identities as free men. The traders also augmented this practice of getting slaves by organizing and instigating slave raiding expeditions against peaceful villages, sometimes alleging to the Indians that such raids were directly commissioned and approved by the government in Charles Town (Klingberg 1956: 41). In this way, whole Indian villages were captured and sold into slavery by other Indians acting, [31]as they thought or perhaps wished to believe, on official government orders. Disorder and chaos were the results for the Indian peoples of the interior, who were repeatedly raided even as far south as peninsular Florida (Cummings 1958: Pl. 45).

As a whole, the traders in the back country feared little the power of the government in far away Carolina and often publicly insulted and abused government representatives and ignored their instructions (Mereness 1916: 137, 544). Traders often spread false rumors among the Indians, much to the detriment of the government's attempts to preserve peace in the back country (Mereness 1916: 512). Personal relations between the traders and their host towns were not often amicable (Salley 1932: 21–22), and physical abuse suffered by the Indians was common enough to warrant direct notice by the Board of Commissioners. In their instructions to their agent in the Indian nations, the commissioners ordered him specifically "to exhort the Traders to be loving and kind to the Indians and not to abuse them by beating or any other Way oppressing them . . . " (McDowell 1955: 31). Treatment of Indian wives by the traders was often very brutal and must have aroused the ire of the Indians, judging from the number of times they sought to avenge such treatment.

Exorbitant prices for trade articles (McCrady 1897: 513) provided yet another reason for the Indians to resent and dislike the traders. Since there was no universal price regulation, the independent trader was in [32]a position to charge as much for his goods as the market would bear. In addition, the goods that were sent to the frontier were very often of inferior quality even during the later periods of government control (McDowell 1955: 142). Some of the goods were diluted to make them stretch further: paint was mixed in weaker and weaker proportions; rum was diluted far beyond the customary one-third proportion of water. Scales and measures in use by the traders were often blatantly dishonest (Gatschet 1884: 193) even to the extent of chopping off the yard measure to give the Indians less and less cloth for the same number of skins (Hawkins 1916). One case brought before the Board of Commissioners concerned a trader who was attempting to collect for goods forced upon the Indians against their wishes (McDowell 1955: 5), and a number of cases of illicit trade in firearms are credited to the traders on the Carolina frontier. Trade in firearms to hostile tribes was forbidden in the best interests of the colony (Rivers 1856: 110), but self-interest encouraged the traders to supply hostiles with arms and powder in spite of the law.

Particularly irritating to the Indians was the traders' practice of plying them with liquor and then cheating them of their skins (Williams 1930: 445). Contemporary opinion not only sanctioned this practice but also encouraged it. Instructions to prospective traders in Carolina contain this illuminating advice: "sometimes you may with Brandy or Strong liquor dispose them to an [33]humor of giving you ten times the value of your Commodities . . . " (Courtenay 1907: 175). David Taitt recorded in 1772 an enterprising trader who, after plentifully supplying the Indians with rum and relieving them of their skins for little merchandise, gave "rum to his wench for to purchase back the goods from the Indians" (Mereness 1916:

505) and increase his profits thereby. Trading liquor to the Indians was several times prohibited by the government of Carolina (Salley 1907b: 56; 1907c: 27), but in spite of this, it became one of the mainstays of the trade.

Other abuses of the Indians included impressing them to act as "burdeners" to carry skins from the Indian nations to Savano Town or even to Charles Town (McDowell 1955: 272). Later, this impressment cost the Carolinians a loss in trade to men from Virginia, who thoughtfully came into the Indian country well equipped with horses and made no demands upon the people for bearers. Extorting "presents" from the Indians for the English governors was another abuse cited by them as particularly offensive (Salley 1939: 21); and petty thieving on the part of the traders added to their unsavory reputation among both the Indians and the Carolinians who sponsored them (Mereness 1916: 509, 510, 521).

One of the most chronic of the ills besetting the Indians under the traders' regime was the accumulation of debts owed to the traders. Several times this practice was declared illegal (Salley 1926:7), but it continued until by the outbreak of the Yamassee War the amount owed by the Indians was reported near 10,000 pounds sterling by [34]one author (Carroll 1836: 2: 145) and nearer 50,000 pounds by another (Klingberg 1956: 159). The amassing of such debts and the fact that "those traders begun to be hard upon them" (Klingberg 1956: 153) were understandably an important factor in causing the Yamassee War. When the war began, the Indians "never paid their Debts, but cancell'd them, by murdering their Creditors" (Carroll 1836:2: 145).

As a general statement, it can be said that the character of the Indian traders in Carolina was of the lowest. Illiterate, greedy, and brutal, they were poor representatives of western European culture for the native peoples of North America to have before them as models and guides. Contemporary public opinion in Carolina and in England, however ineffective it was in stimulating reforms, was universal in condemning the public and private behavior of the men whose labors were enriching the colony and in turn the mother country. Francis Yonge in a description of the Yamassee War stated conservatively that the traders were "not (generally) Men of the best Morals" (Carroll 1836: 2: 145) while another somewhat later opinion described them picturesquely and accurately as a "monstrous Sett of Rogues for the major part of whome the Gallows groans" (McDowell 1958: 263). James Adair, the exceptional deviation from the normal pattern of trader, described many of the traders of his time as "abandoned, reprobate, white savages" (Williams 1930: 306) while another observer among the Creeks [35]noted that the character of most the traders was very miserable and that they were as a whole "abandoned wretches" (Schoolcraft 1855: 282). In 1700 the Commons House itself was moved to comment on the unjust actions of the traders and to exclaim piously that "by the Lewdness and wickedness of them [they] have been a Scandall to the Religion wee Profess" (Salley 1924: 22). Concerning the traders' packhorse men and assistants, contemporary comment puts them in the same category as their employers: "in General a loose Vagabond Sort of people [who] will not Stick out to say or do any thing among the Indians for the Lucre of a few Skines . . . " (Mereness 1916: 107).

Thus it was that the Carolinians, used to the evil name associated with their traders and the perennial abuses accompanying their tenure in the Indian country, were not overly alarmed when word came into Charles Town on April 12, 1715, that " . . . the Creek Indians were dissatisfied with the Traders that ware among them . . . and that they had made severall Complaints without Redress and that they said upon the first Affront from any of the Traders they would down with them and soe goe on with itt" (McDowell 1955: 65). And so used were the Carolinians to the terrible conditions in the Indian country and so confident that the Indians would do nothing about them, that when the news of the impending Yamassee War was given to a favored few, "it was totally disbeliev'd" (Carroll 1836: 2: 145).

At the time of the war, the trade from Charles Town [36]to the Indian nations originated for the most part from Savano Town, where goods arrived by canoe from the coast. The traders themselves were of two kinds, independents or employees of Charles Town merchants. The independent traders purchased their goods from merchants and sold them to their own profit in the towns. Those traders in the employ of the merchants carried goods to the towns and sold them to the Indians usually at a specified commission. Few of the Charles Town merchants themselves ever lived among the Indians or acted as their own traders in the back country. A common form of trade management between the city and the frontier was a trading company, formed by several men in partnership. Before the Yamassee War, the records cite a number of such companies operating among the Ochese Creeks as well as in other areas, and this kind of trading company was apparently the type of organization in effect at the Lower Creek town at Macon (see Chapter 6).

Since the customary route of trade materials to Savano Town was by boat, it was at this point that they were first packed and started over the long roads to the Indian settlements. The trade route lay southwest of Savano Town to the Ogeechee River, where the road forked into the Upper and Lower trading paths. Following the Lower Path, the trade first reached Oconee Town on the river of the same name and then the other towns and villages of the Lower Creeks on the upper Ocmulgee River, called then Ochese Creek by the English. Goods were carried along these famous trails by Indian bearers or by [37]horse pack trains and deposited in the trading houses erected by the English in the Creek towns.

Many of the Creek towns seem to have had their own special traders who spent most of their time trading with that single clientele. Usually the traders did not operate alone; each one had one or two packhorse men or assistants who were most commonly also Carolinians although the records from the early period contain a few mentions of half-breeds employed in this capacity. Worries that beset packhorse men and traders on the long overland journeys from the comparative civilization of Savano Town included not only hostile Indians and inclement weather but also poor roads and an interminable number of barely fordable rivers (Harper 1958). Once the traders had seen the goods safely stowed in the towns and the skin trade profitably functioning, they were plagued by water spoilage of the skins or by armies of rats or worms seeking to feed on them (McDowell 1955: 143). The Indian trade, romantic in retrospect as the instrument of empire, was hardly such to the men who actually engaged in it.

When the Yamassee War began, one of the first actions taken by the Indians was to loot the trading houses and kill the traders. The *Boston News Letter*, reporting the event on June 13, 1715, noted that "we had about a hundred traders among the Indians, whereof we apprehend they have murdered and destroyed about Ninety Men . . . " (Carroll 1836: 2: 572). The traders and trading houses in the Ochese Creek settlements were among the primary targets [38]of the uprising, and it is likely that the trader or traders at the Ocmulgee National Monument site shared the fate of the "Ninety Men" destroyed in the first few days of the war. A few of the traders did escape with their lives and were sheltered by certain of the Indians, but there is no record that any of these came from the Ocmulgee town. After the Yamassee War, the Carolinian trade no longer used Ochese Creek as the first stop in its constant westward march. The first stop became then the Creek settlements on the Chattahoochee River, and the old fields along the Ocmulgee became simply camping sites on the way to a frontier that had forever moved beyond them.

# PART ONE
Archaeological Evidence

# 2
# Excavations at Ocmulgee

[40]The trading house and the Creek town site at Ocmulgee National Monument in Macon, Georgia, are geographically part of the Macon Plateau, one of the most familiar and most excavated Mississippian sites in the southeastern United States (Kelly 1938; Fairbanks 1956a). Directly on the fall line, this large site overlooks the Ocmulgee River and the low plain that extends southeast from the Appalachian piedmont to the coast. Several factors have made this area a favorable one for human habitation. At one time, it was plentifully supplied with game animals and other wild life, including a variety of edible wild plants. The land itself is reasonably fertile, the growing season is long (six to nine months at present), and the rich river bottoms are productive even with the most primitive agricultural methods. Water sources and waterways are abundant today, dried-up stream beds and springs indicating that they were formerly more plentiful than at present. Rainfall in the area is fairly heavy, and the humid sub-tropical climate has no really severe winters. Rich in these natural resources and advantageously situated with regard to river communication, this part of central Georgia was an attractive one to [41]aboriginal settlers and remained such for the Europeans and present-day Georgians who followed them.

The long series of human occupations on the Macon Plateau extends in time from that of the very earliest hunting groups (Kelly 1938: 7) all the way through the present, encompassing almost the entire range of historic and prehistoric culture types in this area. The most extensive pre-contact occupation was that of Mississippian peoples (the Macon Plateau component), whose temple mounds and village debris form the most conspicuous physical features of the site. The other principal prehistoric remains belong to a simple-stamped ceramic horizon while minor amounts of material represent less extensive occupations by Swift Creek, Napier, Lamar, and others (Kelly 1938). The historic Indian artifacts, which comprise a significant part of the total cultural assemblage, are those from a town of Hitchiti-speaking Lower Creeks, the last known Indian occupants of the area. As was mentioned above, the site was abandoned permanently as a habitation spot by Indian groups shortly after the Yamassee War although specific title to the Macon Plateau region was retained for many years by the Creeks. Ocmulgee Old Fields, traditionally the place in Georgia where the Creeks first "sat down" (Harper 1958: 35) after their original migration in prehistoric times, remained in their possession, at least in name, until the early nineteenth century.

Evidences of historic white occupation include not [42]only the trading house, representing the earliest phase of intense white contact, but also the debris from many generations of purely non-Indian settlement. The Georgia government factory, later known as Fort Hawkins, was moved to the area in 1806 and remained there as a trading house and government outpost until 1817 when it followed the retreating frontier into Alabama (Mattison 1946: 178). After the Fort Hawkins period, the Macon Plateau site was known locally as Halsted's Old Fields after John Halsted, the government factor at Fort Hawkins. Soon after the city of Macon was founded in 1823, Ocmulgee Old Fields became part of a large farm, and much of the site remained under cultivation for many years. During the Civil War, a very minor skirmish was fought near the mounds, and Confederate trenches and field fortifications crossed the plateau. One of these trenches cut directly across the site of the colonial trading house, and military items from this period are present in the collections. In later years, parts of the site seem to have been used as a private or public dump, for a large amount of nineteenth and twentieth century refuse forms a heavy overlay on the earlier materials. Since 1936, the site has been a national monument, administered by the National Park Service.

Lying almost midway between mounds A and D (see Figure 2), the trading house proper occupied only a small part of this extensive site. The land on which it formerly stood is now a section of a narrow strip isolated between [43]the present bed of the Central of Georgia Railroad and an abandoned railroad cut (Macon, Dublin, and Savannah Railroad) running almost parallel to it. During the excavations, this artificially segregated segment of the site was treated as a unit and called the Middle or Central Plateau, a designation which will be retained here for easy reference. It must be remembered, however, that this division is based solely on man-made lines and does not reflect any original geographical separation. To the west, a small creek, running roughly north and south, crosses both railroad cuts and is parallel to the trading house at a distance of about 350 feet. The southeastern portion of the site slopes gradually in a series of poorly defined

Excavations at Ocmulgee / 27

terraces toward the old railroad cut, which is now a National Park Service road. At least one small spring is present in this section today, and there were apparently others in aboriginal and early historic times. The Creek town site shared the area with the trading house or occupied it before and/or after the tenure of the stockade there. Other town remains attributable to the Lower Creeks were found in the land around Mounds C and D and elsewhere within the monument boundaries; but judging from the number of burials and other signs of habitation, the Middle Plateau was the major occupation area.

The Lower Creek Trading Path (Gatschet 1884: 152) crossed the Middle Plateau practically at the trading house gates and may be traced in one direction back around Mound D and in the other down to the Ocmulgee River, where [44]signs of it are no longer visible on the river flats. This road, one of a number of crucially important paths that criss-crossed the early Southeast, was for a long time the main route of communication from the English settlements to the Ochese Creek towns and the major means by which English goods and English political influence spread throughout the territory. From the fork at the Ogeechee River, the Lower Path followed the fall line and arrived at the Ocmulgee River after first crossing the nearby Oconee. Westward, the path crossed the Chattahoochee River and in later years was a main throughfare to the Lower Creeks when their towns were located on that river. Many early travelers followed this path through Ocmulgee Old Fields and even camped there, but few of them were impressed enough to leave descriptions or comments on the site. Such descriptions as do exist (Harper 1958: 241; Hawkins 1916: 88; Mereness 1916: 219; Williams 1930: 39) are of the mounds and make no mention of a trading house there or discuss ruins that could be attributed in any sense to Europeans. Despite their silence on this matter, these early comments and accounts are very valuable. They clearly connect the conspicuous Ocmulgee temple mounds, and indirectly the Carolinian trading house and Lower Creek town, with the Lower Creek Trading Path and provide an unmistakable point of reference for finding the site on early maps of the Carolina back country.

[45]The first program of excavation of the site was likewise prompted by the presence of the extensive Mississippian remains and not specifically because of the historic component. Under the direction of the Smithsonian Institution, this entire project was under the immediate charge of A. R. Kelly, with labor provided through the Civil Works Administration. Later, labor was furnished by the Works Progress Administration and the Civilian Conservation Corps. Actual excavation continued at Ocmulgee for eight seasons, from 1933 to 1941, although the main part of the work on the

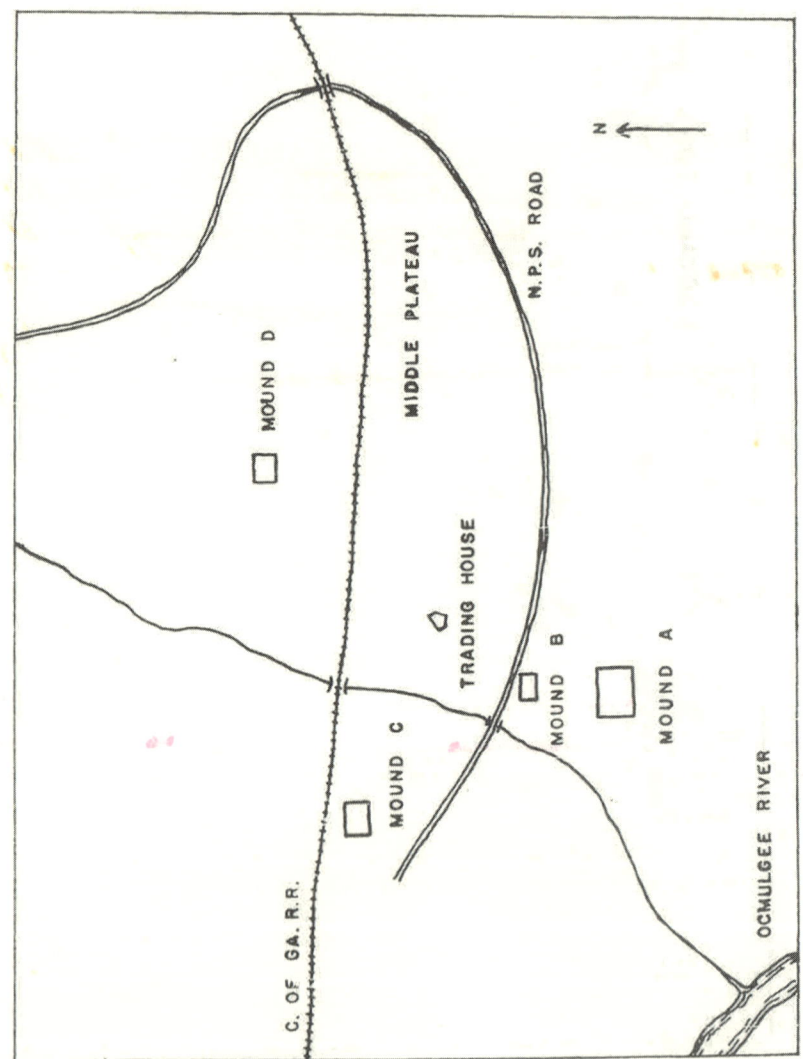

Figure 2. Map of Ocmulgee National Monument.

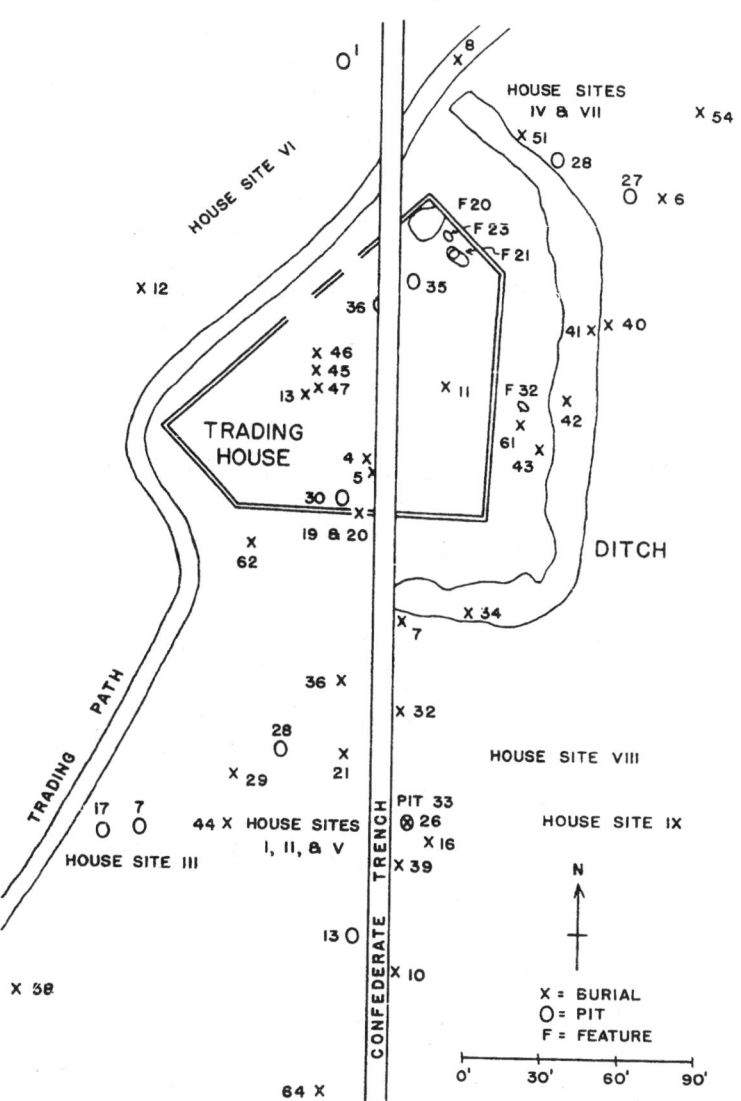

Figure 3. Map of the Middle Plateau.

Middle Plateau itself lasted only from August, 1935, through October of the following year.

A second excavation of this section of the site took place nearly three years later and lasted through part of 1940. The later excavation was first undertaken to locate burials to be used as field exhibits, and part of the area outside of the trading house ditch was stripped back for this purpose. Work continued in 1940 in order to expose the line of the trading house stockade and record all available data before the Middle Plateau was sodded and drainage facilities installed. Although relocation of the five corners of the enclosure for the sake of the National Park Service's interpretative program was the main concern of the final excavation, a concerted effort was made to answer some of the questions left by the first excavations in 1935 and 1936. Primary among these were several concerned with details of construction and [46]architectural design, problems of importance to interpretation of the nature of the structure itself. The second excavation at the trading house site was made by Jesse D. Jennings and Charles H. Fairbanks.

Like the rest of the Macon Plateau, the Middle Plateau was first excavated in a series of parallel control trenches, thirty inches wide, which could be expanded in any direction to include features encountered during the trenching. Ninety feet apart, four main exploratory trenches totalling almost 3500 feet were placed across the plateau parallel to the railroad cuts. Nine others ran the length of the terrace slope, and a number of miscellaneous trenches were run across other parts of the area. Although this Middle Plateau operation was only one small part of the larger excavation plan, it was itself subdivided into a number of smaller spheres of interest, only some of which concern directly the trading house and Lower Creek town. Those which will not be discussed here include sections of the Macon Plateau fortification ditches and the spring sites, both of which were considered important projects during the excavations on the Middle Plateau proper. In addition to the line of the trading house stockade, strictly historic remains on the site included a large number of burials, several houses, and many historic refuse pits (Figure 3).

# 3
# The Trading House

[47]It has been common knowledge in the Macon area for many years that the Ocmulgee National Monument mound group was once an Indian town during the earliest days of white penetration into the Southeast. For many years, it has been customarily called the "Old Fields," a designation used by many white settlers as well as by the Indians to refer to a once-occupied town or village site. The existence of an English trading house within that town was not known locally or even suspected by historians until the Middle Plateau exploratory excavation trenches cut across the old wall lines (Kelly 1939; Kelly and Friedlander 1939). Written records dealing specifically with this part of the frontier in the important pre–Yamassee War period are quite scarce, and no remains of walls or even an outline of them were present on the surface to provide any kind of clue as to the structure's existence. When it had been fully exposed, the size of the building as well as its carefully aligned pentagonal shape and its evidently close relationship to the trading path made construction by Indians improbable. The further discovery of quantities of English trade materials within the walls and in the immediate [48]vicinity of the structure pointed to a connection with the then widespread Carolinian trade. Final identification of the trading house as to who specifically owned and operated it is dependent upon what material has emerged from the scattered historic sources from this crucial early period. As has been mentioned before, sources dealing with the area at the proper time are very scarce, and no really precise mention of this particular outpost appears in any of the usual ones. Enough evidence is available, however, to be sure of the nature and the function of the outpost itself and to be reasonably sure of who was for a time the trader in residence there (see Chapter 6).

The important Mitchell map of 1755 states that "the English have Factories and Settlements in all the Towns of the Creek Indians of any note, except Alabamas, which was usurped by the French in 1715 but established by the English 28 years before." From the *Boston News Letter* article on the outbreak of the Yamassee War, the estimate of the number of traders in the Indian towns was a hundred men (Carroll 1836: 2: 572). What kind of "Factories" and "Settlements" these hundred men maintained in the Indian country is nowhere really explicit for the period immediately before the Yamassee War, and the Ocmulgee National Monument site may or may not have been the usual type of establishment. After the Yamassee War, the situation is little better, for as Crane has pointed out, descriptions of trading houses in the Southeast are [49] "practically non-existant" (Kelly and Friedlander 1939: 4).

It is clear, though, that the construction of European-type trading houses within the Indian towns was common procedure in the immediately post–Yamassee War period and was most probably the continuation of an already established pattern in that area. In the post–Yamassee War period, one centrally located store and warehouse served as the base for the operations of satellite traders in neighboring towns. At one time, for example, the factor to the Cherokee, Theophilus Hastings, had one main store with five helpers situated in nearby villages (McDowell 1955: 123). This, of course, was during the period of government monopoly of the Indian trade when the Commissioners of the Indian Trade were the sole operators and hired factors "in the publik interest."

When European trade was first extended to any one Indian town, the people were apparently expected to provide sufficient labor for constructing the trading house and warehouse and also for keeping these buildings in repair. Desire for trade in the towns was enough motivation to organize them for this type of labor although they often tired of the continual demands of the Carolinians. In 1717, the *Journals of the Commissioners of the Indian Trade* record the fact that the headmen of the Cherokee were scolded for not "building or repairing the Trading Houses . . ." (McDowell 1955: 236) as well as for neglecting to keep the traders supplied with food. Further comment on the [50]fact that the Indians were customarily expected to provide the labor for erecting the buildings from which the trade operated comes from several instances recorded in these same journals. When the Creeks requested a post and factor at Hillabees in 1718, they "said they would prepare a Trading House for him" (McDowell 1955: 282). Traders to the same Indians were told "to get the Indians to build you a good Trading House" (p. 307). When the Carolina trade factory was established at the Congarees in 1716, the factor had some "eighty Indians to assist them in erecting the buildings" (p. 73). Likewise when trade was opened with the Chickasaws, the formal pronouncement read that "the said Goods should be lodged at a town called Talassee, and a sufficient Trading House provided . . ."

(p. 238), presumably by the natives. All of these examples are from the immediately post–Yamassee War period; and then, of course, the government at Charles Town was by law the chief and only merchant in the trade. There is no reason to believe, however, that the government would have been instituting a drastically new policy by requiring the Indians to help in the construction of the trading houses. It was probably only continuing a pattern already established by the traders and merchants of the preceding period, a pattern that was certainly much to its advantage to maintain and one that eliminated the hiring and transport of labor from Charles Town.

It does seem that professional help was utilized in construction in some cases. In discussing the [51]establishment of a new trading station at Savano Town, the comment was made and recorded that "there is not any Store House, nor any Possibility of making one, unless two Sawyers and a Carpenter are hired and sent up . . . " (McDowell 1955: 99). Savano Town was not only an Indian settlement but also served as a trade center intended to draw the Indians from their towns to trade with a well-defended and permanently European-occupied outpost. Eventually, though, even Savano Town was supplied in 1716 with "several Houses" (p. 127) which were built by Indian laborers supplied with "Rum out of the Cargo, for Payment" (p. 127).

The kind of trading factories built by these Indian crews were of a design supplied by the European traders and almost always consisted of at least two buildings, a store and one or more warehouses for skins. The records at Savano Town indicate that provision was to be made for two buildings only, "the one for Skins and the other for Goods, as usual . . . " (McDowell 1955: 99); but the records further report the building of "Storehouses and a Magazin for the Goods" (p. 127). Other less important trade stations apparently had a lesser number of buildings. Adair, in the last half of the eighteenth century, stated that the traders then had the same pattern of storehouses for skins plus houses for the storage of goods. He also added that the traders' many houses were necessary for their many children and attendants (Williams 1930: 443), a factor that must have varied from trader to [52]trader.

The buildings themselves were made of logs although no real description of them exists. At Wineau Bay, the factor is reported as having "Built a log House of twelve Feet by Ten, at that Place, to secure the Trade there . . . " (McDowell 1955: 132). Further information comes from the trading house at Santee, where in 1716 the Commissioners of the Indian Trade allowed the new factor " . . . fifty pounds for building of a logg House . . . of twenty-five Feet length and fourteen Feet wide" (p. 80). A few comments in the contemporary accounts record the presence of stockades surrounding the stores. A somewhat later trading house (*ca.* 1763–1784) in north Florida,

Spalding's Lower Store, seems to have had several buildings enclosed in a palisade (Goggin 1949: 36). The settlement at Savano Town is credited by Crane (1956) as having palisaded warehouses (p. 44) or "trader's stockades" (p. 132). Henry Woodward was reported as erecting a "stockade" among the Lower Creeks for the purposes of trade in 1685, and a second type of structure, called a blockhouse by Bolton, was also built among them later the same year (Bolton and Ross 1925: 50, 51). Colonel Chicken also mentions a "Fort" that is further identified as a "private fort and trading house" (Mereness 1916: 100) used in the Indian trade.

Within the towns themselves, the trading houses apparently had no usual position with regard to the town square or any of the homes of the people. The temporary nature of most Indian dwellings would have made it impossible [53]for the more permanent trading house to maintain any kind of constant position with regard to them even if such a thing were desirable or customary. The only comment available on the position of the trading houses is a general one from Adair. He stated that in towns where the Indians were at war the traders tried to locate themselves in the middle of ihe towns for greater security. In time of peace, he reported that both traders and Indians preferred to live at a little distance from each other for the sake of the traders' livestock, which were preyed upon by the young men of the village (Williams 1930: 442).

The narrow ditch outlining the trading house stockade line at Ocmulgee was first encountered during the general trenching operations across the Middle Plateau in 1935. Clearing revealed a five-sided enclosure measuring one hundred and forty feet on the longest "base" wall, forty feet on each of the parallel short walls, and one hundred feet apiece on the two walls forming the apex or gable end of the pentagon (Plate I). The long line of the "base" wall ran northeast and southwest while the gabled end formed a right triangle whose long arms ran directly north and east. The outline of the stockade was very clear and distinct, leaving no doubt at all as to the structure's original dimensions. The narrow ditch formed an almost continuous dark line throughout its course and was easily traceable in the ground. The only gaps in the wall line found during the excavations were a pair of gateways giving access to the interior of the stockade through [54]the long "base" wall (Figure 4). The longest of these was a thirteen foot blank space containing no remnants at all of the dark footing ditch; it was apparently an original hiatus in the stockade wall. The other probable gateway was only five feet wide and was situated a few feet north of the large gap in the same "base" wall. Nothing remained of gateposts or other possible supports for gates in either one of these gaps. If gates were at one time present on the stockade, they must have been swinging doors attached to one end of the

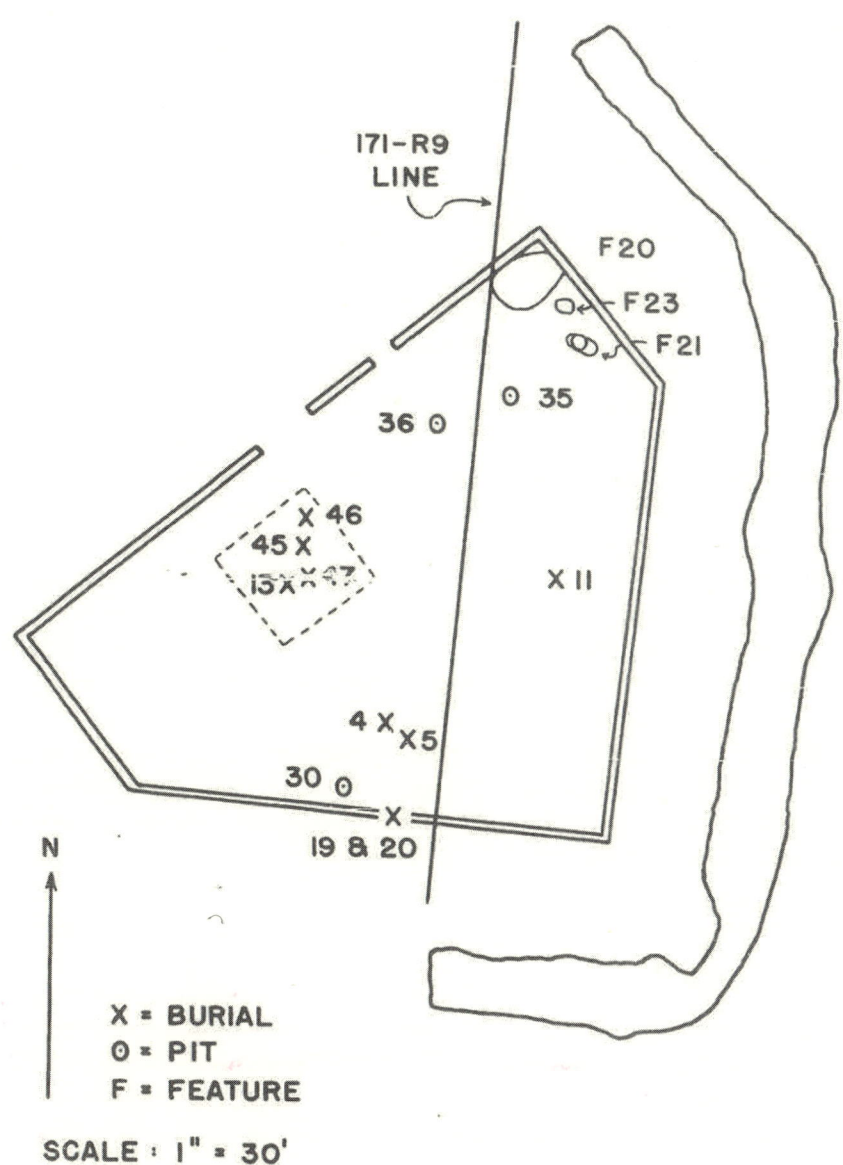

Figure 4. The trading house.

stockade line itself. One of these gateways might have been for pedestrian traffic while the larger of them permitted entrance of the horse trains that were such a familiar part of the Indian trade in the Southeast.

As originally reported, the narrow ditch outlining the stockade enclosure was found to be about two feet deep and filled with a dark waterlaid soil occasionally laminated with lighter sand. There was no evidence of any postmolds anywhere within the ditch itself; it was simply a continuous dark brown stain with no possibility of differentiating it into postmolds. This fact, plus the presence of the light-colored laminated sand, formed the basis for considering that the stockade originally had been built of horizontally-laid logs whose deterioration would leave no postmolds, only vague lines of waterlaid sand deposited under and around the decaying logs. The long horizontally-laid log walls were considered then as having [55]been pegged together and partially supported by an earthwork thrown up against the interior of the structure. Later excavations at the site (1939–1940) directed particular attention to uncovering further information about the construction of the stockade, but few helpful details were forthcoming. No evidence was found to support the original interpretation of horizontally-laid logs with an interior earthwork nor was any obtained to indicate how the stockade had been constructed. As before, no postmolds were found along the entire length of the footing ditch or in its base. During this latter series of excavations, the stockade trench was found to be only one foot deep and filled as before with dark waterlaid sand. The discrepancy in the reported depths of the footing ditch is owing to the amount of overburden removed during the clearing operations that originally uncovered the pentagonal stockade in 1935.

The complete lack of evidence in the ground makes it difficult to comment accurately on the original appearance of the stockade when it was in actual use. Of the two possible types of construction, however, that consisting of logs set vertically into a footing ditch excavated into the ground seems most compatible with such information as is available on early frontier architecture. Throughout North America, the horizontally-laid "log cabin" type of construction (proposed by Kelly 1938: 52; 1939: 330) seems never to have been used for large stockaded areas where economy of effort was a primary concern. Simple structural difficulties in building and supporting long [56]walls of horizontally-laid logs are tremendous even granting the hypothetical presence of an interior combination ramp-support against the walls. In view of the lack of evidence to prove the existence of horizontally-laid log walls and the known extensive use of vertical logs, both from a historical and from a structural standpoint construction of the Ocmulgee stockade of vertically-set logs is a more probable interpretation.

If the stockade were constructed of vertically-set logs, then there must be some explanation for the total absence of postmolds in the footing ditch. The most reasonable explanation and the only one supported by even scanty evidence is that the logs forming the stockade wall were removed or destroyed before they had time to decay, and the subsequent refilling of the ditch left no indications of their presence. The burials intrusive through the line of the stockade (numbers 19 and 20) indicate that in the period between the time of abandonment of the trading house by the Carolinians and the Yamassee War removal of the Lower Creeks from the area for good, nothing whatsoever remained of logs or stumps to impede the digging of graves through the stockade trench. Since the trade materials and the historic records date the trading house nearer in time to the critical year of 1715 than to the earliest years of Lower Creek occupation on the upper Ocmulgee River, there does not seem to have been enough time between the last Carolinian use of the stockade and the Creek exodus from the area for these walls to have decayed away, even [57]in Georgia's moist climate. Somehow, then, in the interval between the trading house's abandonment and the shortly following—probably immediately following—Yamassee War, the disappearance of the stockade walls was effected so completely as to offer no impediment to the excavation of graves in that area. Since there was no evidence found to indicate that the stockade had been burned, the remaining alternative is that it was dismantled rather than destroyed, removed rather than allowed to decay. Dismantling the log enclosure could have been the work of fleeing Carolinian traders in order to avoid leaving any kind of defensible structure behind them in a potentially hostile town although firing the stockade would seem a simpler solution. If the traders themselves had for some reason voluntarily abandoned the stockade, it is very much out of character for them to have destroyed it unless it was to prevent other traders from utilizing it in the future. If this particular trading house was in fact in use up to the Yamassee War, then the Creeks themselves were directly responsible for whatever befell it and its inhabitants. Swanton has cited the scarcity of firewood in the Creek towns as one reason for their continual movement from place to place (Swanton 1928b: 726). Perhaps after the start of the Yamassee War, the logs were removed from the stockade and used by the Indians for this purpose. Several explanations for the removal of the stockade walls and the consequent lack of postmolds in the footing ditch can be considered, but none is completely unassailable.

[58]Throughout the entire stockade area, there are many small postmolds apparently belonging to aboriginal buildings of several different culture periods. In the immediate trading house vicinity none of these form any distinguishable patterns. However, several small and discontinuous lines of

38 / Part I. Archaeological Evidence

them can be traced across and through the palisade line itself; in all cases, these lines were intruded upon by the stockade and not vice versa. Many of the single postmolds may be unrecognized refuse or storage pits since they were often reported to have contained corn and in one instance the remains of a reed mat. Apparently, some dark areas first catalogued in the field as postmolds later turned out to be pits although their original designations were not changed. There is also the possibility that some of these postmolds containing corn might actually have been postmolds from corn cribs used by the Lower Creeks. Within the trading house enclosure itself, there are additional postmolds, and some of these form recognizable patterns in spite of the fact that any such patterns were unnoticed or unnoticeable in the field. The most conspicuous of these is a roughly circular arrangement almost ten feet in diameter in the southeastern corner of the stockade. It is certainly a suspiciously symmetrical patterning, but no evidence was found there to indicate that it was any sort of structure or shelter nor was there any unusual accumulation of debris from any of the historic or prehistoric groups.

[59]Within the stockade there should have been traces of the "Storehouses" and "Magazins" used by the Carolinians during the course of the trade. The best candidate for such a building is directly opposite the larger of the two gateways where a small section of the stockade floor was originally reported to bear traces of decayed wood. These were interpreted as the remains of a fallen log cabin until further clearing revealed unmistakable evidence of upright rather than horizontally-laid walls. The postmold pattern indicated the presence of a square cabin (11.2 by 11.2 feet) whose front wall was on a line with the larger of the two entrances to the stockade. Small and mean, this hut was built Indian style of interlaced posts and contained much the same debris—with the significant exception of any concentration of aboriginal ceramics—as the rest of the trading house stockade floor: deer bones, corn cobs, and other organic refuse. The clear alignment of this hut with the gateway indicates that the two were directly related and that the building was somehow connected with the trade. Beneath the floor of this small structure, there were four burials irregularly grouped within a very restricted area. The burial pits were specifically reported to have been beneath the floor and not intrusive through it. Their suspicious clustering in this one spot is apparently only a coincidence in spite of the widely-reported Creek custom of burial within houses.

[60]Other postmolds adjoining this square hut are possibly further evidences of construction within the trading house. A group of them just southwest of the first cabin can be resolved into a rectangular building (25 by 15 feet) that was built of upright poles. The reason for suspecting that

this, too, was part of the trader's establishment is that its dimensions are almost exactly the same as those recommended by the Commissioners of the Indian Trade for the trading house built at Santee in 1716 (McDowell 1955: 80) and perhaps represent a standard-sized warehouse. Another less distinct group of postmolds seems to be a lean- to or addition of some kind to the original square hut. Evidence noted in the field for these two possible buildings is next to non-existant, and the presence of a small complex of European-built structures is not insisted upon here. Suggestive postmold patterns do exist on the flat maps made of the stockade floor, but no real evidence at all was observed in the field to support their interpretation as auxiliary buildings. From what little is known of the physical plant of the trade at other factories, it is certain that such buildings did in fact exist at this one, but the evidence is not present to confirm it.

Five pits were located within the confines of the stockade enclosure, and all of these are refuse pits assignable to the Ocmulgee Fields (historic Creek) occupation. One of this group (feature 20) was in the very disturbed northwest corner of the trading house and was [61]itself intruded upon by another smaller storage pit. The main pit was 8.5 feet long and 6.3 feet wide and quite shallow (12 inches deep at maximum); at least part of it extended well under the stockade ditch, indicating the pit's precedence in time. The smaller intrusive pit was circular, about ten inches in diameter, and had been dug into the north shoulder of the main pit. This smaller pit had been lined with reeds and contained only charred corn cobs and ashes. The dark, discolored soil of the main pit fill contained deer bone, lenses of charred corn cobs at scattered intervals, a few flecks of mica, a single trade pipe stem, and thirty-three historic aboriginal sherds. As usual on this site, the pit contained sherds from several prehistoric horizons. Two small, roughly circular pits (pits 30 and 35), one near the southern wall of the trading house stockade and the other in the northeast section, were without distinctive characteristics and contained but little midden material. Pit 36, which was intruded upon by the Confederate field trench, was reported to have been capped by a layer of prepared yellow clay. The fifth refuse pit of this group from the trading house (feature 21) was similar to feature 20 (above) in that it was shallow and elongated (6.6 feet long, 3 feet wide) and contained a small round pit intrusive into it much in the same manner as the small pit intrusive into feature 20. In this instance, however, no differentiation of the two pit contents was possible, and the case for two separate pits is less secure. Except for the first, none of these pits can be [62]definitely pinpointed as far as their relationship to the surrounding trading house is concerned, but in view of the extreme paucity of English trade goods in them (two pipe stems from the entire five), probably all of them likewise antedate the period of real availability of such artifacts. Three of this group of five pits contained quantities of river mussel *(Elliptio hopetonesis* Lea) as well as deer bone and indicate that as late as the eighteenth century, river mussels were plentiful enough in the Ocmulgee River to have figured in an everyday diet.

The whole section of the Middle Plateau in and around the trading house was the site of Indian occupation for almost as long as the region had any human inhabitants at all, and the historic occupation was not the least of these. Judging from burials and the heavy concentration of historic Indian artifacts, the very land upon which the trading house was built had been an important living area for the Lower Creek town before the Carolinians moved in. After the removal of the stockade, the same land was reoccupied by the Creeks for the brief interval before the Yamassee War forced them to settle again along the Chattahoochee River. There seems to have been an interval of almost nine months between the start of that war and the actual Creek removal (Crane 1956: 183) for the people to have utilized the trading house site for burials, at least, if not for actual living.

One other aspect of the excavation of the trading [63]house stockade itself deserves mention at this point. Since the original discoveries at Ocmulgee, there have been many attempts to identify the trading house remains with one of a number of strictly military forts—Spanish, English, and even French—that were built in parts of the Southeast by these different national groups during the early years of discovery and colonial expansion. Forts of this early period were usually rectangular with small pointed bastions at each corner. The Spanish fort erected in the Apalachicola country in 1689 was just such a structure (Bolton and Ross 1925: 48, 53) as was Fort Loudoun, erected by the Carolinians at a somewhat later date (Kunkel 1960: Pl. 1). Attempts to make a fort out of the Ocmulgee stockade have persisted for many years in spite of its small size, unusual shape (for forts), the large quantities of datable English trade materials that have clearly placed it too late in time for identification with any of the early forts, and the documented presence of Carolinians traders in the Indian towns at the proper time. One of the points frequently cited in this matter (Harris 1958: 36) is that not enough excavation has been done at Ocmulgee to indicate whether or not corner bastions, the principal architectural feature of the early forts, were present on the stockade enclosure. During the two series of excavations at the trading house, the stockade line was exposed twice, and no bastions were present on the corners of the clearly defined enclosure. In the 1939–1940 excavations, postmolds were found in profusion around [64]both the northeast and the southwest corners of the stockade; these were mentioned at the time as possible evidence for some kind of additional structures on the trading house itself. However, they are similar in type and spacing to the many hundreds of other postmolds found throughout the Middle Plateau and cannot be resolved into any sort of pattern. They can in no way be cited to support the existence of possible bastions on the stockade. It is most likely, in view of the great clarity of the rest of the trading house outline, that had bastions formed part of the original structure, they would have been an integral part of the continuous stockade line and would hardly have been overlooked in two long seasons of excavation. Much of the regret expended over the lack of bastions on the Ocmulgee stockade seems to have its origin in a desire for a more romantic interpretation than that of a somewhat prosaic trading house.

The stockade was surrounded on three sides by a shallow ditch that encircled the "gable" end of the structure and the short northeast wall but did not cross the front or impinge upon the southeast wall (Plates II, III, Figure 4). This ditch was in places almost twelve feet wide although it averaged somewhat less (about seven or eight feet) and varied irregularly over the length of its course. At its deepest, the ditch was nearly three feet, but it averaged about a foot less throughout. Since the ditch was roughly saucer-shaped in cross-section, these reported depths are in some measure deceptive and [65]give an impression of actual size that is not accurate. Along the whole length of it, the ditch was very shallow and sloped in from the sides very gradually.

The ditch's regular alignment with the walls of the stockade as well as a liberal fill of historic refuse indicate clearly its temporal relationship with the trading house, but the precise nature of that relationship has yet to be determined. Because of its small dimensions and because it does not completely encircle the stockade, the ditch seems hardly practicable as a moat or fortification trench in an era when moats even around outposts sometimes reached very respectable sizes (see Goggin 1951:160 for an example). For an interpretation of the trading house as a military fort, the partially encircling ditch must be treated as a moat left unfinished at the structure's abandonment or destruction. Judged strictly within the context of the trade itself, the ditch is even more puzzling since no entries in the brief trade records specifically mention moats, ditches, or other earthworks in connection with the operations of trading houses. The original excavators of the site treated the ditch as a possible barrow pit from which earth was taken to provide the supporting ramp against the interior of the trading house walls (Kelly 1939: 331) although the difficulties with an equidistantly placed, regularly aligned barrow pit were appreciated even then. The ditch has also been interpreted as a barrow pit for dirt subsequently heaped against the exterior walls as a partial support for them. There [66]is some archaeological evidence for this interpretation, but it is only of the flimsiest. The 1939–1940 excavations located a zone of redistributed sand and clay around the stockade trench, which could have been thrown up from the excavation of the ditch but could not be established as positively coming from there. Again, the problem of the regularity of the proposed barrow pit is a major one, and this interpretation of the ditch remains highly conjectural.

It is possible that the ditch may have been dug to provide better drainage for the stockade and hence safer storage for perishables. The original selection of the trading house site on fairly high ground shows some concern for a dry locale, and perhaps the enigmatic ditch was simply another precaution against the effects of the moist climate. The *Journals of the Commissioners of the Indian Trade* (McDowell 1955) contain a sufficient number of pleas and commands to those engaged in the trade to be careful of the skins and protect them especially from moisture that such a consideration was a major one in both pre– and post–Yamassee War times. Losses of skins through water spoilage could be a critical factor in determining profit from the Indian trade.

Since the ditch does not intrude at all upon sections of the site that were actually approaches to the trading house and since it does encircle the more vulnerable rear of the stockade, it is probable that the ditch was in some measure defensive, at least to the extent of keeping the Indians at a distance and providing a rear [67]guard to the structure. Its small dimensions and the fact that it is not complete make its classification as an effective fortification or moat rather difficult—at best it could have provided only token defense from any determined attacker. Certainly, considering the long record of abuses of the Indians by the traders and the equally long record of retaliation by the Indians, fortification of the trading stations in some way would be a necessary precaution. One of the very few direct comments available on the fortifying of trading houses in the extant records of the trade is from a 1718 notice to the chief factor among the Cherokee informing him of steps he should take to secure his post from an expected foray by the French. This notice stated that "you are further to desire the Indians to assist you in building Forts at your trading Houses, for the security of yourselves and Goods" (McDowell 1955: 312). Colonel Chicken's fort and trading house at Coronado Sanelo in the Cherokee country is also relevant here (Mereness 1916: 100) as is Thomas Nairne's advice for the construction of traders' "forts" on the Tennessee River (Salley 1947: 198).

The ditch exhibited all along its course a series of strata that provides some information about the occupation of the trading house and the relationship of that occupation to the ditch itself. At the very base of the ditch was a dark blue clay that was almost totally barren of any artifacts. The lack of artifacts in this zone argues against the interpretation of the blue clay as having [68]been water-laid during the period of the ditch's use (Kelly 1939: 331); this blue clay seems rather to have been a natural stratum into which parts of the ditch were originally dug. Over the blue clay there was a thin layer of tan sand that was itself almost entirely free of historic trade goods but contained occasional sherds of historic pottery as well as sherds from preceding occupations. Above the tan sand was a layer of mottled dark tan sand that represented the real historic midden. This layer contained trade goods, historic Indian ceramics, bones, charcoal, shells, and other debris in profusion. Over this lens of historic material was a thick layer of water-laid tan sand and over this tan sand, the heavy layer of modern plow-disturbed historic occupation materials. The thin layer of mottled dark tan sand represents the period when the ditch was open, and historic debris from the surrounding area was dumped or sloughed into it. After this period, the ditch was allowed to fill of its own accord during a time when—judging from the comparatively few artifacts in the water-laid tan sand—there was no occupation of the trading house and were no Indians living nearby.

Like the stockade itself, the ditch contained refuse pits and burials in addition to compact lenses of historic debris. Burials made in both the base and shoulders of the ditch indicate that some of the Lower Creeks were buried there both before its excavation and after it had fallen into disuse (burials 41, 42, and 43). [69]Evidence for burials in it after the abandonment of the trading house, however, is much less satisfactory than that indicating use of the site as a burial area before the stockade's construction. The ditch cut through a number of refuse pits when it was originally dug (pits 48, 49, 50, 51, and 54), but in no case was it possible to determine whether any one of them was actually of historic date or not. In almost every instance, some historic material was present in each pit, but the clearly intruding ditch made accidental inclusion too much of a possibility to ignore. In addition, in almost every one of these pits, numbers of sherds from either simple-stamped or plain Mississippian vessels were present, and historic sherds were in a scarce minority.

Cutting across the Middle Plateau almost to the very walls of the trading house were the hard-packed remains of an extremely narrow trail. This trail could be traced more or less completely over most of its length through Ocmulgee Old Fields (Plate VI). Sections of it were picked up during the excavations not only around the trading house proper but also down toward the Ocmulgee River, where erosion and flooding had completely destroyed all traces of it on the river bottoms. This path, only slightly over three feet wide on the Middle Plateau, was the Lower Creek Trading Path, which was used by generations of Indian traders and by travelers crossing the Indian

44 / Part I. Archaeological Evidence

nations. Among the latter was William Bartram: "about seventy or eighty miles above the confluence of the [70]Oakmulgee, this trading road runs nearly two miles through ancient Indian fields . . . " (Harper 1958: 34). During his visit, Bartram made no mention of the remains of a trading house on the site nor did he refer to any former occupation of this area by the Carolinians. He did describe the conspicuous mounds and other features of the Macon Plateau, and he must have passed right by the abandoned site of the trading house. During the excavations, the path was picked up directly south of the stockade and again northeast of it. Apparently it approached the trading house quite close to the southwest wall and then turned to cross in front of the gates before swinging away to the northeast. The relationship between the stockade and the trading path is unmistakable, and they were for a time contemporaries, co-existing adjuncts of the expanding Indian trade.

The European trade artifacts found within the line of the trading house palisade were the second largest single concentration of such artifacts found anywhere on the Macon Plateau. Their distribution within the trading house offers the only possible way, short of a complete floor plan, of confirming the identification of any of the various postmold patterns as possibly representing buildings of Carolinian origin. The section of the stockade floor in and around the most probable European structure, the small square hut aligned with the main gate, was checked to determine whether or not any large concentration of trade goods occurred there; such a concentration would [71]normally be expected on the site of any kind of European house. However, the number of European trade artifacts in this restricted section is quite small if it were indeed the house of the trader. A few pipestems and bowls, a single sheathed knife, lead shot, blue seed beads, an unidentifiable lump of rusted metal, several gun parts, and a single sherd of English ceramics comprise the total. This small sample of trade artifacts assumes more importance when compared to the overall distribution of such items within the stockade enclosure. Of the seventy-eight early eighteenth century European artifacts found in the humus inside the walls of the trading house, half could be pinpointed within it with reasonable accuracy. These artifacts clustered in three separate areas, one of which was the "log" zone where the small square house had stood. Concentration of trade materials within the next distinguishable level followed a similar pattern, using ninety of the available one hundred and sixty-seven European artifacts. The area of greatest concentration of historic trade artifacts within the trading house (69% of the total) was slightly above the southeast corner, where no clearly discernible postmold patterns occurred. This might mean that the Carolinians had additionally used that particular area for storage or that they had thrown trash there.

The concentration of trade goods in the southeast corner might also mean that there had been heavy Indian occupation of this particular spot before and/or after the [72]construction of the stockade. An examination of the distribution of aboriginal artifacts from the trading house indicates that the whole east half of the enclosure (using the 171-R9 line as a rough divider) contained over 2.3 times as many historic Indian ceramics as the west half, and any accumulations of historic trade goods there may simply be a function of Indian occupation rather than representing any specific occupation by the Carolinians. In direct contrast to this situation, the area containing the square postmold pattern does not show a similar concentration of historic Indian sherds. Hence, the trade artifacts there cannot be interpreted as possibly dependent upon an associated concentration of Indian artifacts. From these two comparisons, it seems that the relatively small number of European trade items found in the cabin or hut do support the contention that it was some kind of European-built or occupied structure. No similar support can be obtained for any of the other possible "Magazins" or "Storehouses" whose postmold patterns are present on flat maps of the site. On the contrary, only a single European artifact came from the suspicious postmold covered area southwest of and adjoining the original hut, and no concentrations of Lower Creek or earlier ceramics hint at an aboriginal origin for them. As before, these postmold patterns remain completely enigmatic.

The small cluster of historic trade artifacts (thirteen) in the very north end of the trading house enclosure may be the result of an aboriginal house site in [73]that area. The whole north corner of the stockade is covered with a very confused mass of postmolds such as might be expected from an Indian house site that had been intruded upon by the subsequent construction of the Carolinian trading house. Several "dark areas" were observed in this sector and burned clay as well as charcoal were reported from there. The postmolds themselves were present both inside and outside the stockade line, and at least one continuous line of them can be traced for a short distance on either side of the wall trench. As was noted above, postmolds were very numerous throughout this whole section of the Middle Plateau although no nearly complete patterns were observed nor were any distinct floors or hearths noted.

It seems likely, in spite of the presence of historic Creek ceramics in very large numbers over one half of the enclosure, that many or most of the trade artifacts found within the trading house pertained to the European occupation and not exclusively to the Lower Creeks. The sheer numbers involved compared with the amounts of similar material from the known house sites argues that the trade goods from the stockade are more likely attributable to a bigger and steadier supply than was available to the average native householder. Acting on the assumption that this indeed was the case, the European trade artifacts (a total of 167) from the sub-humus levels within the enclosure were segregated according to type and enumerated to see if any gross [74]differences could be observed between this inventory and a similar one from the house sites (see Table 1, page 103). The most common item of the trade on the site—clay pipes—were most numerous within the trading house (45.1% of the total) while English ceramics (10.5%), glass fragments (7.8%), Spanish ceramics (5.2%), tools (7.8%), gun parts (10.5%), and ornaments (7.2%) comprised most of the rest of the artifacts that could be identified. Copper scrap was very plentiful within the stockade (5.9% of the total) but was excluded from this comparison since no finished pieces were present. European trade objects from houses I, II, and V (a total of 95) were also separated by type, and a slightly different arrangement was obtained. Pipes comprised only 35.1% of the total while gun parts decreased to 8.8%; glass fragments increased to 14.0% of the total and ornaments to 14.0%. English ceramics remained the same while Spanish ceramics and tools decreased to 3.5% and 5.3% respectively. Copper scrap was slightly more plentiful in the house sites (8.8%) than it was within the trading house. A series of *chi square* tests performed on this information indicates that a similar distribution could have arisen by chance alone and that no actual significant difference in the over-all types of European objects found in the house sites as opposed to those found in the stockade obtain. The only real difference lies in the larger quantity present within the stockade walls.

[75]The picture of the Ocmulgee stockade that emerges from the physical evidence found on the Middle Plateau is clear in its outlines with no evidence available to indicate that it was anything other than a trading outpost. Liberally sprinkled with typical trade artifacts of the early eighteenth century and lacking the ground plan and fortifications of the military establishments of the period, it was situated directly on an important trade route during a time of intense trade with the Indians of what is now Georgia and Alabama. Most likely built of vertically-set logs, it was a pentagonal enclosure with one, possibly several, interior huts or cabins. Its tenure on the Middle Plateau was a brief one, brief enough to have been almost entirely unmentioned in the traders' records of the period and unimportant enough to have been completely forgotten by the time William Bartram passed by its vanished doors.

# 4
# The Lower Creek Town Site

[76]The Lower Creek town that supplied the trading house with skins was one of eleven Indian towns settled on or near Ochese Creek after 1690. The land that was chosen for this particular village after its removal from the Chattahoochee River was already an "old fields" when the Lower Creeks arrived there; and in their legends, at least, they believed it to be the site of their own ancestral home (Harper 1958: 35). Certainly they had no dread of ancestral ghosts and spirits such as were later attributed to the site by the Indians (Williams 1930: 39), for they built their houses within the shadow of the temple mounds and even occasionally buried their dead in them.

Most of the town itself was located directly on the Middle Plateau and on the land around Mound C in what is now a National Park Service parking lot (see Figure 2). It is in this area near the site of the trading house that the bulk of actual physical remains of the town was found. These remains consisted of houses, burials, and refuse pits.

## HOUSES

[77]By 1791, at least some of the Lower Creeks were living in log cabins with chimneys, windows, and doors much like those of their white neighbors on the frontier (Schoolcraft 1855: 294). At the same time, however, houses of an older aboriginal architectural style continued to be built and used by both the Upper and the Lower Creeks. These houses were described in an account of 1739, which stated that "their Houses or Hutts are built with Stakes and Plaistered with clay mixed with Moss which makes them very warm and Tite" (Bushnell 1908: 573). Swan described Creek houses at a somewhat later date as being

> commonly from 12 to 18 or 20 feet long, and from 10 to 15 feet wide; the floors are of earth; the walls, 6, 7, and 8 feet high, supported by

poles driven into the ground, and lathed across with canes tied slightly on, and filled in with clay. . . . The roofs are pitched from a ridge pole over the centre, which is covered with large tufts of the bark of trees. The roofs are covered with four or five layers of rough shingles, laid upon rafters of round poles, the whole secured on the outside . . . by long heavy poles laid across them and tied with bark or withes at each end of the house. (Schoolcraft 1855: 692)

In the interiors, Swan mentioned sleeping platforms on either side of the fire and a single door in one wall near the center of the house (p. 693).

William Bartram (Fundaberk 1958: Pl. 125) differentiated between Upper and Lower Creek habitations, but apparently his Upper Creeks are what are known as Lower Creeks today while his Lower Creeks are the Seminoles. [78]His sketches of either of these two habitations are not detailed enough to show very much of floor plans or any significant interior features of the houses. Other than his comment that the houses were very large and oblong and his drawing of rectangular houses within the Creek towns, he offers very little in the way of structural details of individual dwellings:

The dwellings of the Upper Creeks consist of little squares, or rather of four dwelling houses inclosing a square area, exactly on the plan of the Public Square. Every family, however, has not four of these houses; some have but three, others not more than two, and some but one, according to the circumstances of the individual, or the number of his family. Those who have four buildings have a particular use for each building. One serves as a cookroom and winter lodging-house, another as a summer lodging-house and a hall for receiving visitors, and a third for a granary or provision house, etc. The last is commonly two stories high, and divided into two apartments, transversely, the lower story of one end being a potato house. . . . The chamber over it is the council. . . . The fourth house . . . is a skin or ware-house, if the proprietor is a wealthy man. . . .

The Lower Creeks or Seminols are not so regular or ingenious in their building, either public or private. . . . Their private habitations consist generally of two buildings: one a large oblong house, which serves for a cook-room, eating-house, and lodging rooms, in three apartments under one roof; the other not quite so large, which is situated eight or ten yards distant, one end opposite the principal house. This is two stories high, of the same construction and serving the same purpose with the granary or provision house of the Upper Creeks. (Fundaberk 1958: 115)

Elsewhere, Bartram further described an Alachua (Seminole) house, which at the time differed but little from the [79]dwellings of the Lower Creeks: "the town of Cuscowilla which is the capital of the Alachua tribe, contains about thirty habitations, each of which consists of two houses nearly the same size, about thirty feet in length, twelve feet wide, and about the same in height" (Cruikshank 1957: 322),

Nine house areas were originally described for the Middle Plateau, but only a small number of this group of nine seem actually to be houses. Some of the reported houses are features belonging to earlier horizons while others are not houses at all. In spite of this situation, it is certain that many other historic houses were at one time present both on the Middle Plateau and around Mound C; the quantity of sherds alone testifies to a heavy occupation during the comparatively short time that the Creeks were present in the area. In addition to this purely archaeological indication, many eyewitness accounts describe the Creek towns in Georgia as being fairly large in terms of the number of houses in them. Somewhat later in time than William Bartram's description of the thirty houses of Cuscowilla, Swan said that "the smallest of their towns have from 20 to 30 houses in them and some of the largest contain from 150 to 200" (Schoolcraft 1855: 262). No other house sites were reported from Ocmulgee, though, not even from the heavily occupied area around Mound C. Years of heavy plowing have apparently eradicated whatever remained of them except in the [80]immediate trading house vicinity. Without exception, these remaining house sites are very near the trading house stockade line although this does not mean that any of them were necessarily contemporary with it. The duration of the town on the Middle Plateau was a short one, but there was ample time for the construction and reconstruction of several generations of impermanent Creek houses.

The usual organization of house clusters within the towns or villages was in terms of matrilineally related families, which lived and worked in the same place (Swanton 1928a: 79). Agricultural lands seem to have been in close proximity to the houses, judging from Bartram's diagram of a Creek town (Fundaberk 1958: Pl. 125). In addition to the information in this drawing, he also stated in his text that there are "few instances among the Creeks, of farms or private plantations out of site of the town" (p. 114). Bartram's Alachua Seminoles, however, planted only small gardens around the houses, and their main "plantation" was about two miles from the town itself (Cruikshank 1957: 324). Part of the lands around the Creek house sites preserved at Ocmulgee might conceivably have been part of the gardens or other agricultural fields of one of the Creek kin segments. The lack of other similarly preserved house remains in the vicinity could then be explained in terms of these lands.

House lands and usufruct of particular agricultural areas were not perpetual, and a certain amount [81]of moving around of both houses and gardens was common. Swan stated that the houses were so lightly constructed that new ones had to be built every few years. Since the new houses were always placed on new ground, "by continually shifting from one place to another, the bulk of some of their largest towns are removed three or four miles from where they stood three or four years before" (Schoolcraft 1855: 693). Thus from the archaeological evidence alone, a small town of twenty years duration could appear to be a very large one spread over a large area.

The major evidence for houses located during the excavations on the Middle Plateau was found immediately south of the trading house and directly on the line of the north-south Confederate trench (Figure 3). This whole section of the plateau was covered with many confused postmolds, which probably represent occupations during several different periods by several different groups of people. In four instances, however, clear rectangular postmold patterns were observable and definitely represent the former presence of houses or buildings of some kind. Dating of these four structures must rely on the rather suspect stratigraphic data given in the original field notes and upon such information as is available from the artifacts found within the houses themselves. The field notes describing the excavation of these features place them intrusive from the "old sod" or "occupation zone," which around the trading house has always meant a stratum [82]of strictly historic age; however, it is sometimes difficult to interpret accurately this "old sod" level, which in actual practice has meant several different things during the course of the excavations at Ocmulgee. Dating the structures through overlapping pits or burials has not been possible in this case since those features that were clearly intrusive through, or were intruded upon by, the walls of the houses were not profiled. For this reason, it is next to impossible to get a clear-cut age assignment for any of them in relation to the walls of the houses themselves.

In spite of the real paucity of good information from the ground on the age of these four houses, a fairly solid dating of them can be made using other kinds of direct and indirect observations. For one thing, features such as refuse pits assignable to both the Macon Plateau and the Ocmulgee Fields occupations were present, but the only refuse pit actually within the walls of one of the houses (pit 13) is clearly historic in time. Artifacts present within the house sites also provide some information since the whole area encompassing the four house sites was one of heavy occupation with sherds, charcoal, and other midden refuse forming a thick overlay throughout. The number of historic Indian sherds found in and around the rectangular postmold patterns is quite large and fully supports the contention that houses of historic date were present. There were 5,528 historic sherds from [83]house V and 13,001 from combined houses I and II. European trade artifacts occurred in some number within the boundaries of the houses and, in view of their scarcity elsewhere, seem to support a historic date for the houses. Several historic burials were in the immediate vicinity of the houses (burials 10, 29, and 32), but there were also four others of unknown provenience in the same area (burials 31, 33, 35, and 36). One instance of infant cremation was present just outside the walls of houses I and II, where a whole Ocmulgee Fields vessel was found inverted over a pile of charred bone and charcoal. On the basis of the trade materials, the tentative "historic level of intrusion" cited in the field notes, the infant cremation, the very large numbers of Ocmulgee Fields series sherds, and the correspondence of the house patterns with contemporary descriptions, the four houses have been treated as historic in age. Considering the amount of plowing that was done on the land before the establishment of Ocmulgee National Monument, it could be argued that houses of historic age would be the first to go and that the house sites on the Middle Plateau must pertain to earlier horizons protected by depth from plow and damage. The survival of the eighteenth century trading house indicates, however, that for some reason plowing was not sufficient to eradicate all historic structural remains on the plateau and the same factors responsible for its survival contributed to the survival of nearby historic house [84]patterns. It should again be noted that no other historic house sites were found anywhere else at Ocmulgee, not even in the land around Mound C, where historic ceramics and other debris were very plentiful.

Houses I and II must be treated as a single unit since they were superimposed almost directly, one upon the other (Figure 5). The houses were originally situated about one hundred feet south of the trading house site, and the eastern corners of both were sliced off during the nineteenth century excavation of the Confederate field trench. There were no floor depressions or prepared floors noticed in either house, and for this reason there was no separation possible in the field between the two. Only after both floors had been removed were the excavators able to resolve the postmold patterns into two distinct structures. House I was an almost square building whose diagonal axes ran roughly north-south and east-west. A very large structure, it measured 47.5 by 46.25 feet, almost double the measurements

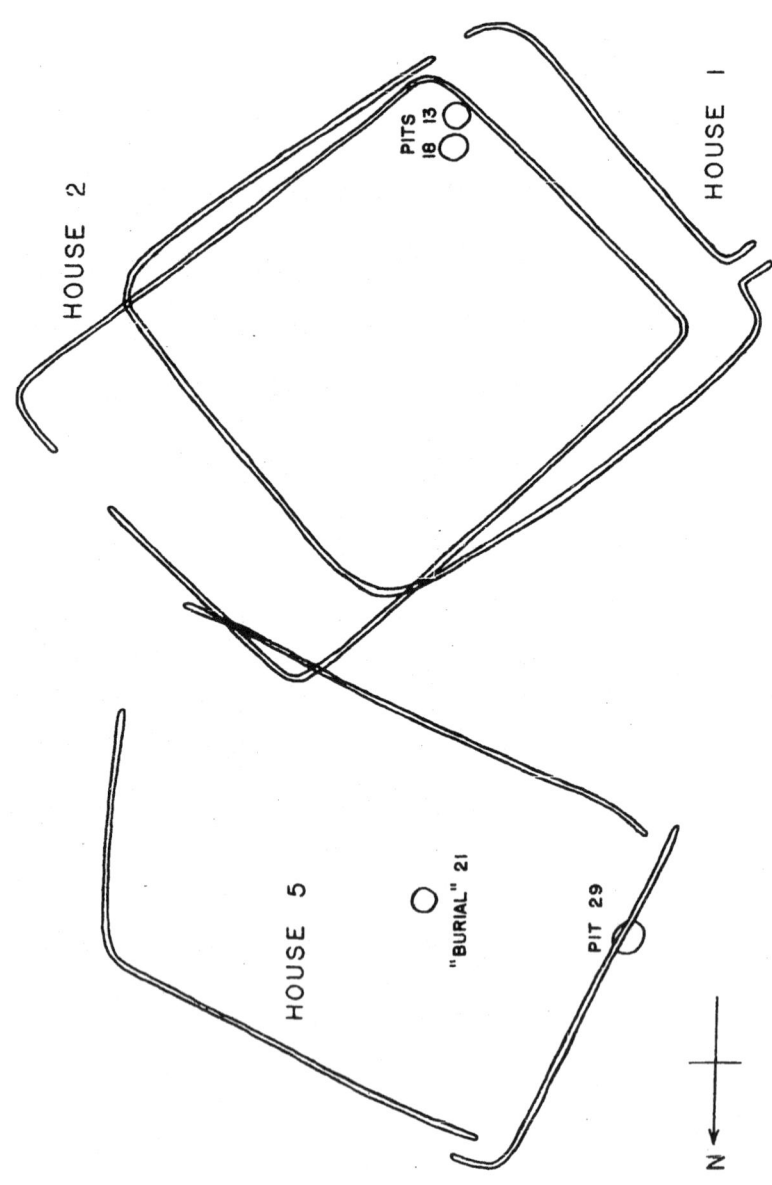

Figure 5. Houses I, II, and V.

recorded by Swan in 1791. It was constructed in the same manner as the houses described by him (Schoolcraft 1855: 692): posts set in the ground, interlaced with cane, and daubed with clay. Throughout the area, debris from these walls was present in the form of lumps of dried (unfired) clay occasionally bearing the impression of a cylindrical object that might easily have been cane. Judging from the size of the postmolds, the house was originally constructed of small trees averaging [85]about six inches in diameter. These poles had been placed in the ground close together in a large square with neatly rounded corners. It is impossible to tell from the postmold patterns inside the structure whether or not interior supports were present for the roof. In view of the size of the building, however, roof supports of some sort seem very likely even though no discernible pattern for such supports is present. Some of the postmolds around the walls inside might represent the sleeping platforms mentioned by Swan (Schoolcraft 1855: 693), but again the evidence for additional interior structures is too confused to be of any value. There are two breaks in the line of the walls that could have served as doorways, and neither of them fits the location cited by Swan ("they have but one door at the side and near the centre of the house" p. 693) and seconded by Bartram (Cruikshank 1957: 322). The first of these possible doors is simply a five foot gap near the lower end of the southeastern wall; the second and more likely candidate is a two and a half foot break near the end of the southwest wall. This latter opening has a long line of postmolds leading out from it for about five feet on either side, almost as if the entranceway were walled for a windbreak or roofed over.

It is interesting to note that this house form, with windbreak, is identical to the Creek hot house in Tuckabatchie described in 1772 by David Taitt. Taitt spoke of the hot house as being "a Square building about 30 feet diameter rounded a little at the Corners; the walls [86]are about four feet high; from these walls the roof rises about twelve feet, terminating in a point on top. The door is the only Opening in this house for they have no window or funnell. . . . there is a small entry about ten feet long built at the outside of the door and turned a little round the side of the house to keep out the Cold and prevent the wind blowing the fire about the House . . . " (Mereness 1916: 502).

Within the house there were two pits (nos. 13 and 18), both of which contained charcoal and other debris. Pit 18 seems to have been a fire pit since it contained ashy soil and large quantities of charcoal, but no sherds or other datable materials were recorded as being found in it. Pit 13 was an oval refuse pit near the presumed hearth; it contained scraps of charcoal and bone as well as enough historic debris to place it definitely within the Ocmulgee Fields occupation. Both pits were located well off center within the house, but they are the only possible candidates for hearths or fire basins. Other floor features included a single historic burial (burial 39), which may or may not have been intrusive through the line of the house wall. This burial was reported to have been forty inches below the present ground surface, a respectable depth for historic burials at this site, while the main house occupation occurred at a reported depth of only about twelve inches. The lack of information about the burial's relation to the house wall may simply be owing to its preceding the house in time and to an originally deep burial pit that was [87]not disturbed by the subsequent erection of the house. The only other floor feature in house I was a roughly circular arrangement of postmolds in the southern end of the house; no unusual characteristics were reported for it in the field, and its suspicious circular shape may be strictly fortuitous.

House II consisted of a rectangular postmold pattern which, while clearly continuous, was more confused and in places very much less well defined than that of house I. It was impossible to determine in the field which of these two superimposed houses was the first to be built, but it is likely on the basis of the far better preservation of the outline of house I that it is the more recent of the two. The two houses shared an almost identical orientation as regards the placement of the walls and were very much alike in size and shape. House II was 47.5 feet long and 42.5 feet wide and had rounded corners like those of house I. In both houses, the wall posts were of the same size. There are several gaps in the line of the postmolds forming the walls of house II, but there is no clear evidence pointing to the location of a doorway and nothing at all approaching the walled or roofed entranceway of house I. For the most part, the two house sites share the same floor features; and it is impossible to determine, for example, which house belongs to which of the two pits.

House V was a very similar structure north of houses I and II and closely adjacent to them (Figure 5). [88]In one place, the wall line of house V overlapped that of house II for a short distance indicating that these two, at least, were not contemporaries. Again the less well-defined outline of house II suggests that it is earlier than house V. Like both of the other houses, house V contained many artifacts within it and scattered unevenly outside the walls all around it. As in the two previous cases, no real concentration of such materials was reported during the excavations except for one refuse pit within the house (see "burial" 21) and a small pocket of midden near the Confederate trench. The house itself was originally rectangular in outline with rounded corners. Wall dimensions were roughly 47.5 feet in length and 39 feet in width, but there was some variation in these figures from one end of the building to the other owing to a rather poor alignment of the walls on the part of the builders. As in the other two houses, no pattern of roof supports can be detected in the many postmolds covering the floor. However, a distinct line of them parallel to the far west wall might have been part of the sleeping platforms that were reported by Swan as a regular feature of these houses.

Since there are three possible places, location of the house entranceway is not quite exact: two of the three possibilities are simply gaps in the wall line, one in the southeast corner and the other in the far southwest end. The third and most likely location consists of a double wall line in the northwest corner. This feature looks as if the walls of the building had simply been [89]overlapped to form a partially walled and/or roofed entranceway about five feet long. The resemblance of this walled entranceway to the walled opening of house I partially supports the former's identification as the doorway to house V even though the two are not identical in execution. Again, none of these possible doors coincide with Swan's and Bartram's middle-of-the-house location.

Several burials were located around house V, but none of historic date was actually found within the walls. "Burial" 21 was the only pit found within the house itself, and it is of unknown cultural affiliation. A single Macon Plateau refuse pit (number 29) was found in the line of the far west wall, but in this case postmolds were specifically reported to be intrusive into the top of the pit rather than the other way around. No evidence at all was obtained for any kind of fire pit except for the brief mention of a baked clay area, which was not further described or even located with certainty.

To the west of house V and occasionally parallel to its walls, there were several lines of discontinuous postmolds which may have been parts of other houses whose total outlines have been obliterated by time and by the subsequent construction of still other houses. In the field these were not treated as separate units since the then existing accumulations of midden around them apparently were not sufficient to stimulate notice of them or to permit their identification as separate houses. They are mentioned here solely because of the presence of [90]suspicious postmold patterns on field maps and not because of any evidence noted during the original excavations.

House VIII was the same type as the three other houses and was located closely adjacent to them (see Figure 5). Smaller than any of the others, it measured only 27 by 23 feet and had squared rather than rounded corners. Its construction was very similar except that this house seems to have had a prepared clay floor. A fire pit, lined with the same clay floor material, was present in the south central portion of the house, but no other pits or floor features were found within the walls. The southwest wall of the house consisted of a double line of postmolds, probably indicating that this area resembled houses I and II in having more than one house superimposed upon another. No clear gaps in any of the walls indicated the presence of a doorway, but a line of postmolds angling off from the house wall in the far west corner might represent some kind of protected entranceway similar to those found in houses I and V. Few artifacts of any kind were reported from within the house or from the area surrounding it, a surprising circumstance considering the quantities of sherds alone from the other house sites. The prepared clay floor itself contained only 168 sherds, and only 18 of these were from historic vessels; a single RT clay pipe was recovered from this clay floor and represents the only European trade artifact found in or around the house. It may well be that the entire collection of artifacts from this house site is not now [91]present at Ocmulgee National Monument and that more material was actually recovered from it than the records show. Certainly, other features of this house site in addition to the artifact collections are unusual and not very precisely reported in the excavation notes. Evidence of some kind of round house was mentioned in addition to that noted for the pattern of the rectangular house, and the nature of the prepared clay floor found in the house site is not clear. As a whole, house VIII is the least satisfactorily described of the known house sites; but it is included here since, like the others from this area, it was reported as being definitely intrusive from the historic occupation level.

The four houses discussed above represent the only really well-defined aboriginal structural remains found during the entire course of excavations on the Middle Plateau. They are, except for size, similar in details of construction to the houses described in the literature for the Lower Creeks at a slightly later date. The closely adjoining houses V and I may have represented part of the four-square arrangement described by Bartram as typical of his time. As far as construction and shape are concerned, these Lower Creek houses have architectural roots in the past: houses of a similar type have been present in the Southeast for many years (Webb 1938).

Several other features were interpreted in the field as evidence for small, oval brush-covered pit-houses made and used by the historic peoples (Kelly 1938: 53; [92]Pope 1956: 49). Since nothing of this kind has been reported by ethnographers or travelers, it is important that their existence be verified if possible and a more complete description be made available. The best record kept for this type of structure was for an area designated "houses" IV and VII, which were treated in the field as parts of a single unit even though they were in fact completely separate features. Both were located at the extreme north end of the shallow ditch around the trading house, and "house"

VII was partly cut through by it. This whole section of the plateau contained innumerable postmolds and refuse pits in addition to the two features designated as house sites. "House" IV was troweled out as a roughly circular midden area about eight feet in diameter with ten postmolds found irregularly placed about the margins. The base of this pit was in fact excavated into the earth although there were no real indications of any floor line or of a definite occupation layer as distinguished from simple pit fill. In places, between the excavated portion of the feature and the surrounding postmolds, there was a narrow ledge interpreted then as a kind of marginal sleeping platform or living quarters around a central domestic pit. "House" VII was northwest of "house" IV and was similar to it except that it lacked the occasional postmold around the margins and was in all respects less distinct. This was probably because the trading house ditch cut through this part of the site and perhaps through [93]part of "house" VII.

Indian and European artifacts were plentiful within both of these features and in the area immediately surrounding them. In this section, there is in fact the greatest concentration of European trade articles (270) found anywhere on the Middle Plateau, including a surprising number of sherds from Spanish pottery vessels (18). The quantity of midden material and the many postmolds over the whole area do indicate that this was indeed originally some kind of house site, but there is not enough evidence to identify the two oval pits as small houses. The large amounts of bone, charred wood, and corn found within the excavated portions of these two features in conjunction with their small oval shape suggest that they were refuse pits rather than being any kind of house sites themselves in spite of the occasional postmold around their margins. The closeness of the trading house and the ditch point to the fact that this entire area was far from being undisturbed, and any features that might have been identified as the actual remains of houses have been obliterated.

A third feature, designated in the field records as house III, was located southwest of the trading house and very near the Lower Creek Trading Path. It was of the same type as the two "pithouses" discussed above although it was apparently somewhat larger. Exact dimensions were not given for it nor are any real details available for comparison.

[94]House IX was found southeast of the trading house and just west of the spring located in that area. Excavation revealed a puddled pile of clay, which was at first thought to resemble the clay floor of house VIII. This floor was quite irregular with no enclosing postmold pattern to give it any outline; because of this, no comments on the shape of the proposed house are possible. Artifacts from the puddled clay area were mainly simple stamped

pottery and Macon Plateau plain wares with only a few historic sherds and no European trade materials present at all.

House VI was cited as being directly opposite the gates of the trading house. No postmolds were observed nor was there any accumulation of midden debris such as might be expected in and around an old house site. Excavations in this area were of an exploratory nature and not enough evidence was obtained during them to justify any attempt at interpreting what was found. A single historic refuse pit was found in the area reported to have contained house VI. This was a large oval pit (eight feet in diameter) whose depth was only about eight inches. The pit was definitely historic and contained many historic sherds as well as English trade goods (eight pipe stems, trade beads, three pipe bowls, and a single gunflint). This refuse pit may very well have been treated as a house site much in the same manner as "houses" IV, VII, and probably III.

During the excavations, the data obtained that have a bearing on Creek architecture and settlement [95]patterns for the first decade of the eighteenth century add very little to the ethnographic picture except to confirm structural details. The only serious discrepancy between these house sites and the descriptions in the literature lies in the matter of size. None of the described houses is nearly as large as the four found on the Middle Plateau around the trading house. If the dimensions as reported in the excavation notes are accurate, then the Lower Creeks in the early part of the eighteenth century were building houses almost twice the size of those described by observers in the last part of the same century. Every since Morgan's pioneer attempts to correlate house type with aspects of social organization, it has been noted that such things as size of family groupings and sometimes even finer distinctions may be inferred from house structure. It is known that the Lower Creeks lived in matrilocal household groups consisting of a man and his wife, their daughters and unmarried sons, and the husbands and children of the daughters (Swanton 1928a: 79). Perhaps a decline in house size reflects a decline in the strength of matrilocality as the political and economic systems were adjusting more completely to the influx of trade goods, the importance of the deerskin trade, and the dominant military pressure from Carolina. It is unfortunate that the sample of Creek house sites at Ocmulgee is too small to be really indicative of such changes, even on a very tentative basis.

Considering the large numbers of historic Creek [96]artifacts found on the Middle Plateau, the real paucity of structural remains is quite remarkable. Nothing at all was found of the usual public buildings or of the square grounds or even of the many more houses that were surely present at one time. It is very likely that years of plowing as well centuries of human occupation have obliterated such traces as did remain of this particular Lower Creek town.

## BURIALS

In striking contrast to the little evidence of houses were the numbers of burials found in and around the trading house and on the rest of the Middle Plateau. This fairly restricted part of the Ocmulgee National Monument site continued to be used for burying the dead from prehistoric through into historic times, a fact consistent with other evidence of occupation by several different groups of people, and as a consequence, a very large number of burials was found. While some of these burials undoubtedly belong to occupations earlier than that of the historic Creeks, others can be clearly assigned to a historic date. Of a total of sixty-seven burials encountered during the excavations, twenty-five are other than historic in origin; ten more are of doubtful origin while thirty-three definitely pertain to the Lower Creek occupation itself. With only a very few exceptions, direct association of a burial with European trade artifacts was the major criterion for assigning a historic date to it. [97]In most cases it is impossible to determine from stratigraphy exactly where in the vertical column burials occurred, and in most cases, artifacts are the only kind of information preserved. Some burials not containing any trade artifacts were further eliminated from a possibly historic category through analysis of burial pit ceramics, when these were available for examination. In most cases this supported the observation that historic burials were almost uniformly accompanied by some kind of European trade materials.

The burials themselves were encountered in almost every part of the Middle Plateau where excavation trenches were run, and it is likely that many more are still present in the unexcavated portions of the site. Specific locations for them included the trading house—within it and even intrusive through the line of the wall and the ditch around it. The occurrence of burials here is probably not a function of the trading house's presence but instead is owing to the fact that the stockade was built in an area previously, and subsequently, part of the original Indian town or village site. Other historic burials were found irregularly over most of the rest of the Middle Plateau. Some of them occurred as late intrusions into Mound C, the Macon Plateau burial-temple mound, and in parts of the historic site around it (Fairbanks 1956a).

Many of the non-historic burials from the site are probably Mississippian (Macon Plateau) or belong to [98]the earlier horizon characterized by simple-stamped pottery (Mossy Oak). In many cases, however, the evidence is not sufficient to make any clear distinction between them. Some of them, certainly, could be historic burials for which there are neither sherds nor European trade artifacts, but most of them seem clearly to be prehistoric in origin.

Skeletal material from the entire group of historic burials is almost completely uninformative. Much of it is missing from the collections at Ocmulgee National Monument, and in most cases where there is bone present, it is too fragmentary for any kind of analysis. A few bone pathologies were noticed, but the very grossest age and sex categories were the only observations possible on the remaining fragments.

With the exception of burials 1, 18, 24, and 38, the following burials are located on Figure 3. Burial 1 was found 390 feet east of the south corner of the large trading house gate while burial 38 was 300 feet east of the same feature. Burials 18 and 24 were found just north of the Macon Plateau fortification trenches, approximately 600 feet east of the trading house stockade.

Burial 1 was one of several multiple burials found on the Middle Plateau. It consisted of three individuals, two superimposed and the third lying slightly to one side (Plate IV). The superimposed pair were clearly within the same pit. Although the general impression obtained from the field notes is that all three were within [99]one pit, the third burial—because of its distance from the other two, its angle of interment relative to them, and the reported small size of the original burial pit—was more likely in a second burial pit intrusive into or intruded upon by the first The superimposed pair were lying south and east in a round or oval pit of about thirty inches in diameter while the third was oriented northwest and southeast in a pit of undetermined dimensions. No information is available as to the level from which any of these burials was originally made, but all three were about two feet below ground surface when excavated.

The three burials were all of adults, and all were accompanied by European trade artifacts. Only one of them, the top member of the superimposed pair, was definitely in a flexed position although the fragmentary burial under it may also have been flexed. The third burial was very poorly preserved, only fragments of the upper half of the skeleton remaining, and it is impossible to determine its position. The top burial contained a large number of red beads with green cores (Cornaline d'Allepo beads, 8 mm. in diameter) as well as a few white porcelain beads (of the same size) in the chest region. The fragmentary third skeleton was accompanied only by five spherical bullets. The second burial, the lower member of the superimposed pair, contained fairly elaborate European equipment: a basket-hilted sword, a small unhafted axe, a badly broken knife, four gunflints, six bullets, a bale seal (Plate XVIII, figure 1, *c*), and two rectangles of glass, which were [100]probably from a mirror. The knife and sword were in the ground parallel to each other with the unhafted axe lying across the sword blade. The bale seal may have been an accidental inclusion since it does not have any readily apparent function in the otherwise coherent complex of burial accompaniments. There was no evidence preserved to indicate that the sword was originally in a scabbard or that the axe was originally hafted.

Other than the fact that it was of an adult individual, burial 3 was too fragmentary for any information to be obtained as to age, sex, or even original position in the ground. This burial was identified as historic on the basis of trade beads and a single musket ball included with it. One conch columella bead was with the burial, but whether it was part of the costume of this individual or only accidentally in the pit fill is unknown.

Burial 4 was found within the trading house and was reported intrusive from the same level as the trading house, "the historic occupation zone." It was also too fragmentary to yield any information as to its age or sex, and since the skeleton is not available for examination, no comments on these details are possible. The burial was reported to have been in a narrow pit about two feet below present ground surface. It was accompanied by ten conch columella beads as well as by blue and white seed beads and a single misshapen bullet.

Also within the trading house stockade, burial 5 [101]was partially disturbed by the excavation of the nineteenth century Confederate trench across the Middle Plateau. Originally the skeleton was lying on its right side with the legs semi-flexed and was oriented in a northeast-southwest direction. The original burial report listed this burial as having been put upright into the pit, implying some kind of "sitting" burial; the extant photograph, however, clearly indicates that it was simply a flexed burial (Plate V, figure 1). The only European trade artifacts present with the burial were white and light blue seed beads scattered in an apparently random manner throughout.

Burial 6 was located northeast of the trading house ditch and between that feature and the narrow channel of an abandoned stream bed. It was found in a small pit just under the humus zone. The burial itself was described in the field as being that of a small female individual who had been buried tightly flexed on the left side (Plate V, figure 2). The skeleton was oriented north and south with the head to the south and the skull facing west. Other than historic Indian sherds in the pit fill, the only historic artifacts were eleven broken blue beads scattered among the bones. A large quantity of flint scrap was present in the pit fill, but this was probably only an accidental inclusion.

Burial 7 was just east of the Confederate fortification trench and at the southwestern tip of the trading house ditch. It was a male individual lying flexed on the [102]right side. Similar in this respect to burial 6, it was facing west and aligned north and south. Several artifacts of European manufacture were in the burial pit, but not all of them seem actually to have been directly associated with the individual interred there: three pieces of glass, probably from a rectangular hand mirror; a rectangular iron nail; one gunflint; a single striped bead; and a small section of rusted iron with inset glass beads. This last rusted item was probably part of a heavily rusted iron implement with glass beads adhering to the surface; it has since been lost and cannot be identified.

South of the trading house stockade and just east of the Confederate trench, burial 10 was made in a deep pit, which must have been intrusive from the historic level. It consisted of an adult male lying on his back with his legs flexed to the right; the skeleton as a whole was oriented east and west with the head to the east (Plate VII). Just over the skeleton, half of an *Ocmulgee Check Stamped* jar had been placed (Fairbanks 1956b) probably as a kind of covering. The closeness of this very large vessel half to the burial and its careful orientation to the skeleton seem to indicate quite clearly that it was a purposeful and not an accidental inclusion. This is the only instance on the Middle Plateau of sherds or vessels being placed deliberately with adult dead, and it has no parallel in contemporary ethnographic descriptions of Creek burials or in any of the more recent accounts. Further protective covering of the [103]burial is indicated by the presence of small bits of a decayed fibrous material in the pit. This may be the remains of some sort of burial wrapping or mat placed around or over the dead. According to the field notes, this burial was also unusual in having an artificially flattened forehead. The Lower Creeks are not supposed to have practiced head deformation (Swanton 1928b: 687) although Samuel Morton, who also denied head deformation among the Creeks, cited it among "some of the Creek tribes on the Gulf of Mexico" (Schoolcraft 1847: 325). Exactly who these Gulf of Mexico Creek tribes may have been is not clear from Morton's account, but conceivably the individual who became burial 10 might have originally come from nearer the Gulf, one of the Apalachee refugees living among the Lower Creeks in the first part of the eighteenth century (Salley 1947: 208). Several European artifacts were found with the burial: hundreds of tiny blue and white seed beads were scattered around the skull, probably once part of a head ornament or covering; eleven bullets of different calibers were found in a group at the waist on the right side where they were in some long-since decayed container. Three of these lead balls were stained with red, the familiar vermillion of the traders' accounts. Twelve large brass bells were strung or sewed on a belt around the waist with three of the smaller copper "hawk's" bells. The bells around the waist can be interpreted as part of a dance costume, for there is one eye-witness account of 1739 which described the residents [104]of Coweta as wearing bells and rattles around their waists during dances (Bushnell 1908: 573).

Another burial from within the trading house stockade, burial 11 was most probably historic in time. The only actual evidence from artifacts, however, is the presence of eighteen historic Indian sherds and a single glass bead in the presumably undisturbed burial pit fill. The burial itself was of an adult male individual who was extended on his back in an east-west direction with his head to the east. The skeleton looks as though it had been hastily pitched backwards into a shallow grave. One arm was thrown back and the feet were fully ten inches higher than the skull. When it was excavated, this burial was just under the humus although the head and shoulders were somewhat lower. The single trade bead in the pit fill was barrel-shaped and of heavily patinated blue glass.

Burial 13, also from within the trading house, was of a young adult. Since the remains were quite fragmentary, nothing definite can be said about position or orientation in the ground. Historic artifacts in the burial pit fill included a single bullet in addition to Ocmulgee Fields ceramics. The burial itself was originally made in a midden scattered with charred corn cobs and other debris. It is one of five burials grouped together in a fairly restricted area within the trading house stockade walls and very near the small hut outline. This grouping does not seem to have any significance relative [105]to the trading house proper or to the probably European cabin and is most likely a pre– and/or post–Carolinian phenomenon.

A flexed burial of undetermined sex and age, burial 16 was unaccompanied by any European material other than a single trade bead found in the pit fill and a single unworked sherd of dark green English rum bottle. The corpse had been flexed when placed in the pit on its left side and was oriented southeast and northwest with the head to the north. This burial is most probably historic although there is the slight chance that the two European artifacts may have been intrusive.

Burial 18 was a cremation which had been placed in a deep, straight-sided pit with quantities of European and aboriginal grave goods. The pile of bone comprising this burial includes not only charred human bone but also deer bones, which may have been part of the debris used to close the pit after the cremation was placed in it. The human bone is that of a very young infant, highly fragmented and charred. Piled on and around the heap of charred bone were a number of artifacts that must be interpreted as actual grave offerings or accompaniments since they are hardly likely to have been the personal property of a very small infant. These artifacts included one flintlock barrel and breech with the gunflint still in place between the jaws (Plate IX, *top*), a necklace of fifteen barrel-shaped conch columella beads, a circular conch shell gorget with three small holes in it (Plate XVIII, [106]figure 2, *a*), a single brass bell decorated with scallops and a pair of initials on the seal, one unworked sherd of dark green rum bottle, a bracelet of coiled iron wire, and eight large barrel-shaped black beads (8 mm. in diameter). In addition to these, there were thousands of purple, red, white and blue seed beads mixed with the cremated bones. Although the burials of very young children ordinarily contained ornaments of some kind, the quantity associated with this cremation is very unusual. Swanton (1928a) quotes from the Hitchcock Manuscript that "'their friends [that is, friends of the dead] frequently throw tokens into the grave'" (p. 393), and something of the sort may have been involved here. Burials of very young infants were not common at Ocmulgee, and it is likely that cremation was the usual type or one of the usual types of burial (see below for analogous examples).

Burials 19 and 20 are particularly important since they were inside the trading house and clearly intrusive into the line of the stockade. They indicate positively that the area once occupied by the trading house continued to be used by the Indians subsequent to the abandonment of the structure and the destruction or removal of the wooden walls. Both of these burials were together in a single pit located just under the humus. Number 20 was an adult, sex undetermined, who lay flexed on the right side with its head to the northeast. European artifacts with this burial were one musket ball, [107]three gunflints, part of a rusted iron knife, eleven white "porcelain" trade beads, a bracelet of coiled iron wire, and a small axe lying near the skull. The other burial was that of a child, who had originally been placed parallel to but slightly below the legs of burial 20. The bones from this burial were too fragmentary for any observations to be made on position in the ground or on actual age except for the fact that it was a child as opposed to an adult or an infant. Artifacts with the child were three tubular conch columella beads (Plate XVIII, figure 2, *c*), an iron knife with no handle remaining, and many seed beads of several different colors (blue, black, purple, red).

Burial 24 was another child. It was lying in an extended position on its back with the head to the north. No information is available on depth or level of intrusion, but the burial is clearly historic on the basis of several historic trade artifacts found in the grave and associated directly with the skeleton. These artifacts of European manufacture consisted of a pair of embossed copper buttons and many seed beads of blue and of white milky glass. Four conch columellas, perforated at one end for suspension, were also with the burial.

Burial 29 was the one burial definitely reported as a "sitting" burial for this site. The legs were doubled, and the upper half of the skeleton was slumped forward somewhat in the manner of the sitting burials described [108]by Webb (1938: Pl. 58) for an earlier group in the Norris Basin. The left humerus was projecting straight up, providing a further reason for labeling this as a sitting burial. Its interpretation as a truly "sitting" burial is very important in view of contemporary accounts describing Creek burials (see below), but as a whole this interpretation fails to be convincing. Burial 29 looks more like a somewhat carelessly disposed flexed burial than like an actual sitting one. The almost complete skeleton was that of a male individual of robust proportions. He had been buried with a number of artifacts: two coiled iron wire bracelets, large blue and white beads (8 mm. in diameter), four gunflints, and a single iron belt buckle. In addition, several hundred red and blue seed beads came from the burial pit fill around the head and shoulders of the skeleton, and a single barrel-shaped purple bead with white stripes came from somewhere in the pit. Other artifacts from the pit fill included a small scraper of dark green glass (probably the familiar English rum bottle) and one very flattened piece of lead shot. This burial was near house V, but its relationship—if any—to that feature is unknown.

Burial 32 was an adult of undetermined sex, who was lying flexed in a northeast-southwest direction with the face toward the southeast. Like the preceding burial, this one was near house V but of no known relation to it. No information about level of intrusion of the burial pit [109]is available, but this burial was definitely historic on the basis of European trade artifacts found with it. Several kinds of beads were found around the neck, presumably parts of a necklace: three blue seed beads and one red bead of the same size, a single long barrel-shaped bead of black glass, and forty large beads that were described as being cylindrical in shape and white, blue, and brown in color. Also in the pit fill were two "hawk's" bells of pewter and two of copper.

Burial 38 was poorly preserved and fragmentary, and no comments can be made about its original position or orientation in the burial pit. The remaining bone fragments are those of a child, and like preceding burials of children, this one was accompanied by beads and other ornaments. Associated with the skeleton were three decahedral beads (one green and two clear glass), eighteen conch columella beads, one copper "hawk's" bell (Plate XIII, figure 2, *top*), two buttons, and four brass wire bracelets. Many other beads of several different kinds were found scattered throughout the burial: red and blue seed beads, light blue seed beads, white milky glass beads, black barrel-shaped beads, and a single white oval bead with olive stripes.

Beads and conch shell ornaments also accompanied burial 39, the partially flexed interment of a young child. This burial was oriented north and south with the head to the south. It was located within house sites I and II and may have been intruded upon by (or intrusive into) the wall [110]of house I. Eleven conch columella beads as well as the ubiquitous multi-colored seed beads were with the burial, and the field notes also mention the presence of eight decahedral beads. These decahedral beads were lost during the excavations, but they were described as of an amber color with a white patina and quite similar to others found on the site. Three pieces of mussel shell were found near the knees of the skeleton, but these were unworked and probably were not a purposeful inclusion.

Burial 42 was found under the trading house ditch. In this case there is a fairly clear profile indicating that there was no burial pit intrusive through the ditch; the ditch was dug right over the burial, badly disturbing it in the process. The burial itself was very fragmentary although enough remained to show that it was an adult individual rather than a child. With the burial were a number of trade artifacts: four bullets, three bells, two buttons, and many beads. The beads included large black beads (about 10 mm. in diameter), purple striped beads, milky glass beads, and quantities of tiny seed beads (light blue, milky blue, white, red), The fact that this burial, definitely historic and very liberally supplied with trade goods, was placed in the ground before the trading house ditch was excavated illustrates that the trading house was not the very first source of trade for these people. The Ocmulgee town clearly had some access to European trade goods a number of years before the [111]stockade was erected among them and the surrounding ditch was dug.

Burial 41 was found in the shoulder of the trading house ditch and, like burials 19 and 20, indicates that burials were made on the site after the trading house had fallen into disuse. The evidence here, however, is not entirely conclusive; the burial may have been made prior to the Carolinian occupation and may have been intruded upon by the ditch rather than vice versa. The burial itself was an adult individual of undetermined sex, who had been interred in a flexed position with the head to the north. European artifacts with the burial were half of a broken black trade bead (originally 10 mm. in diameter) and two sheets of copper rolled into what are apparently some kind of cuffs. Each cuff, almost twelve inches in length, was laced together through perforations in the metal along the edges. Both of these cuffs are presumably arm ornaments, but they could also have functioned equally well as ankle or leg decorations. Both of them were found slightly above the fragmentary skeleton, and their exact anatomical relationship to the bones is unknown.

Also probably pre-ditch in time, burial 43 was made in the west shoulder of the ditch between it and the northeast wall of the trading house. The ditch seems to have cut through the pre-existing burial pit although the field notes are not sufficiently explicit to be entirely certain of it. The skeleton was that of an [112]adult, sex undetermined, who was buried extended on its back with the legs flexed to the left. The burial was oriented northwest and southeast with the head to the northwest. European artifacts found in the pit associated with the skeleton consisted of part of a rusted iron knife blade, a triangular piece of copper scrap, and several trade beads. A single tomato red bead with a green glass core (Cornaline d'Allepo) was also found in the pit fill.

Burial 45 was also made before the construction of the trading house. It was found within the stockade and directly under the area reported to have contained the remains of the presumed European hut or cabin. This burial was specifically noted to have been well beneath this section and not intrusive through it. The burial was of an adult female individual interred on her back with both legs flexed. The skeleton was lying with its head to the west and its feet to the east. Of special interest was the fact that the skull was moderately deformed frontally and occipitally (Fairbanks, 1958 personal communication). With the burial, there were light blue and purple seed beads at the neck and waist as well as scattered throughout the pit fill. A number of black beads with white or silver inlay were also present in the burial but were removed by vandals during the burial's long career as a field exhibit at Ocmulgee National Monument. Other beads present included Cornaline d'Allepo beads (about 8 mm. in diameter) and white "porcelain" beads. Decahedral beads were mentioned in the field notes, but they were not [113]described nor are they presently in the Ocmulgee bead collections.

Burial 46 also came from the section of the trading house stockade near or perhaps under the supposed European cabin. It was reported to have been covered with some kind of clay capping, a unique feature which was not further described or discussed in the field notes. The burial itself was an adult, who had been placed fully flexed in a narrow pit; the head of the skeleton was west while the feet were east. Accompanying European artifacts, all of which were lost during excavation, included an iron knife, some sort of "brass" artifact, part of a flintlock rifle or perhaps a pistol, and the only complete kaolin trade pipe ever found on the Middle Plateau. In addition to these, two gunflints, light blue seed beads, and milky glass beads (about 10 mm. in diameter) were recovered from the pit fill.

Also from within the trading house, burial 47 shared the same general location as burial 46. In this case, too, there seems to have been no direct relationship between the burial and the small cabin located in the same area. The burial itself was an adult, sex undetermined, who had been buried in a flexed position, face down, in an east-west direction. Personal ornaments consisted of light and dark blue seed beads as well as slightly larger milky glass beads.

Burial 51 was in an oval pit on the edge of the trading house ditch in the general area containing [114] "houses" IV and VII although of no known relation to them. It was the burial of an adult of undetermined sex lying fully flexed on the right side (Plate VIII). Accompanying European artifacts were a silver-butted pistol (Plate IX, *center* and *bottom*), six brass buttons, two brass buckles, fragments of cloth, and seed beads of many different colors. A broken piece of metal, presumably the pistol barrel, and lead shot of a size no larger than the seed beads were also present in the burial pit.

Burial 61 was found east of the trading house stockade, between the wall trench and the ditch. It was an adult, sex undetermined, who was lying flexed on the right side with the head to the north. The skull was reported in the field notes as being artificially deformed, but the type of deformation was not recorded nor is the skull itself presently available for examination. The only European artifacts with the burial were numbers of assorted trade beads: light blue seed beads, slightly larger purple beads, a single purple bead of an elongated barrel shape, and one oval milky glass bead.

Burial 62 was that of a child, who had been buried south of the trading house stockade. Only slightly below ground surface when found, the burial showed the results of severe plow damage. For this reason, no comments are possible on its original position other than the general observation that the skeleton seems to have been extended east and west. With the burial were a mussel shell spoon, an iron wire bracelet around the right wrist, and beads at [115]the neck and ankles. Trade beads from the burial included large green-cored red beads (Cornaline d'Allepo, 8 mm. in diameter), white "porcelain" beads, and light blue beads; seed beads of light blue, white, and black; and large white and blue beads, each color striped with red and/or white in pairs or single lines (these beads are also about 8 mm. in diameter). Four tiny coils of copper wire were also in the burial pit and appear to have been strung with the beads; evidence for this comes from a small piece of fiber string found through one of the striped beads and stained with copper salts, presumably from one of the small copper wire coils since no other copper was present in the burial pit. Similar copper coils have been found elsewhere unassociated with beads of any kind (Goggin, Godwin, Hester, Prange, and Spangenberg 1949) so they apparently have been used for several different purposes (Brannon 1935 identifies them as hair coils).

Another infant cremation was found in a small oval pit very near the walls of houses I and II. The cremated bone and associated charcoal were placed under an inverted pottery vessel, probably the base of an inverted *Ocmulgee Fields Incised* olla or jar (Plate XXII, figure 2). Four small stones were found resting on the vessel, but no grave goods or other artifacts were present.

The above twenty-nine burials are those of almost certain historic date. Others may be historic, but the evidence is less convincing. Discussion [116]of these burials is included here for the sake of completeness of the record.

Burial 8, because of its reported location, should be included in this group of possible historic burials. It was described in the field notes as definitely intrusive through the Lower Creek Trading Path and hence of a fairly recent date. There was no European material of any sort with the burial nor were any historic Indian sherds—with the exception of one *Walnut Roughened* sherd—present in the pit fill. The almost total lack of historic artifacts as well as the burial position (fully extended) make the proposed historic date questionable. In addition, the Lower Creeks, however casual they might appear by modern standards in their choice of burying grounds, do not seem likely to have buried their dead right in the middle of what was then a very busy thoroughfare. The burial itself was a middle-aged male extended on his back with his head to the east and his feet to the west (Plate VI).

Burial 12, found just northwest of the trading house entrance, was an adult lying extended on the back with the head to the east and the feet to the west. The skeleton was surrounded by twelve postmolds aligned in pairs around it. This arrangement of paired postmolds suggests that a scaffolding of wood or a little "house" had been erected over the burial. This type of thing has been reported for the historic Creeks (Swanton 1928a: 394), but in this case, unfortunately, no confirmation of it for the early periods can be made. No historic date can be [117]confidently assigned to the possible scaffold since no historic trade artifacts were present in the burial. Although two historic sherds were reported from the pit fill, the predominantly plain ware in the pit was *Bibb Plain,* a type belonging to the Macon Plateau occupation. It is most likely that this burial with its surrounding postmold pattern does in fact belong to the prehistoric rather than the historic horizon at Ocmulgee.

Burial 21 has been cited as evidence that the historic Creeks at Ocmulgee Town regularly practiced cremation of adult dead (Kelly 1938: 52). The burial consisted of a heap of broken bone, animal and human, that was found mixed with other debris in a small circular pit. The pit itself was within house V, reportedly intrusive from the historic occupation level. There are only a few fragments of human bone in this collection of broken and charred bone, and it is most likely that their inclusion in this pit is only accidental. The animal bone, mostly deer and some small vertebrate, is ordinary refuse and was mixed only incidentally with the very few scraps of human bone. This "burial" is better interpreted as a refuse pit, and the human bones in it are the result of disturbance and redeposition long after original interment.

Burial 26 is another example of what was first thought to be a cremation. The bones from the feature are not in the trading house collections at Ocmulgee National [118]Monument, and it is not possible to ascertain for sure whether or not they were actually burned. The extant photograph of the burial does indeed show some human bones, evidently those of an adult; but none appear from the photograph to be at all charred or burned. It is also quite possible that not all the bones from the pit are actually human bones. The bones themselves were in a small pit in the base of refuse pit 33, but it is not known whether the burial pit constituted a separate pit or was simply part of the refuse pit. The evidence available is not adequate to treat these bones as a cremation. The most that can be said is that they are likely to have been part of the disarticulated reburial of a skeleton originally disturbed by the excavation of historic refuse pit 33.

Burial 34 was found in the southern arm of the trading house ditch, It is most probably historic, but there is no really concrete evidence to support the dating. There is no information available as to whether the ditch cut through the burial or the burial was made into the ditch, and no European trade artifacts were found in the burial although historic Indian sherds were present in the burial pit fill. The skeleton was that of an elderly individual, sex unknown, who was buried flexed on the left side with the head to the southeast. If this is indeed another post-ditch burial, then it is further support for the contention that the site was occupied by the Lower Creeks for a time after the tenure of the trading house within the town.

[119]Burial 36 was found just outside house V, but there is no known connection between the burial and the house site. There was no European material in the pit although there were historic Indian sherds present in the pit fill. The whole burial had been badly disturbed, however, and cannot be satisfactorily dated one way or another. Except or the fact that it was an adult, no observations could be made on age, sex, original position, or orientation in the ground.

Burial 40 was found in the east shoulder of the trading house ditch. This is another burial whose position relative to the ditch is unknown, and it is impossible to determine which preceded the other in time. The burial itself was very fragmentary, but it seems to have been that of a child interred in a flexed position with the head to the north. It was unaccompanied by any native or European ornaments.

Four other burials (nos. 44, 54, 58, 64) from the same general area are also very probably historic. In each of these cases, however, information is so limited as to make any discussion of them unwarranted.

During the excavations at nearby Mound C, five historic burials were found, four in the village area and one intrusive into the mound itself (Fairbanks 1956a). Three of the village burials were of children. The first of these was partially flexed on the right side with the head to the southeast; it was directly associated with conch shell beads, a blue glass pendant, and trade beads [120](including three decahedral beads). The second child, also found with conch shell beads and trade beads, was partially flexed and lying face down with the head to the north. The third, represented by only a skull, was found with glass beads and a single olivella bead. The adult burial from the village area was a fully flexed female individual interred with the head to the west; small amounts of iron oxide were present on some of the bones, and an iron trade knife (probably the source of the iron oxide) was found in the grave. The historic burial found intrusive into Mound C was another adult female, who was flexed on the right side with the head to the east; a single red trade bead was the only historic artifact found in the pit. Other burials from this Mound C area were also undoubtedly historic in time, but, as at the trading house, provenience is often impossible to determine.

This entire group of burials constitutes one of the largest available samples of early historic Lower Creek burials and should provide enough information to fill out some of the details of historic mortuary customs in the Southeast. In a number of instances, however, the burials fail to confirm details as stated in early descriptions and mentioned in ethnographic sources on the Creeks. This lack of close coincidence may simply reflect expectable variation within a normal permissible range by this particular group of Lower Creeks, or it may point to the existence of much more fluid patterns of behavior in regard to disposal of the dead than is ordinarily present. [121]In other instances, the burials echo strikingly details of costume and oraments as they are described in the literature and appear in paintings of historic Indians in the early Southeast (Fundaberk 1958).

Many of the early observers of Indians commented on burial position and almost uniformly used terminology that can only be interpreted as referring to flexed burials. Bartram (Harper 1958: 328) described the corpse as being placed "in a sitting posture, as if it were alive." Romans (Swanton 1928a: 392) spoke of the dead as buried "'in a sitting posture,'" and Swan (Schoolcraft 1855: 270) also spoke of burial of the dead in a "sitting posture." Swanton (1928a: 390, 396) quotes sources describing similar "sitting" burials for the neighboring Alabama and Chickasaw. In addition, one of his Creek informants, Jackson Lewis, stated that burials were arranged in that position even within his own lifetime (Swanton 1928a: 395). Undoubtedly these descriptions were all referring to flexed burials, but there are only a few clues in them to indicate exactly what the authors really meant by "sitting" burials, and none of these hints is very explicit. Bossu (Swanton 1928a: 397) intimated that the dead were actually buried "upright" among the Alabama while Swanton, at least, accepted uncritically the literal meaning of "sitting" burials. Thomas (Hodge 1907: 945), apparently following Swan and accepting sitting burials as just that, cited sitting burials for the Seminoles as well as for the Creeks. Of the historic burials at Ocmulgee, [122]only one (burial 29) might be referred to as sitting upright although this one is a very doubtful case. The remainder were uniformly flexed on the back or side except for two fully extended burials of children and a somewhat questionable fully extended adult (burial 11). Notwithstanding the one possible "sitting" burial from the Middle Plateau, it is most probable that the early descriptions did in fact refer to flexed burials when they mentioned sitting ones and that flexed burials were the customary type throughout the historic period. Confirmation of this assumption comes from the Upper Creek site at Childersburg, Alabama, where flexed burials were the dominant type within the town (DeJarnette and Hansen 1960).

Regarding the direction in which the dead were placed, the burials at Ocmulgee do not agree with the few bits of information present in the literature. Very early records do not comment on direction at all, perhaps indicating that orientation of the burials in any one particular direction was not significant. The only precise statement available on this matter is a contemporary one from Swanton's Creek informant Jackson Lewis: "the body was . . . facing east, because that quarter is associated with the renewal of life" (Swanton 1928a: 395). Swanton does observe, however, that facing east and later orientation of the extended corpse with the head to the west was "the custom of most of the Southeastern Indians" (p. 390, footnote). If this was the custom, it was a very [123]late one, judging from the information obtained from the Ocmulgee burials. These have no definite preference for any special direction at all. Of the burials whose head direction was observed in the field, eight were to the north, eight to the south, and three apiece to east and west. Where both directions were recorded, five were north-south, six were east-west, and three others were oriented northwest-southeast.

Since not much information remains about shape of the burial pits, the evidence from the Ocmulgee burials cannot be used to support or refute the data from the written records. Bartram (Harper 1958: 328) mentioned a square pit while Swan described a "round hole" (Schoolcraft 1855: 270) as the typical grave type. There were no rectangular or square pits of any kind reported for Ocmulgee; and where pits are described, they are round or oval ones. All of the historic burials at the Childersburg site were similarly in oval pits (DeJarnette and Hansen 1960).

Many of the historic sources cited burials under the floors of the houses. Like those giving information on burial position, these sources extend in time from the last half of the eighteenth century to the last part of the nineteenth. Bartram (Harper 1958: 328), Swan (Schoolcraft 1855: 270), Gregg (Thwaites 1905: 316), and Swanton (1928a: 393-395) all referred to burials made directly under the house floors. At Ocmulgee, no historic burials at all occurred within any of the known house sites [124]although several were made just outside the walls of house V.

Special treatment of the burial pits themselves seems to have been frequently observed by those attending Creek burials. Bartram (Harper 1958: 328) reported lining of the grave with cypress bark while Swan (Schoolcraft 1855: 270) described an elaborate cane roof and clay cap placed over the burial. Speck (1907) reported the placing of elm bark over the body for the historic Creeks of Oklahoma, and, most recently, Swanton's informant stated that "the grave was lined with split planks, and a rug or else some cloth was placed on the bottom" (Swanton 1928a: 395). Speck and Swanton both reported the construction of a "little house" over the grave, a feature which might be present in burial 12 if it is actually historic in time. Few indications of special treatment of the burial pits were noticed during the excavations on the Middle Plateau. Perhaps the only one was a clay cap possibly present over burial 44. DeJarnette and Hansen (1960: 30) report a possible sun-baked or burned floor for burial 9 at the Childersburg site, but this feature has no analogues at all at Ocmulgee.

A few comments from Swan (Schoolcraft 1855: 270) indicate that the dead individual was wrapped in a blanket and occasionally had the legs bound together. No instance of tying of the limbs was present among the thirty-three historic burials, and the only evidence of burial wrapping [125]was the remains of a fiber covering from burial 10. A few bits of cloth were found in burial 51, but these could have been the remains of clothing rather than a burial wrapping as such. Burial wrappings may have been present at the Childersburg site, where cane matting was reported from two of the burials (Dejarnette and Hansen 1960). The dead seem to have been buried fully clothed as the occurrence of buckles and buttons in the graves indicates, but one modern source (Swanton 1928a: 393) states that shoes or moccasins were removed so that their friends "could not hear them walking about."

Three of the burials from this site were described as having artificially deformed skulls (burials 10, 45, and 61). Other instances of head deformation may have been present but not observable because of extremely poor preservation of the skeletons. Of the three examples present, one was reported as a frontal deformation and another as frontal-occipital; the third was not described. The available evidence is not sufficient to completely refute Swanton's blanket statement (Swanton 1928b: 687) that the Creeks did not practice head deformation in historic times, but is sufficient at least to challenge it and to suggest qualification. As a whole, head deformation among eastern groups did tend to disappear as acculturation proceeded, but probably more of them practiced it than is evident from modern ethnographic sources.

There is little information in the historic sources [126]about the burials of individuals other than "warriors," and it is difficult to interpolate from this any data on the dress or ornaments or differential treatment of the burials of other segments of the society. Specific burials at Ocmulgee (burials 1 and 51) contained, often in very close detail, remains of personal artifacts described by Romans, Bartram, and others as accompanying the burials of warriors, and this paraphernalia seems fairly common as everyday articles of dress among many of the historic tribes of the southern frontier (Fundaberk 1958). Not enough data are available from the burials to describe with any accuracy differences in dress and ornaments between men and women, those in their prime and the aged.

There is, however, one correlation between a special age group and an artifact type that is particularly striking. The burials of children were distinguished by the presence of conch shell ornaments. A total of seven of the nine burials of children were accompanied by conch shell beads or pendants. These ornaments seem to have been the exclusive property of children judging from their almost complete absence in the burials of adults. Conch shell beads occurred with only two burials (burials 3 and 4) other than the seven burials of children mentioned above. Only one of these, however, was surely an adult (burial 3), and in this specific case, the direct association of the single conch columella bead with the skeleton is questionable.

[127]The importance of conch shell ornaments among the Indians of the Southeast has a very long and respectable history, and the demand for conch shell extended from earliest prehistoric times well into the historic period. James Adair mentioned the importance of conch shell beads among the Chickasaw and stated that conch shell was once highly valued: "formerly, four deer-skins was the price of a large conch shell bead" (Williams 1930: 179). The association of conch shell ornaments at Ocmulgee with children illustrates the progress made by European ornaments in competing with native-made ones. As native-made ornaments began to lose ground, they were replaced first among adults and last among the children, who became

heirs of what was beginning to be stylistically outmoded. Interestingly enough, a similar situation obtains at the Childersburg site, for the only conch shell beads found in burials there were also found with the burial of a child (DeJarnette and Hansen 1960: 29).

Only two of the burials from the Middle Plateau were multiple burials. One of these (burials 19 and 20) could have been the burial of mother and child although, since the sex of the adult member is unknown, there is no evidence to support such an interpretation. If this is the case, however, it is the only example; all other burials of children are single ones. The other multiple burial (burial 1) was of two adult males who died at the same or nearly the same time. It is known from Adair (Williams 1930) that the Chickasaw, [128]similar in so many ways to the Creeks, regularly brought home the bones or bodies of those who died at a distance. He does not say, however, that all of those thus returned were interred in the same pit, something that certainly might have happened, considering the resulting economy of effort. Burial 1 could have been an example of this sort of thing as well as simply the consequence of several local deaths at the same time, but its interpretation one way or another cannot, of course, be substantiated.

Swanton, discussing the burial of infants, stated that "among all of the Creek tribes a miscarriage, a stillborn child, or a very young child was laid away in a hollow tree where it was nicely ceiled [sealed?] in" (Swanton 1928a: 398). There is no evidence preserved at Ocmulgee to support this statement, but a number of factors indicate the presence of a pattern other than, or in addition to, that cited by Swanton for the disposing of infant dead. There are two definite infant cremations among the thirty-four historic burials from the site. One of these cremations (burial 18) was simply placed under an inverted pottery vessel. Two other similarly inverted historic vessels were found in the site, but in neither case was the debris under them checked for bone or charcoal nor was any of this material saved for later examination. In two of these three cases, the inverted pots were themselves weighted down with stones, and in the third, sherds from another larger vessel seem to have served the same function (Plate XXVIII). There are enough [129]data present to indicate that cremation of infants was practiced among these people and that such cremations were at least occasionally—perhaps usually—placed under inverted, weighted pottery vessels. It is tempting to consider this a survival of traits from the days of urn burial in the Southeast, but if there is any connection, it is too tenuous to trace for sure.

The quantity of artifacts buried with the historic dead at Ocmulgee is quite considerable when compared to the amounts found in graves of earlier horizons on the same site. In most cases, material interred with the dead is personal property rather than offerings or conspicuous waste at death. The artifacts found in the graves are things in daily use by the individuals buried there and are by extension simply aspects of their personalities, inseparable from them at death. In only one instance, burial 18, do European and native artifacts seem to be offerings or gifts rather than the personal effects of the dead: this is the cremation of an infant and seems to be somewhat of a special case. Apparently by the time European observers recorded burial customs, personal effects were still the only burial accompaniment although two of Swanton's sources cited the inclusion of domestic animals (chiefly horses and dogs) with the dead (Swanton 1928a: 392).

Some of the burials from the Middle Plateau have provided valuable information on the relative dating of other features. Burials in and around the trading house [130]proper indicate very clearly the time relationships between it and the Indian settlement in the same area. Burials 42, 43, and 45 show that there was extensive occupation of the trading house site prior to its erection while burials 19 and 20 confirm the fact that settlement continued there for a time after the destruction, dismantling, and/or abandonment of the trading house by its builders.

## REFUSE PITS

Many pits identified as refuse pits (a total of 58) were located during the excavations. Separation of these and assignment of them to their proper cultural context has not always been possible. In some cases, the pit contents have been lost or mislaid and the surviving information is simply that of the pit's existence. In other instances, disturbance and intrusion have rendered the otherwise adequate information suspect. As a general statement, it can be said that few of the refuse pits from this site yielded any really trustworthy or usable information.

Seventeen pits of completely unknown cultural affiliation came from the double line of the Macon Plateau fortification trench, which once encircled parts of the Mississippian ceremonial center. These refuse pits were located in the shoulders, floor, and on the banks of the trenches. In no case was the contents of these pits available for examination, and in at least some [131]instances, the "pits" themselves were only discolored areas first given pit reference numbers and then retained as pits in the field catalogue when in actuality no refuse pits were present at all. It is highly unlikely that any of these pits were historic refuse pits since the Mississippian fortification trenches were apparently filled in by the time the Lower Creeks arrived on the site in the late seventeenth century. Most of these pits were probably made during the Macon Plateau occupation but fairly late in the sequence after the trenches ceased to be an important functional part of the town site.

Twenty other pits from the Middle Plateau were attributable to some horizon other than the historic one. Six of these pits contained large quantities of simple stamped sherds (*Mossy Oak Simple Stamped*). Three of them (feature 25, pits 2 and 44) were certainly Early Woodland in time, but two others—although containing numbers of simple stamped sherds—also contained several fragments of a refired Mississippian style vessel with an incised and punctated design and a small shoulder node (pits 3 and 48). Similar fragments, apparently from the same vessel, came from a third refuse pit (pit 47), which contained Macon Plateau material as well as numbers of simple stamped sherds (*Mossy Oak Simple Stamped*). This refired (burned?) Mississippian vessel is unlike the Macon Plateau ceramic series in decoration, but because of the burning which has reduced the sherds to little more than cinders, no comparisons can be made as far as ware characteristics are [132]concerned. Its apparent Mississippian style is solely the product of over-all shape and the presence of the single distinctive shoulder node. One other probable Early Woodland pit (pit 49a) was located in the trading house ditch and was cut through by the original excavation of the ditch. This was a small oblong pit (38 by 20 inches) whose contents were entirely simple stamped sherds.

Eight of the total number of pits were Macon Plateau refuse pits (pits 12, 29, 50, 51, 52, 54, 55, and feature 35), but in three instances (pits 12, 29, and 50) small numbers of historic Creek (Ocmulgee Fields) sherds were also present in them. In two of these three cases (pits 29 and 50), this was most likely the result of intrusion by house V and by the trading house (respectively). The third case (pit 12) could have resulted from mixture in the field during excavation or from actual disturbance and intrusion by unknown agents. Four other pits that could be definitely identified as Macon Plateau refuse pits came from the Mississippian fortification trenches. Two of these (pits 19 and 22) were reported from the base of the trench, and two others came from its shoulders (pits 38 and 45). One other non–Ocmulgee Fields pit from this area was modern (refuse pit 43), containing twentieth century trash.

Seven historic refuse pits (pits 1, 8, 11, 27, 33, and features 23 and 32) were totally unassociated with any other major site features. There was also no pattern [133]observable in their distribution nor any conspicuous clustering of them in any one spot. One of these pits (pit 11) was similar to the large elongate pits from within the trading house (about 7 by 3 feet) and quite shallow. Like the trading house pits, it contained animal bones (chiefly deer) and charcoal as well as numbers of historic aboriginal sherds. Five others of this same group of refuse pits were roughly circular or oval and ranged in diameter from thirty to thirty-six inches. Their depth averaged about seventeen inches with a range from a shallow ten inches to a deeper twenty-eight inches. Each of these pits contained historic and prehistoric sherds, occasional small bits of bone, charcoal, trade goods, and in one case, conch and mussel shell as well.

Pit 8 contained an inverted *Ocmulgee Fields Incised* cazuela (Plate XXI, figure 2), which had been weighted down with small stones. The soil under this vessel was not examined for carbonized bone or charcoal, so it is not possible to state that this was an instance of an infant cremation's being disposed of under an inverted, weighted vessel. This is, however, an additional example of the "inverted, weighted pot" trait and lends some support to its interpretation as an actual pattern of behavior rather than an accidental occurrence. The inverted vessel in pit 8 was placed in the very bottom of the pit, weighted down with four small stones, and then covered with rubbish. The refuse heaped over it included twenty-one fresh water mussel shells as well as many historic [134]Indian sherds.

Pit 33 was reported to have contained in its base a small pit which was not clearly part of the main pit nor could it be distinctly separated from it in the field. This small pit contained part of disarticulated burial 26, a burial of unknown time or culture. Burial 26 was either the original occupant of the ground and was intruded upon by the excavation of refuse pit 33 or it was actually interred in a smaller pit in the base of the refuse pit. The absence of any similar burials within refuse pits and the disturbed condition of the burial argue that the interment actually preceded the pit in time and was disturbed by it. Pit 33 was a historic refuse pit, oval in shape and about thirty-six inches in diameter; it contained historic aboriginal sherds and a single gray gunflint.

Other historic refuse pits occurred within the walls of the trading house (pits 30, 35, 36, and features 20 and 21), within houses I and II (pit 13), and elsewhere on the Middle Plateau. There is no real clustering of any of these pits except at the north end of the trading house ditch in the area designated as "house" sites IV and VII (not to be confused with separate refuse pits bearing the same numbers). These two "houses" were part of a very disturbed area whose major feature was a number of refuse pits, some of which were found in conjunction with postmolds. It seems obvious from the amounts of refuse and pottery as well as from the large numbers of [135]scattered and confused postmolds, that there once was a structure or house, perhaps even several houses, present in this area at one time. There is no real justification, however, for considering that the refuse pits also found in the same area were in actuality those houses. It is extremely difficult to comment on the contents of the two refuse pits designated houses IV and VII since the whole section at the north end of the trading house ditch was treated as a single unit without much separation of what was obtained there. Within this large section at the north end of the ditch, there were three historic refuse pits ("houses" IV and VII and refuse pit 28). One of them ("house" VII) was partly intruded upon by the trading house ditch, thus establishing a primacy in time for this one over the Carolinian stockade. Pit 55, cited in the field notes as intrusive from the floor of "house" IV, may be a Macon Plateau refuse pit or at least part of one.

"House" III seems to be another historic refuse pit although information on it is less adequate than for the two similar features mentioned above. It occurs in an occupation area of some sort, but the concentration of historic materials is less than would be expected from an actual historic house site, and the almost total lack of European trade artifacts from the supposed floor is surprising. Postmolds were present in the "house" area, but no patterning of any kind was observable. Two clearly defined historic refuse pits (pits 7 and 17) occurred [136]within the general area of the proposed house site. The original location of one of these, pit 7, may have provided the stimulus for interpreting the whole area as a house site since some soil discoloration was observable for a distance in and around the pit. Pit 17 was a very shallow pit, five inches at its deepest, and was almost circular, with a diameter of about forty-three inches. This particular pit was reported to have been purposefully lined with clay although in this section of Georgia, clay in the pits should have been a natural feature and an almost constant factor. Pit 7 was also very shallow and measured only four inches in depth when completely excavated; in shape, it was elongate rather than round, measuring sixty by twenty-three inches. Pit 7 contained a variety of European trade artifacts including a ramrod worm, an iron knife, trade beads, part of a swingletree, and a single European button. Pit 7 also contained aboriginal sherds of both historic and prehistoric types. Both pits 7 and 17 as well as the whole section including "house" III are immediately adjacent to house sites I, II, and V and are in such close proximity that they might well be considered part of that complex rather than an entirely separate area.

Somewhere within the area designated as "house" site III, another inverted vessel was found, this time a globular *Walnut Roughened* bowl (Plate XXV) that had been weighted down with four large sherds from a second *Walnut Roughened* vessel (Plate XXVIII). There is no information on a pit containing this weighted bowl, nor was the soil under [137]it checked for the presence of charcoal or burned bone. However, in spite of the lack of evidence, this seems to be another instance of a similar trait present in pit 8 and near houses I and II.

Pits attributable to the Ocmulgee Fields occupation occurred throughout the Middle Plateau; and, although data are nowhere complete on all of them, a summary statement can be made for those where sufficient information is available. Historic refuse pits ranged in size from long oval pits over eight feet in length to small circular pits only thirty inches in diameter. Many of those excavated were quite shallow, sometimes only four or five inches in depth, although in at least some cases this was owing to former deep plowing in parts of the area and to subsequent removal of the upper portions of the pits. An occasional straight-sided pit was described (pit 1, for example), but the usual shape was more of a bowl shape with gently sloping sides. Pits used for refuse and for corn storage were both reported, but no association of shape or size with proposed function could be determined. Refuse pits were not localized in any one particular area, but they seemed to occur wherever sufficient excavation had been carried out on the Middle Plateau. At most, they occurred in rare groupings of two or three, never in sufficient numbers to indicate a really dense population or an area occupied for any real length of time.

Charred corn cobs from one of the pits described in the field notes as a "corn storage" pit were sent to [138]the Ethnobotanical Laboratory of the Museum of Anthropology at the University of Michigan for analysis in 1949. The report, issued in 1951, described the corn as having from eight to fourteen rows (with an average of 9.8 rows) and being little over one centimeter in diameter (averaging 1.5 cm. with a range from 1.1 to 2 cm.). All of the examples sent to Michigan fall within the Eastern Maize complex range, the kernels apparently being typical of that type. No information could be obtained as to whether the corn was of the flour or flint variety.

The occasional occurrence of charred corn still on the cob in so-called corn storage pits presents a real problem in interpretation in the Southeast. It is difficult to understand how so much corn could have been burned accidentally in storage pits or why corn was ever stored in pits at all when the familiar Southeastern corn crib was so widespread. It is also difficult to understand why charred corn or cobs in these supposed storage pits seem to have been accorded special treatment as regards their disposal. Dan F. Morse (1960) has pointed out from recent work in Georgia that not only burned corn-on-the cob but also shelled corn cobs have been found in specially prepared pits, treated in what was apparently a special manner: "there were four rows of corn cobs on top of a stratum of wood fragments and shavings, bark, and a few corn cobs. Each row consisted of cobs laid side by side and oriented so as to be perpendicular to the cobs of the row above or below" (Morse 1960: 4). There are sufficient [139]references in the ethnographic literature on the ceremonial firing of corn in the busk of the Southeastern Indians (Swanton 1928a: 555, 578, 580–581, 588, 595) to support Morse's contention that the caches of burned corn frequently encountered on sites in the Southeast "indicate a special ceremony connected with corn and fire" (p. 4). He further advances the thesis that "this is why there is so much evidence for agriculture in Mississippian components [compared with] . . . very little direct evidence of agriculture in Woodland sites; that is, certain peoples purposely burned corn kernels or cobs in Green Corn ceremonies or something similar, hence leaving it preserved for hundreds of years afterwards" (p. 4). The several pits on the Middle Plateau containing large quantities of charred corn-on-the-cob would fit easily into this hypothetical framework since the Creeks participated in elaborate Green Corn ceremonies well into modern times.

# 5
# Artifacts

[140]Because the Macon Plateau is a multi-component site with no really air-tight stratigraphic separation of cultures, it is often totally impossible to determine whether a given artifact belongs to the Lower Creek occupation or not. Only in the cases of pottery, a few other aboriginal tools and ornaments, and, of course, the articles brought into the town by trade can artifacts be unquestionably assigned to the historic period. This situation means that the artifact inventory presented here is not as complete as is ideally desired nor as truly representative as it might be. Because of the influx of trade goods, however, the sample of Creek artifacts is less unrepresentative than it would be for any prehistoric component on the same site. Substitution of European artifacts for native-made ones reduced considerably the scope of aboriginal manufacture and eliminated many kinds of native-made artifacts that would normally be present. The severe atrophy of Indian handicrafts is illustrated more easily on unmixed sites in other areas of white contact. This same situation obtains, and native-made artifacts other than pottery and an occasional [141]projectile point are very few in number (Boyd, Smith, and Griffin 1951).

## TRADE ARTIFACTS

The course of the Indian trade moved a tremendous amount of European goods into the Indian country to be incorporated into the native culture. The extent to which these innovations really represented alterations in the basic technology of the society has yet to be assessed in all its detail, but certainly they caused changes. More important to the culture as a whole, perhaps, as an instrument of social change was the immediate juxtaposition of a primitive method of production and distribution with the exploitative, money-based system operated by the traders. This is probably a classic example of such a meeting since it was totally unhindered by the ameliorating influence of the clergy (see Klingberg 1956: 111 for relations between one

Carolina clergyman and the traders) or the regulative influence of a strong government. The total effect produced in the economic system cannot be considered here since at this point the artifacts themselves are the major focus of attention.

One very early discussion of the Indian trade as a business divided the articles traded to the Indians into two separate categories, those destined for neighboring groups and those directed at the Indians in the interior. This discussion recommended that "if you barely design a home trade with neighbour Indians . . . your best truck is a sort of coarse Trading Cloth . . . as also Axes, [142]Hoes, Knives, Sizars, and all sorts of edg'd tools, Guns, Powder, and Shot, etc., are Commodities they will greedily barter for; but to supply the Indians with Arms and Ammunition is prohibited in all English Governments" (Courtenay 1907: 175). The Indians in the interior were to be supplied with less utilitarian goods: "to the remoter Indians you must carry other kind of truck, as small looking glasses, Pictures, Beads and Bracelets of glass, Knives, Sizars, and all manner of gaudy toys and knacks for children . . . " (p. 175). The prohibition on trading arms and ammunition to the Indians did not survive for very long the realization that greater profits could be obtained from the trade if the natives were provided the means for killing deer on a large scale. This, coupled with the fact that the Indians themselves developed an insatiable appetite for guns, soon made firearms the important staple in the trade. Guns, incidentally, were among the most expensive items available to the Indians with each rifle bringing the traders the exorbitant price of thirty-five skins in 1716 (McDowell 1955: 89).

In addition to guns and ammunition, a number of other tools found their way to the frontier through trade: hatchets, broad hoes, knives, axes, and scissors. Significantly, though, much of the bulk of the "truck" brought to the frontier consisted of apparel and ornaments—hats, coats, girdles, beads, paint, and shirts (McDowell 1955: 89). By 1751 the list of ornamental [143]attire had grown to include such exotics as galix shirts, "osnbrigs," hose, handkerchiefs of India, fine "rufel" shirts, fine ribands, gartering, and even worsted caps (McDowell 1958: 146). This list is an important indication of the expansion in material needs occurring among the Indians. No longer were their desires limited by the traditions of their society, but they were expanding to include a larger and larger number of ornamental nonessentials.

### *Gun parts*

Guns and gun parts were among the most numerous of the English trade materials recovered from the trading house and Lower Creek town site at Ocmulgee. This emphasizes once more the notorious importance of guns in the Indian trade and illustrates the speed with which the Indians learned to appreciate firearms once they were made available. In the Southeast, guns not only provided the Indians with an obvious advantage, or at least an equal opportunity, in warfare but also gave them the means for participating in trade on a far grander scale than was possible on a bow and arrow basis. Firearms made the deerskin trade practically an assembly-line affair. All during the history of the trade in the Southeast, guns moved into the area at a prodigious rate while deerskins moved rapidly in the opposite direction.

As a group, the guns brought to the frontier through the trade were not of a single uniform type. The [144]English flintlock was undergoing a fairly rapid evolution during the seventeenth and eighteenth centuries; and many minor variations in cock shape, sear attachments, lock shape, and so on occurred during that time. Because of these minor variations, flintlocks may often be very accurately dated, sometimes to within ten or fifteen years. In spite of this close dating, however, flintlocks must be handled carefully when used to date the sites upon which they are found. This is because the minor variations in the parts of the guns, when treated as a complex, pinpoint only the date of *manufacture* of a particular piece. Guns used for the Indian trade did not always reach the frontier immediately after their manufacture, and in many cases a long time lag was likely to be present. At any one place in the Carolina back country, arms from a number of periods may be found, depending upon the rapidity of distribution from the English manufacturing centers and upon the vagaries of a trade in which the old and outdated were often sent to be sold to the Indians.

Recognizable gun parts from the Middle Plateau consisted of fifty-nine pieces: three lock plates with almost complete mechanisms, seventeen mainsprings, six frizzens, five lock plates, thirteen cocks, two frizzen springs, three gun screws, four tumblers, two sears, one trigger, one pan, and two flint screws. In addition, several barrels and broken sections of barrels were recovered, but they were too rusted and fragmentary for [145]any descriptions of them or comments on them to be made. Generally, most of the gun parts are from light fowling pieces, which the Indians preferred to heavier guns such as those used by the military. Many of them also appear to be of good quality, a characteristic usually conspicuous by its absence in items destined for the Indian trade. Most of the gun parts from this site were recovered from the trading house and its immediate vicinity although guns and gun parts were also found in and around the houses and in several of the burials.

Two of the lock plates with almost complete mechanisms were from burials. One of these (Plate XI, figure 1, *a*) was from burial 18, the cremation of a young infant. It is a true dog lock from a pistol or light fowling

Artifacts / 85

piece and dates from 1625 to 1645. A frizzen of the proper size to fit this piece was also found and with the lock plate forms the earliest English arms from the site (Plate XI, figure 1, c). The other lock plate was from burial 51 and is a pistol plate dating from between 1700 and 1710 (Plate IX, *bottom*). This piece has an elaborate silver butt ornament decorated with four female heads, which seem to represent classical figures, and four floral forms, which resemble fleurs-de-lis (Plate IX, *center*). There is only one small hallmark on the butt ornament; and since European hallmarks of this period usually consisted of two or more marks, it identifies the piece as probably of American manufacture (Wyler 1937). The mark itself is a heart with the initials "IH" inside. Beneath the two initials [146]is a small indistinguishable raised design, and what appears to be a small circle lies between them. There are two American silversmiths known to have used this hallmark: John Hastier and John Hull, perhaps the most prominent colonial silversmith of the period. Hull worked in Boston around 1645 and continued operations for most of the rest of the seventeenth century. Hull's later products are not likely to be very helpful since after 1652 they were usually signed with the hallmark of his partner, Robert Sanderson, in addition to his own heart-shaped hallmark. John Hastier lived in New York and made silver artifacts around 1726. Judging from the date of the lock plate, Hull was too early to have made this particular piece while Hastier's single date as given in the hallmark lists is too late (Okie 1936). This is one instance in which archaeological data can provide supplementary information for the hallmark lists. John Hastier is known only for the 1726 date, which may actually be late in his productive career. The 1700–1710 date on the silver-butted pistol combined with the date of the site itself indicates an earlier working date for him and provides evidence for a more exact temporal range for his products.

Three of the gun parts—a lock plate, cock, and frizzen—belong in type to a heavy English military dog-catch flintlock. The dog-catch flintlock was the predominant English military weapon in the area through the Fort Frederica period (1736–1742), at least, and was probably in use for an even longer span of time. This [147]particular dog-catch assemblage (Plate X, figure 2, *c, d, g*) dates between 1690 and 1720 and is typical of the military flintlocks. The frizzen (Plate X, figure 2, *d*) is heavy, crudely made and almost lopsided while the cock (Plate X, figure 2, *c*) is squat and flat with the tumbler screw fused to its obverse side. The lock plate itself (Plate X, figure 2, *g*) is broad and heavy. Military weapons of this kind were often poorly made and at this site, at least, offer a sharp contrast to the lighter, more gracile trade guns.

As a whole, trade guns from the Middle Plateau fall into the first part of the eighteenth century, a dating consistent with the information obtained from historic records. The guns are as a group very uniformly made with little real variation from piece to piece. Some of the cocks are feathered (Plate X, figure 2, f). indicating guns of better than average quality, but the majority are completely plain. Most of the guns were light fowling pieces, the most popular type of trade gun, although at least one of them (Plate XI, figure 1, e) was a flintlock pistol. Only one of the gun parts falls outside of the time range set by the other pieces. This is a feathered cock (Plate XI, figure 1, f), which was dated between 1725 and 1740. It may have been early enough to have been contemporary with the trading house, but it would have been brand new in 1715.

On the other end of the time scale, a small iron artifact was tentatively identified as a matchlock pan cover (Plate XVIII, figure 1, d). Because only a small fragment [148]of it remained, positive identification of this artifact was impossible, and it cannot be taken as unassailable evidence of the presence of matchlocks on the site. Although matchlocks seem unlikely in the Ocmulgee area in the early eighteenth century, they are certainly not entirely out of context there. Matchlocks had two possible sources: the Spanish used them in the early days of exploration, and as late as the founding of South Carolina, matchlocks still appeared in the lists of equipment to be used by the settlers (Salley 1928: 8).

The only positively identified ornamental hardware from firearms was a single brass side plate from a trade gun (Plate XVIII, figure 1, e). It was made in the usual stylized serpent design, but it is completely plain and very simply arranged. It has none of the customary embellishments at all. Like the other trade gun parts, it dates from the first part of the eighteenth century. One other brass artifact, a rear gun sight, might also be considered ornamental hardware although its primary purpose was certainly a functional one. This piece (Plate XVIII, figure 1, g) also dates from the first part of the eighteenth century.

Although three pieces from the site belong to a military type of weapon, the guns from the trading house and Creek town were, as a whole, light trade guns. Almost all of them were long guns, or fowling pieces, with an occasional pistol among them. With but one possible exception, the feathered cock discussed above, the gun parts date from [149]the very first part of the eighteenth century or earlier, and in no case does a date very much later than that seem to be supported by them.

Associated with the firearms were gunflints and musket balls, necessary adjuncts of the gun trade proper. Many of the gunflints (Plate X, figure 1, h, i, j) recovered from the site were of black (probably English) flint or taffy-colored waxy flint (also probably English in spite of the traditional identification of tan flint as being French). Gunflints of native material and native manufacture, however, were not uncommon. Even though they were often considerably worn and fractured before being discarded, gunflints were occasionally reused as scrapers (Plate XIV, figure 1, *j*).

Musket balls of many sizes were found all over the area (Plate X, figure 1, *d*). They ranged in size from extremely tiny shot (3 mm. in diameter) to large lead balls of five times that size (up to 17 mm. in diameter). Many of these were certainly imported into the area, but others may have been made on the frontier itself. While no bullet molds were recovered at Ocmulgee, small hand molds have been found in other Creek towns in Georgia (Willey and Sears 1952: Pl. I). Some of the musket balls were intact when found, even to the original mold marks; others were in all stages of flattening, from completely flat to only slightly misshapen.

Only one ramrod worm was found on the entire site (Plate X, figure 1, *c*), testifying, perhaps, to the kind of [150]care given the guns by the Indians.

## Majolica and olive jar sherds

The most positive evidence for some kind of Spanish contact with the Creeks of this town site is the group of olive jar and majolica sherds that was found on the Middle Plateau and around Mound C. The greatest concentration of these artifacts was at the north end of the trading house ditch in the area designated as "houses" IV and VII. Since one of these features is most probably pre-ditch in time, it seems to indicate that the Spanish material in it may also have been deposited there before the digging of the ditch and the construction of the trading house. However, this is not a necessary conclusion, for Spanish majolica and olive jar sherds on this site have two possible sources. They could have been acquired by the Indians during their residence on the Chattahoochee River before the Creek removal to the Ocmulgee River area or they might have been brought from Florida as loot from the many raids conducted by the English and the Indians against the missions and the mission Indians of Apalachee. The latter seems more likely in view of the fact that the Spanish were not trading with the Lower Creeks and apparently had few but military or clerical contacts with them. There is also the slight possibility that the majolica may have been brought to the frontier by the Carolinians. European ceramics were scarce in the early days of colonization, and majolica has been found on [151]English sites where there is no evidence of direct Spanish contact (Cotter 1958).

The majolica included seven sherds of *San Luis Polychrome* (Plate XII, figure 2, *c, d, e*), one of *Castillo Polychrome,* one *Abó Polychrome* (Plate XII, figure 2, *f*), four *Puebla Polychrome* (Plate XII, figure 2, *g, h, i*), and six unclassified sherds (Plate XII, figure 2, *a, b*). The unclassified group contains two white glazed pieces, one gray-green sherd, two black-on-white striped, and a large blue-on-white striped sherd with a strap handle. This last sherd may have been of Spanish rather than Mexican origin as were the others. As far as dates for these type of majolica are concerned, *San Luis Polychrome* and *Castillo Polychrome* date roughly between 1660 and 1720 while *Abó Polychrome* and *Puebla Polychrome* date from the last half of the seventeenth century. Since the sherds are so small, little can be said about vessel form in this collection. One of the *San Luis Polychrome* sherds, however was part of a plate ring foot while several rim sherds seem also to have been from broad plates or bowls.

Majolica from the village area around Mound C included one unclassified sherd that had been perforated and made into a crude disc (Fairbanks 1956a: Pl. 20, b). None of the sherds from the immediate trading house area were so treated, and the majolica disc remains a unique occurrence.

In addition to the majolica, twenty-four sherds [152]of green-glazed Spanish olive jars were found. These were recovered from almost every section of the site with only nine from the vicinity of the trading house itself. The sherds are too small to provide any information about body size or shape, but the original vessels were probably the typical globular or elongated globular jars. Fairbanks has pointed out (1958 personal communication) that the fact that all these sherds are glazed contrasts with the situation on Florida mission sites, where both glazed and unglazed olive jar sherds are found. This suggests, at least, that only the better olive jars—the glazed ones—found their way into Lower Creek hands, presumably as selected loot from the missions.

## Beads

Trade beads were once destined to become the currency of the Carolina frontier by the Lords Proprietors (Rivers 1856: 368); and in spite of the failure of this scheme, the beads themselves remained a vitally important part of the Indian trade. They are usually the most ubiquitous of European trade artifacts on contact sites, and such is the case at Ocmulgee, where large numbers of trade beads of many different kinds were found. In spite of their volume, however, trade beads are one of the least satisfactory of the European artifacts to date. Only a few minority types can presently be dated within short enough time spans to be useful while the great majority are datable only within the limits of a century or so. [153]To complicate the matter even further, some kinds of trade beads have remained in production until the the present and are worthless for dating purposes. Opaque blue seed beads, for example, are made in Venice today and have not changed in style and color for over two hundred years.

For purposes of rough classification, the beads from the Creek town and trading house at Ocmulgee were grouped into five general size categories, which were quite uniform for all colors of beads. The first was a category of the largest beads found on the site, averaging ten millimeters in diameter; the second group consisted of somewhat smaller beads averaging eight millimeters in diameter while the third category averaged six millimeters in diameter. The fourth bead group averaged five millimeters in diameter, and the fifth category included all beads three millimeters in diameter or smaller. It is this last category that is referred to in this paper as "seed" beads. The "seed" bead category could further be subdivided into three very uniform size classes: three millimeters, two and one-half millimeters, and two millimeters. As far as sheer volume is concerned, this last general grouping, seed beads of all three sizes, was the most plentiful on the site while the largest sized beads, ten millimeters in diameter, were the least common.

In color, the beads are white, blue, purple, black, turquoise, and tomato red with green glass cores. This last type, the familiar Cornaline d'Allepo or Hudson's [154]Bay bead (Plate XIII, figure 1, *bottom*), is often longitudinally striped black or white over the red surface. Occasionally a milky white or "porcelain" bead is similarly striped in blue and/or red over the white surface (Plate XIII, figure 1, *top left*). The Cornaline d'Allepo bead type ranges from New York throughout the middle South and extends in time from the seventeenth through the nineteenth centuries. At this site, it is found in several different size categories, including seed beads. In the north, at least, seed beads of this type seem to be principally post-1677 (Pratt 1961: 14).

Minority bead types found during the excavations include a number of decahedral beads. Thirteen of these were reported although eight of them were lost or stolen during excavation (find 3605). Several others were mentioned for burial 45 but never seem to have been properly catalogued, and eight more were found in the village area around Mound C. The decahedral beads now present in the trading house collections are all amber in color except for one green bead (Plate XIII, figure 1, *top right*), a single bead with a milky whitish surface (Plate XIII, figure 1, *top*), and one clear glass bead (Plate XIII, figure 1, *bottom right*). Some hand-pressed decahedral beads seem to be among the earliest of trade beads, and the transparent hand-pressed decahedral beads have been considered the bead type of Desoto's time. As a group, though, the decahedral beads are thought by some to be generally confined to the seventeenth century (DeJarnette and Hansen 1960: 57, 58). [155]According to this dating, the decahedral beads from Ocmulgee, if they are to fit in with the rest of the chronology, must date from the very end of the period of popularity of decahedral beads in the Indian trade of this area unless they are heirlooms from early Spanish contact. In New York, however, beads of this type are considered to be post-1710 (Pratt 1961: 19). With but one exception, all the decahedral beads from the Middle Plateau were found in burials.

In addition to the decahedral beads, a number of other distinctive types were recovered. Among them was one red glass tubular bead with a green core that was found on the surface. Large black barrel-shaped beads, ten millimeters in diameter, occurred in very small numbers; these barrel-shaped black beads have irridescent, patinated surfaces and are the only beads at all affected by soil chemicals. A number of black beads with white or silver inlay (or paint?) were mentioned as stolen from one of the burial exhibits near the trading house (Fairbanks, memo on file, Ocmulgee National Monument). These beads seem to have been unique since no other similar examples were found anywhere else on the plateau. Another group of missing beads was also described as being very unusual: these were forty large blue, white, and brown cylindrical beads, which were mentioned in the field catalogue but never appeared in the laboratory.

[156]Twenty-six of the burials at the trading house and town site were accompanied by beads, but these provide only a few clues as to how the beads were actually worn. In a few cases, distribution of beads in the neck region indicates that some were worn as necklaces, perhaps the most common use of beads up to and including the present day. Many of the portraits and sketches of southeastern Indians confirm this fact not only for the Lower Creeks but also for many of their neighbors (Fundaberk 1958). In one instance (burial 10), blue and white seed beads were found scattered around the skull, perhaps indicating their use as part of a head covering or head-dress. Burial 29 had thousands of large white beads, light blue seed beads, and Cornaline d'Allepo beads scattered around the head and shoulders, perhaps also as a head covering or ornament. In one case (burial 62), beads were used as ankle ornaments as well as for necklaces. One burial (burial 45) had beads around the waist, probably part of a sash or belt. Seldom was any one bead type favored to the exclusion of others, and bead types were mixed in making ornaments without much apparent regard for size, shape, or color. Conch shell beads were strung with the glass beads, and even small copper coils were used as beads and strung along with the others (burial 62).

### Kaolin pipes

There were many broken kaolin pipe stems and pipe [157]bowls recovered from the Ocmulgee site. Analysis of variation in European clay pipes as a means for dating post-contact sites is a widely used tool in historic research. Like pottery, pipes are a sensitive index to change since over fairly short periods of time they are subject to many minor but significant variations in shape, size of spur, angle of bowl rim to stem, and so on. Sometimes more helpful than change in silhouette are the initials and makers' marks that were occasionally placed on the bowls and on the stems. In some instances, these can be traced to point of manufacture and directly to a specific pipe-maker. Clay pipes provide a more sensitive temporal indicator than flintlock parts, for example, since the clay pipes were inexpensive, easily broken, and very often replaced.

Of the pipe bowls found at Ocmulgee, most were unmarked, but several bore unadorned initials and/or rouletted lines around the rims of the bowls (Plate XIV, figure 2). Five of the broken bowls were marked with the incuse initials "RT" and one with "RB." The "RB" pipe may have been made in Hull, England, sometime after 1683 when a pipemaker with those initials, Robert Burrill, was first entered on the freemen's rolls of that city. Robert Burrill and his heirs of the same name continued to manufacture pipes in Hull through at least 1774 (Sheppard 1912) although the custom of marking pipe bowls with makers' initials was discontinued early in the eighteenth century in Hull (p. 16) and not resumed until much later. The "RT" pipes may have been [158]made by Richard Taylor (or Tylor) of Bath; by Thomas Roden, who operated around 1654; or by Timothy Risbett, who was admitted to the freemen's lists in 1669 (Oswald 1951). Other possible makers of the "RT" pipes are Robert Tippet and his son and grandson, all of whom made kaolin pipes in Bristol in the late seventeenth and early eighteenth centuries (Kurjack 1961: 22). The "RT" pipes have such a large number of possible makers that they are particularly difficult to tie down in time.

Pipes from the Middle Plateau, judging mainly from their silhouettes (Oswald 1951), fall within a 1680–1720 time range although there is the possibility that one or two of them might be slightly earlier. The sample of pipes used to determine this time range was quite small (only nine specimens) since only exceptionally was enough of the bowl and stem present to determine the lines of the silhouette with any accuracy. Seventy-one other bowl fragments proved to be of little or no diagnostic value in determining original pipe shape.

The diameters of the holes in the pipe stems were measured in order to determine whether the date obtained from this method would confirm that arrived at by examination of bowl shape. There has been considerable discussion of this as a dating technique (Harrington 1954; Chalkey 1955; Omwake 1956), and in this case a study was undertaken partly as an independent check of the method. A collection of 437 pipe stems, all those that could be measured accurately, was used; and as far as this site is [159]concerned, the use of pipe stem hole diameters was very successful, the date obtained being precisely within the time range determined by the dating of other artifacts and the use of historic sources (Irwin 1959). The year of mean deposition of pipe stems at this site is 1709.9 or 1710, a date in close agreement wlth other information on the date of the trading house and town.

In addition to the group of white English trade pipes, there was a small number of mold-made clay pipes of similar shape and clearly of non-native manufacture. These pipes are distinctive in being of a reddish brown or terra cotta color. They never have makers' marks or decorative rouletting on them, and from the few pieces of bowls recovered it is possible to say only that they are not spurred and seem to be as large or larger than the largest of the white kaolin pipes. In keeping with their size, the stems of the pipes are also more massive than their white counterparts with stem hole diameters of 6/64 or 7/64. Because of these differences, the terra cotta pipes were omitted from the analysis of hole diameters and were not classified as to time period by the silhouette chart for white clay pipes (Oswald 1951). There seems to be no really clear information available on the origins of these unusual pipes although brownish pipes apparently like them have been found at Jamestown (Cotter 1958), where they were thought to have been of local manufacture. According to Smith (1956: 93), however, pipes of [160]Spanish make may also be of a similar reddish-brown clay.

*Coins*

Only two coins were recovered from the trading house and Lower Creek town site. This could be considered peculiar in a site whose most salient characteristic is its commercial nature, but in this early period the common currency in use beween the Indians and the Carolinians was, of course, deerskins. The prices set for the trade goods were in number of skins rather than any number of coins, and it is doubtful that the traders ever had the occasion to use very much actual coined money during the course of business on the frontier (see McDowell 1958: 89 for some common equivalences of trade goods and deerskins).

The first of the two coins is part of a Spanish silver piece that was found within the trading house stockade. There is only a very small part of the coin remaining, and it seems to have been originally cut in half and then pounded out and ground smooth. On both faces of the coin, the metal bears minute striations resulting from the smoothing process. What is left of the obverse of the remaining section of the coin bears part of the word "Philip" (PHIL) encircling a quartered shield of arms. The only devices that can be identified in the quarters are rampant lions, which are probably coupled with small castles, the arms of Leon and Castile. To the left of the quartered shield, there is part of a capital letter "F," which may refer to a coin series printed in [161]a particular place. The reverse of the coin bears two fire-crowned pillars, the Pillars of Hercules, emerging from the sea; and across the pillars there are two distinct lines of letters. In the top line, only the single letter "I" is visible, but the second line is more complete, containing the letters "SVL" and "T." All of these letters are part of the phrase "PLVS VLTRA" (Plus Ultra), which occurs on many coins of Spanish make. There may be additional letters (or numerals) beneath this line, but they are indistinguishable. The Pillars of Hercules symbol with the shield of arms on the obverse is an early type of Mexican (or South American) made issue which was discontinued as far as silver coins are concerned after May 10, 1570, when Philip II decreed that the coinage of the Spanish colonies should thenceforth resemble that of the mother country (Director of the Bureau of the Mint 1912). The Pillars of Hercules symbol appears again in a stylistically more sophisticated version in 1732, a version that is quite unlike that on the Ocmulgee specimen. The Ocmulgee coin, then, must date from the reign of Philip II (1556–1598) in the period before the decree of 1570 and the replacement of the Pillars of Hercules symbol.

The presence of an ancient Spanish coin in the Ocmulgee area is consistent with the position of Spanish coinage in the world market at that time. In Carolina, as well as in the other British Colonies in America, the greater part of the gold and silver coins in use were of foreign make. Not many nations were able to provide [162]themselves with sufficient currency; and Spanish coin, readily available and abundant, functioned as an international medium of exchange. The Journals kept by the Commons House of Assembly in South Carolina devote space year after year to describing in detail the exchange values of Spanish coins then current in the colony (Salley 1925, 1932, 1947). Even as late as 1775, "Spanish Dollars" were important coins in circulation (Williams 1930: xxii).

The mutilated condition of this particular Spanish silver coin and the fact that it had been hammered out may mean that it had been in possession of the Indians and had been used as a source of metal for ornaments. A more likely reason for its condition, however, is that it had been legally halved or quartered during circulation, making it a half or quarter "dollar." It may also have been illegally tampered with in order to make it stretch further as money. Clipping and defacing the current coin of the province was widespread enough in Carolina to require specific legislation against it (Salley 1913: 5).

The second coin from the site is a small round silver coin (Plate XVII, figure 2, row *c, center*) whose surfaces are too worn and defaced to provide any means of identification. It has two holes drilled in it, one on each edge, and was probably used as some kind of ornament. Similar treatment of metal discs (some of them medals) perforated near the margins and strung around the backs has been reported from a historic site in Maryland (Ferguson 1940).

## Metal tools

[163]Among the articles brought to the Ocmulgee River area through the deerskin trade were many kinds of objects destined for the tasks of daily life, which somehow managed to continue in spite of the changing political and economic scene. Axes, hoes, nails, chisels—all of these things became part of the everyday pattern of existence. Although the new tools wreaked havoc on the native industries and handicrafts, they were undoubtedly welcome labor-saving devices.

Four different kinds of axes were recovered from the excavations on the Middle Plateau. The first of these types (represented by four specimens) is the common "trade" axe with a slightly flaring bit end and a loop eye haft hole (Plate XV, figure 2, *bottom*). These axes were made by doubling over a long metal strip and using both ends as part of the blade. One of those found at Ocmulgee had been continually trimmed down until the remainder was only a short stubby tomahawk. There were no observable makers' marks on any of the axes from this group. The second axe form is a fairly large and heavy axe, slightly flared at the bit end and with a haft that was formed by looping over one end of the original metal strip until it touched the blade (Plate XV, figure 2, *top*). The third type of axe is represented by one axe with a broken haft hole. It is distinctive because of a widely flaring bit and blade that contrast with the rather narrow bits and blades of all the other axes. One other axe form that occurred [164]at Ocmulgee was a long parallel-sided specimen with a broken haft hole (Plate XV, figure 1, *b*). This long axe has manufacturers' marks on the blade: the Initials "RB" or "RR" set within a circle. There are two of these marks, one beneath the other, and they appear to be exactly the same except that one of them is slightly less distinct than the other. Many of the axes used in the trade were brought from England, but some were manufactured in Charles Town by the gunsmiths (Salley 1907a).

Four hoes or pieces of hoes were recovered from the excavations, and these, too, represent several different kinds. The commonest is a sturdy iron hoe with a broad rectangular blade (Plate XVI, figure 1, *right*). It has a small heavy eye socket with a projecting spur on it opposite to the eye's attachment to the blade. The other hoe style, represented by only one specimen (Plate XVI, figure 1, *left*), has a thinner blade and a large eye socket with no projecting spur. The whole tool is less well made and of a much lighter construction than any of the other hoes.

Other metal tools include a die for stamping metals which was found inside the trading house stockade (Plate XVIII, figure 1,*f*). The stamp consists of the Roman numeral "VII" and is of the type used to stamp gun parts. It is so cut that impressing it would produce a reverse image of the numeral in the metal. This particular tool is hardly usual as an article of commerce in the Indian trade since it is an implement involved in the manufacture of goods [165]rather than being a good itself. However, it could have been part of the tool kit of one of the itinerant gunsmiths who regularly visited the trading houses and outlying towns for the purpose of repairing guns.

The only other iron tool found at Ocmulgee was part of a chisel or "hollowing adze" (Plate XV, figure 1, *c*).

## Seals

Many of the bales of merchandise that moved from Charles Town to the frontier were sealed with lead seals that attested to the quality and quantity of the goods inside. A few of these seals were found at the trading house, but none bore recognizable dates, names, or any of the other information usually impressed in the lead. On one bale seal (Plate XVIII, figure 1, *c*), the letters "AND" can still be seen, possibly the end of "England," but the portion commonly bearing the date is missing. One other seal (Plate XVIII, figure 1, *a*) was impressed with lettering, this time a monogram letter "S" in combination with what appears to be a letter "T." Who or what this monogram refers to is unknown, but it may be some kind of shippers' seal. Considering the number of glass bottle fragments found on the site, some of the seals were very probably from rum or wine bottles although most seem to have been on bales of merchandise.

## Knives

Knives, scissors, and other similar cutting implements were among the most popular items in the Indian [166]trade. They are usually mentioned in the same breath with arms and ammunition by observers commenting on artifacts destined for the trade although they figured less spectacularly in the history of white contact with the Indians. Twenty-three small knives and three large ones were found in the Middle Plateau area. Five of the small knives were from burials, and nine others were found within the line of the trading house stockade. Many of the small knives had tangs for the attachment of handles (Plate XVI, figure 2, *top*) while only a few were made for screw attachments. The three large knives are all very similar in general size and shape (Plate XVI, figure 2), and all three have screw type handle attachments.

96 / Part I. Archaeological Evidence

One of the large knives was found in a sheath under or in the floor of the small hut within the trading house. The sheath was made in part of a coarsely woven fabric that covered the tip of the knife. While the central part of the blade was apparently encased in wood decorated with metal brads, none of the handle survived at all.

One scissor blade and handle was found inside the stockade. This piece was made of iron and resembles in general shape the scissors of today.

One section of a sword blade and an almost complete sword were the only large edged weapons found. The nearly whole sword, found with burial 1 (Plate IV), has a basket hilt and a slightly curved blade. A bone handle was described by the field crew, but no trace of it [167]presently remains on the sword. There are no observable identification marks on either the blade or the handle, but this type of basket-hilted sword was in use in the New World after about 1650 and was the standard English sword form for most of the eighteenth century (Peterson 1956: 84).

*Ornaments*

Decorative artifacts of many kinds besides beads were brought to the frontier through trade. Purely non-utilitarian decorations—bells, copper ornaments, wire bracelets—were immensely popular if sheer number is any indication. In addition, as articles of European dress became more common for the Indians, the hardware of colonial clothing appeared more often among the trader's wares (Salley 1941: 24) and in the debris at post-contact Indian sites.

Bells in particular seem to have been very popular among the Indians. Both the large harness bells and the tiny "hawk's" bells were common in the excavated areas of Ocmulgee Town. The large harness or "horse" bells were often elaborately decorated and sometimes stamped with initials, a practice that should aid in eventually producing some usable dates for them. Several kinds of signed and decorated brass harness bells occurred on this site. The most elaborately decorated of them were impressed with scallops, fine line designs, and sometimes small seals with initials on them. The initials on these bells are [168]always on either side of the slit opening in the bell and sometimes face away from it. The initials on the brass bells consist of the letters "CI" or "CL" (Plate XIII, figure 2, *top left*) and the familiar "KW." The "KW" bells have been found on historic sites in the Southeast that have a fairly long range in time and apparently were used as trade goods over much of this long time span. Copper bells of the same size as these brass bells also occurred at Ocmulgee but were never decorated with any kind of designs. The completely plain copper harness or "horse" bells, however, often bear single stamped initials, "D" in one instance (Plate XIII, figure 2, *bottom left bell*), "N" in another (Plate XIII, figure 2, *bottom right bell*). The very smallest copper bells (Plate XIII, figure 2, *center bell*), those called "hawk's" bells, occurred in small numbers but bear no identifying marks or decorations at all. These small copper bells were versatile costume ornaments and were worn in many ways. Catlin, for example, illustrated them worn at the knees, sewed on decorative shawls, and attached to trouser cuffs (Catlin 1913). In addition, the bells were even strung as beads and worn as part of a necklace (burial 32). James Adair mentioned them as ornaments on moccasins and hunting boots and as decorative additions to "war pipes" (Williams 1930: 8, 179). From the evidence obtained at Ocmulgee, there was only one use of the large harness bells; twelve of them were found around the waist of burial 10 as part of what was probably an ornamental dance belt.

[169]Buckles and buttons from the eighteenth century occupation were difficult to identify because of the frequency of nineteenth and twentieth century forms on the site. Confederate soldiers lost an amazing number of buttons during military activities on the Macon Plateau, and subsequent visitors to the site have been equally obliging. The buckles and buttons illustrated on Plate XIII, figure 2, *right* and *bottom left,* are those for which a good association, usually presence in an undisturbed burial, is available.

The Indians made considerable use of sheet copper for ornamental purposes. The sheet copper may have been brought to the frontier in the form of copper kettles (McDowell 1958: 85) although leftover pieces such as bails and bail hoops are not at all common. There are, however, large numbers of odds and ends and small scraps of copper sheeting which look very much like the debris of *in situ* manufacture, and at least some of the copper ornaments can be proved to have been made at Ocmulgee (see below). Whether or not the people bought the raw materials and made all their own ornaments or whether or not some of the copper ornaments were brought to them in finished form cannot be answered from the information available here. The most that can be said is that some of them were made by the Indians, but perhaps not all of them. The lists of merchandise carried to the Indian towns (McDowell 1955) certainly support the idea that the copper ornaments were all Indian-made, for they do not mention any kinds of copper ornaments except buttons. The lists do, however, [170]continually contain references to the familiar copper kettles, which, by the way, were sold to the Indians by the pound.

Most of the copper ornaments were tinklers and copper tubular beads of various lengths (Plate XVII, figure 2, *e, d*). The tinklers vary in size from a tiny specimen of only eleven millimeters in length to one almost fifty-five millimeters long. They functioned as ornamental noise-makers much in the same way as bells and were worn in a similar manner. The copper tubes were most probably used as beads: Ferguson (1940) found them strung with glass beads, and other archaeologists have usually treated them as a kind of bead Early portraits of Creek Indians, however, show tubes of this kind stuck through the ear lobes and used as holders for feathers (Fundaberk 1958). Quimby (1960: 91) has reported prehistoric copper tubes of a similar kind used as hair ornaments in the Great Lakes region. Some of the tubular copper artifacts found at Ocmulgee may have had functions other than the traditional one of beads while others of extremely large diameters may have had still other ornamental uses.

Although not as common as copper tubes and tinklers, a number of other ornaments were made of sheet metal. A pair of wide cuffs (or anklets?) was found with burial 41. These cuffs (6.5 by 12 inches) consisted of a pair of metal sheets, each of which had been rolled into a cylinder and then secured by lacing the edges. Another sheet copper piece was apparently a gorget, which originally consisted [171]of a roughly circular section of copper with two arcs cut away and a hole put through the center (Plate XVII, figure 1, a). One of the missing arcs of copper was found elsewhere on the site, proving that the gorget had been worked there rather than having been imported as a complete ornament. Small metal discs (Plate XVII, figure 2, c) were found with holes drilled near the edges much in the same manner as the silver coin described above. These were probably used in the same manner as the coin as some kind of decoration. Other sheet copper artifacts of no apparent function occurred in some number in every section of the site (Plate XVII, figure 1, b).

Wire of both brass and iron was used for ornaments, always on this site for bracelets. Nine wire bracelets were recovered from burials (burials 18, 20, 29, 38, and 62), and of these, four were brass wire and the remaining five were iron. The four brass bracelets (Plate XVII, figure 1, d) are tiny ovals in shape and were found with the burial of a child. All the iron wire bracelets (Plate XVII, figure 2, b) are in the form of coils of wire and were recovered from the burials of both adults and children. Both types of bracelets were noticed by early observers of the Indians, and an account of around 1714 stated that "they often wear bracelets made of brass, and sometimes of iron wire" (Lawson 1860: 314). Confirmation of the fact that the Indians did actually wear bracelets of iron wire has been helpful for this site since the iron wire bracelets were originally interpreted as part of a burial binding [172]rather than as ornamental wristlets.

Three small rectangular panes of glass were also recovered from burial pits. These were originally parts of mirrors, common items of dress for the Indian dandies of the frontier (Williams 1930: 458). Nothing at all is left of the backing or of the handles, but mirrors of this kind were most often set in wooden frames with wooden handles (Greenman 1951).

Very little archaeological evidence was obtained from the excavations at Ocmulgee of clothing and similar ornamental attire sent to the Lower Creeks during the course of the trade. Evidence from written records indicates that a wide variety of such items and related articles made their way to the frontier and, judging from their very volume, must have had serious and immediate effects on the dress of the natives. Constant items on the lists of goods available from the traders are "strouds" and "half-thicks," types of coarse cloth sold to the Indians by the yard. Complaints about the prices of strouds and half-thicks and the shortness of the yard measure dot the journals kept by the Commissioners of the Indian Trade (McDowell 1958) and point to the real importance of these articles to the native peoples. Since these were yard goods as opposed to ready-made clothing, some limited fashioning or sewing must occasionally have been done, resulting in new techniques and re-orientation of crafts done in the home. These new techniques, however, were apparently of the very simplest since wrap-around [173]skirts and untailored robes were very much in evidence across the Southeast (Williams 1930: 9). White, blue, or red Duffield blankets were also sold to the Indians, and cloth of "double stripe" was traded by the yard (McDowell 1958: 269).

In addition to yard goods, coats of half-thicks, broadcloth, or double striped cloth were frequently mentioned as popular items in the trade. These coats could be bought plain or with lace, depending upon the number of skins to be traded. Laced and plain hats are also present in the traders' lists as well as on lists of gifts given by the government to those Indians they wished to impress the most. Shirts of "course linnen" completed the attire available to men. For women, the lists include calico petticoats and red girdles (McDowell 1958: 89) as well as flowered calico and scarlet "Caddice," both sold by the yard. The only remains of cloth found at Ocmulgee were found in burial 51 and consisted of tiny shreds of some non-native material.

Paint was also traded to the Indians and was one of the dearer items sold. Shortly after the Yamassee War, face paint was offered to them at a rate of sixteen skins per pound (McDowell 1958: 269), compared to an identical number of skins for a gun. The only evidence of this item of the trade was a scattering of red paint found in burial 10.

Two small blue glass pendants were recovered from the town area around Mound C. One of these was in a burial [174]and was associated with decahedral beads. These blue glass pendants (Fairbanks 1956a: Pl. 20, g) are of particular interest since a number of them have been found at various places in the Southeast and especially in widely separated sites in Florida (Laxon 1959: 4; Sleight 1949: 28; Willey 1949: Pl. 58), where they appear to be somewhat earlier than at Ocmulgee Town. Judging from their distribution in Florida, the pendants are Spanish in origin as are perhaps the decahedral beads with which one of them was associated at Mound C. No similar blue glass pendants were recovered from anywhere on the Middle Plateau.

### Miscellaneous metalware

A small number of miscellaneous metal artifacts were recovered from the site. Many of these are not included in the traders' lists of regular merchandise traded to the Indians while others would be of limited use to them even if they were included in the trade. Door hardware, for example, would be of no use to people living in houses of typical southeastern construction although it could have been used within the trading house. Door hardware found on the site consists of one large rectangular lock plate (Plate XV, figure 1, *a*), a single hinge (Plate XI, figure 2, *b*), and a heavy iron key (Plate XI, figure 2, *a*). Other household metalware includes an iron kettle bail loop (Plate XVIII, figure 1, *i*), a broken strike-a-light, and part of a kettle handle.

Three conical points of iron and one of heavy [175]brass were found in and around the trading house stockade. Similar conical points of copper have been described as projectile points (Berry, Chapman, and Mack 1944; Speck 1907: 108), but all four of these seem to be too heavy to have served as points. Speck records points of rolled metal specifically as tips for fishspears, not ordinary projectile points. Both brass and iron tipped arrows are mentioned in historic sources (Salley 1941: 45), but no description of them is available.

A number of pieces of hardware from wagons and harnesses were found in the area, but not all of them can be unequivocally assigned an eighteenth century date. Among these are several swingletree attachments, including a swingletree hook and a double ring for attaching the swingletree to a wagon or perhaps to a plow (Plate XI, figure 2, *c*). This last piece was in an apparently undisturbed refuse pit (pit 7) in company with unquestionable seventeenth or early eighteenth century material and is fairly certainly of an early date. There is no good early association for any of the others, and they could have just as easily come from the nineteenth century: swingletrees and swingletree attachments have changed little over long periods of time. Since most of the transporting of trade goods to the frontier was by means of pack trains, both human and animal, why swingletrees or any other wagon hardware should be here is a mystery.

Harness equipment includes two ornamental bridle bosses (Plate XVIII, figure 1, *h, j*) and an iron harness ring. [176]The bridle bosses are undistinguished as far as workmanship is concerned although one of them resembles in style the plain hemispherical bridle bosses found at Jamestown (Cotter and Hudson 1957: 86).

*Ceramics and glassware*

European ceramics and glassware form a significant part of the non-native debris recovered from that part of the site immediately in and around the trading house proper, particularly from the north end of the ditch and in the area designated as "houses" IV and VII. Few sherds of European ceramics, especially, were found elsewhere on the site in areas of heaviest purely Indian occupation. This fairly limited distribution of European ceramics in other parts of the site may indicate that few of the European-made stoneware and china articles were available for use as common trade items. Certainly the native ceramic industry here shows no signs of having atrophied in the face of serious competition from the kilns of Europe. In addition, the fact that the native potters occasionally imitated European forms indicates their desirability and underlies their scarcity as trade goods.

Several different kinds of European ceramics were found other than the Spanish majolica and olive jar sherds discussed above, and not all of these were specifically English in origin. Of four sherds of tin-glazed earthenware recovered from the site, two are possibly of seventeenth [177]century Dutch origin. These two were originally from a deep bowl with a slightly flaring rim (Plate XII, figure 1, *g, h*). Four sherds of Staffordshire combed ware (Plate XII, figure 1, *d, e*) were from a vessel originally imported from England. The quality of the combing on these sherds indcates an early eighteenth century date for them. All four sherds have a very distinct curvature with the combing on the exterior, and the original vessel or vessels may have been cylindrical mugs, an unusual form for this particular ware. Also from England was part of the base of a tankard of brown stoneware. This base (Plate XII, figure 1,*f*) is part of an early eighteenth century jug type that frequently bears the excise stamp of Queen Anne on it. However, no identifying marks appear on the part of the base recovered at Ocmulgee.

Salt-glazed stoneware was the most common type of European ceramics found. The sherds recovered are uniformly gray in background color with occasional decorative designs in blue or purple. The decorations usually consist of alternating blue and gray stripes (Plate XII, figure 1, *k*), purple areas with raised crests, incised lines, or raised lines. Some of the sherds were from mugs or jugs although in most cases vessel shape is impossible to determine. One sherd was identified as part of a Grenzhausen bulbous jug (Plate XII, figure 1,*j*) of the kind commonly bearing the arms of William III or of Queen Anne. Another, of a coarser ware, bears part of a royal coat of arms or medallion and is of a similar late seventeenth or early eighteenth [178]century date (Plate XII, figure 1, *i*).

Other types include three body sherds from lead-glazed earthenware vessels of seventeenth to eighteenth century date. One of these, a chamber pot with a white slip and a red core, was probably West English in origin (Plate XII, figure 1, *b*). The other two sherds of this same ware were of similar manufacture and may have come from the same area (Plate XII, figure 1, *a*). A number of sherds with a green glaze and a soft, chalky white core (Plate XII, figure 1, *c*) are also present in the trading house collections, but no identification of them has been possible up to the present time. They have been suggested as perhaps of Spanish origin (Fairbanks, personal communication, 1958), but no real comparative data have been found for them. The sherds themselves are presently quite small and undistinguished by any really diagnostic features. The green glaze tends to flake badly on the surfaces, exposing the very soft white core. As far as thickness is concerned, all the sherds from the site are as thin as the lead-glazed earthenware discussed above. Since no rim sherds were found, it is impossible to even venture a guess as to body shape or size of vessel. The only unusual characteristic of these sherds is the presence of heavy, crude throw marks (like those found on the interiors of Spanish olive jar sherds) on the inner surfaces.

Glassware that could be definitely assigned a trading house date was seldom present in large enough [179]pieces to provide any information on the body size or shape of the original vessels. Most of the glass sherds are probably from the squat, hollow-based rum or wine bottles that are commonplace on many colonial English sites. Only one good basal sherd was present, and it was a typical hollow base. A few sections of bottle necks were recovered, all of them fairly long and thin. All of the glass sherds were of a dense dark green glass, and nearly all were heavily patinated and iridescent. Some of the sherds had been worked into small scrapers that subsequently acquired the characteristic golden surface and iridescent sheen (Plate XIV, figure 1).

A few other sherds are of a very thin green glass that appears to be from tall rectangular bottles. These sherds may represent the familiar "gin" bottles that also occur on colonial sites of this period.

### *Distribution of trade artifacts*

Since the problem of stratigraphic control at Ocmulgee was such a difficult one, it was often necessary to use sheer distributional data to interpret certain ground features reported in the field notes. One of the most helpful in comparing these features has been the use of trade artifacts, which occur in conjunction with them and tend to be concentrated in these specific areas. Within the trading house stockade, the distribution of trade goods was used to aid in interpreting some of the less distinct floor features. In addition, comparison [180]between percentages of trade goods in the house sites and in the trading house were made to see if any differences between these two kinds of features were present. Some interesting differences in numbers and percentages occur when the trade goods in several different areas are compared. Three such areas—the trading house, house sites I, II, and V and "houses" IV and VII—were chosen to see if comparison of the types of trade goods found in each would yield any information on the nature of enigmatic "houses" IV and VII. House sites I, II, V were treated as a unit since two of them are superimposed and the third overlapped one of the other two. Some differences in distribution could be expected because of the time differences among the three houses, but variations within a twenty-five to thirty year time span cannot have been really significant.

Historic trade artifacts from the three areas were enumerated and sorted into type categories: pipes, glassware, ornaments, gun parts (including gunflints), Spanish ceramics, English ceramics, sheet copper, iron tools, and a miscellaneous category (Table 1). The collection of pipes includes all pieces of both bowls and stems while the ornament category includes tinklers, bells, bracelets, buttons, and buckles. Spanish ceramics includes both majolica and olive jars while English ceramics includes sherds from vessels made in England and those from other countries brought to Ocmulgee by the English. Artifacts not fitting into these types comprise a miscellaneous group.

[181]TABLE 1
PERCENTAGES AND TOTALS OF TRADE ARTIFACTS

| area | pipes | glass | orna. | E.cer. | guns | S.cer. | cop. | tools | total |
|---|---|---|---|---|---|---|---|---|---|
| Numbers of artifacts (total) | | | | | | | | | |
| tr.h. | 95 | 22 | 14 | 31 | 21 | 10 | 13 | 17 | 223 |
| IV,VII | 116 | 42 | 7 | 48 | 14 | 18 | 17 | 4 | 266 |
| I,II,V | 28 | 13 | 9 | 14 | 8 | 2 | 5 | 4 | 83 |
| Percentages of artifacts (total) | | | | | | | | | |
| tr.h. | 42.2 | 9.8 | 6.2 | 13.8 | 9.3 | 4.4 | 5.8 | 7.6 | 99% |
| IV,VII | 43.0 | 15.6 | 2.6 | 17.8 | 5.2 | 6.7 | 6.3 | 1.5 | 98.7% |
| I,II,V | 33.7 | 15.7 | 10.8 | 16.9 | 9.6 | 2.4 | 6.0 | 4.8 | 99.9% |
| Numbers of artifacts (excluding humus) | | | | | | | | | |
| tr.h. | 69 | 12 | 11 | 16 | 16 | 8 | 9 | 12 | 153 |
| IV,VII | 98 | 37 | 6 | 38 | 13 | 17 | 13 | 4 | 226 |
| I,II,V | 20 | 8 | 8 | 6 | 5 | 2 | 5 | 3 | 57 |
| Percentages of artifacts (excluding humus) | | | | | | | | | |
| tr.h. | 45.1 | 7.8 | 7.2 | 10.5 | 10.5 | 5.2 | 5.9 | 7.8 | 100% |
| IV,VII | 42.8 | 16.2 | 2.6 | 16.6 | 5.7 | 7.4 | 5.7 | 1.8 | 98.8 |
| I,II,V | 35.1 | 14.0 | 14.0 | 10.5 | 8.8 | 3.5 | 8.8 | 5.3 | 100.0% |

[182]The latter category was excluded entirely since it contained very few items, each of a different type. Two separate series of totals were considered, the first a count of strictly sub-humus artifacts and the second of all historic trade artifacts, ignoring such stratigraphic information as was available. Separate *chi squares* were run on these sets of data, and no significant differences between the lumped and the stratigraphically separated material were present for any of the three areas in any one of the categories of trade artifacts. This is considered justification for using the collections from specified areas, completely ignoring such stratigraphy as was reported to be present for each of them.

*Chi squares* were then run comparing the total collections from the three areas with each other in order to determine the extent of the difference in distribution of different kinds of European trade artifacts. Significant differences in distribution were observed between the trading house stockade and "houses" IV and VII (*chi square* = 22.054; d.f.= 7), but no significant difference was observed between house sites I, II, and V and the trading house (*chi square* = 6.3707; d.f. = 7). This points out again the atypical nature of the area designated as "houses" IV and VII; and while it cannot provide any solution to the problem, distribution of trade artifacts also cannot lend any support to their interpretation as actual house sites.

Comparison of the percentages of artifacts from [183]the three different locales yielded some interesting information. All three areas have similar percentages of copper artifacts, but some striking differences obtain in the other categories. The trading house has the largest percentage of tools (7.6%) while the percentage of the same artifacts in area IV, VII is almost negligible (1.5%). Area IV, VII is similarly deficient in its percentages of ornaments and gun parts but has a decided edge in the numbers of sherds of Spanish pottery found there. In fact, this one area has the greatest number, both absolutely and relatively, of Spanish artifacts found together on the Middle Plateau. Glassware and English ceramics are also most plentiful in this same area although the advantage is a small one. Area IV, VII, judging from the many postmolds and the quantities of debris there, may very well have been a house site, but there is no real evidence to suggest that the house was in fact historic. The Spanish ceramics could have been part of a pre–trading house, Spanish-influenced historic Creek household, but they could also be trash dumped in a convenient area by Carolinians who had acesss to Spanish materials through raids on Apalachee.

## PROJECTILE POINTS

The 821 projectile points recovered from the Middle Plateau represent all of the occupations at Ocmulgee including examples of earliest Archaic types up to the tiny triangular points associated in this area with the historic Creeks. In no case was it possible to obtain any kind of [184]clear association of any of these points with corresponding ceramics or any other definitive artifacts or features. They have been identified as historic solely on the basis of what has been found at other sites in the Florida-Georgia area on a similar time level.

Twenty-one of the 821 projectile points are of a small triangular type associated with historic occupations over most of the eastern United States. From region to region, these points are strikingly similar: Creek projectile points, specimen for specimen, do not differ from Iroquois points or from small triangular points from such distant places as Texas and the Plains except in material and perhaps very minor details of workmanship. Within the general classification of "small triangular point," there are several variations which do not as yet appear to have a real significance although they are sometimes treated as chronological markers within one specific area (MacNeish 1952: 56) There are three different kinds of small triangular points in the group of twenty-one from the Lower Creek site at Ocmulgee. While these kinds may actually represent parts of a continuum rather than clear-cut types as such, they are sufficiently distinct to be easily segregated and sufficiently marked to warrant separation.

The first group, consisting of six points, is one of narrow-based isosceles triangles with serrated edges and concave bases. They average 27.5 millimeters in length (with a range from 22 to 33 mm.) and [185]13.6 millimeters in width at the base (ranging from 11 to 16 mm.). Blades are thin (about 3 or 5 mm.) and workmanship is uniformly excellent. The sides of the points are straight but slightly incurvate at the base. Material is variable and includes chert, jasper, and chalcedony.

The second kind, represented by only four specimens, is a broad-based isosceles triangle with a uniformly straight base and sides slightly incurvate at the base. Points in this group average 20.5 millimeters in length (ranging from 16 to 24 mm.) and 15 millimeters in width at the base (with a range from 13 to 17 mm.). Blades are thin, between 3 and 4 millimeters, and the whole point is approaching a distinctly more equilateral shape than is present for the points in the first group. None of the points in this second group has serrated edges or any kind of concave base. Chert is the predominant material with a single point made of jasper.

The third category contains eleven points. They are broad-based triangular points that range from true equilateral to squat isosceles triangles. The bases and edges are uniformly straight without the slight curvature that characterizes the preceding groups. In size, these points average 20 millimeters in length (with a range from 14 to 25 mm.) and 15 millimeters in width at the base (ranging from 13 to 20 mm.). Blades are thin and workmanship is variable, ranging from fully flaked points to some that are only slightly retouched flakes. [186]Two of the points grouped in this class have serrated edges and were included here on the basis of distinctive over-all shape. The total range of suitable materials available in central Georgia was employed for the manufacture of these points with no apparent preference for any one of them. These materials included jasper, chert, flint, chalcedony and even quartz.

The small number of historic projectile points from this site (only 2% of the total) can probably be considered as evidence that aboriginal weapons were being rapidly replaced by European firearms during this earliest period of intensive trade with the English. The early Spanish embargo on supplying arms to the natives, which must have affected these people at one time in their history, left them no lasting hesitance—moral or practical—to prevent them from buying arms from the English traders as fast as they became available. Other known Creek town sites show a similar paucity of projectile points, again illustrating the rapidity of the conversion to firearms. Interestingly enough, Spanish mission sites in Florida also show a real scarcity of projectile points (Boyd, Smith, and Griffin 1951) in spite of the fact that there was for a long time no appreciable influx of arms and ammunition to the mission Indians.

Other stone work attributable to the Creek occupation at Ocmulgee are small thumbnail scrapers. These were very often made from gunflints or from dark green rum bottle glass in addition to native flints. These [187]scrapers seldom exceed 35 millimeters in length and are most often much smaller. Occasionally they are round rather than oblong, and they always have a steeply beveled working edge. Similar scrapers, including the glass ones, occur at other contact sites in the Southeast, but the shape, at least, is not confined to the historic period.

Stone tools of many kinds were recovered during the excavations, but there is no really usable information from context or association to tell precisely from which of the many mixed occupations a particular artifact derives. From the volume of European tools—axes, hoes, knives, etc.—it seems that many of the everyday appliances of the Lower Creek household were of non-native manufacture, but it is impossible to assess from the data found here the extent of such replacement or the extent of persistence of aboriginal handiwork.

## POTTERY

Sherds of the Ocmulgee Fields ceramic series were among the most numerous of the artifacts recovered from the Middle Plateau and form a respectable percentage of all the pottery from the extensive Macon Plateau site. Sherds of this series and related types are found throughout the range of Lower Creek settlement in Georgia and Alabama and show up in Florida in Seminole and Apalachee sites as well. The Ocmulgee Fields series as defined at this site contains five sherd types: *Ocmulgee Fields Incised,* [188]*Ocmulgee Fields Plain, Walnut Roughened, Kasita Red Filmed,* and *Ocmulgee Checked Stamped.*

*Ocmulgee Fields Incised* (Jennings and Fairbanks 1939) occurs in three different shapes: a cazuela bowl, a large flaring-rimmed bowl, and a narrow-necked globular olla or water bottle. Of these three forms, the cazuela is the most common, comprising 95.6 per cent of all the *Ocmulgee Fields Incised* sherds. Both the flaring-rimmed bowl and the globular olla are minority types occurring respectively as 2.5 per cent and 1.9 per cent of the total.

In general, the cazuelas have sharply angled shoulders with fairly narrow rim areas above the shoulders. Bases of the bowls are both round and flat although it is impossible to say in what percentages since very few basal sherds were available for examination. Judging from the whole vessels in the Ocmulgee collections, the cazuelas tend to be small, averaging 20.6 centimeters in diameter (with a range between 12.0 and 31.8 cm.) and 9.0 centimeters in height (ranging from 5.5 to 13.3 cm.). In cross section, the sharply angled rims usually exhibit some sort of protuberance or pronounced thickening at the lip. Where this lipping does occur, it varies from an almost unnoticeable thickening to a pronounced outward flare. Often an observable lipping occurs on the interior as well as or in place of an extrusion on the exterior. In 67 per cent of the cases, lips are flattened, and the remaining number are rounded. In 15 per cent of the cases, there is no lipping at all with lips of a simple rounded [189]or flattened type being present.

Method of manufacture of the cazuelas was by coiling; coil fractures occasionally occur, and sometimes the coil structure can be felt in the vessel walls. Temper is usually grit or sand and ranges from very fine to very coarse. In some sherds, temper is so scarce as to be almost non-existant, and in others it is very plentiful. In addition to sand and grit, shell temper is also occasionally present. The paste is usually even and compact with a smooth surface, but the texture ranges to very coarse and uneven. Surface color is as varied as ware characteristics: buff-orange, gray, black, or a combination of these colors. Often the surfaces are mottled or there is extensive fireclouding. Surfaces of the vessels are usually smoothed, sometimes on both the exterior and the interior, and marks from the smoothing tool are commonly present.

The cazuelas are incised on the rim area above the shoulder of the vessel.

The bases below this band of incising are usually smooth and plain although rarely an example occurs of an incised cazuela with a brushed or stippled base similar to *Walnut Roughened*. One almost complete vessel of this brushed base variant is illustrated on Plate XXI, figure 2. Design elements on the cazuelas are sometimes confined to the rim area by a row of rectangular, circular, or triangular shoulder punctations or a series of small notches along the shoulder. Occasionally this row of punctations is repeated just under the lip [190]producing an effect of isolating the incising within a band. In one case the shoulder punctations were replaced by a notched strip added to the shoulder. Shoulder punctations are quite rare and are present in only one per cent of the incised rimsherds examined.

Range in incised designs on the cazuelas is quite broad although a small core of designs was most often used by the potters. Predominantly curvilinear designs are the commonest, comprising almost eighty per cent of the total. Strictly linear designs comprise the remaining twenty per cent of the sherds. All or almost all of the major design motifs, of course, contain both curvilinear and straight line elements, and the classification made here was on the basis of whether or not any curvilinear elements at all were present in the designs. The complete lack of any curviliniear motifs was the basis for calling any one particular design linear.

For the purpose of classifying designs, 2572 rimsherds from *Ocmulgee Fields Incised* cazuelas were examined. Of this number, 465 sherds bore sufficient design for accurate identification. The small number of sherds bearing identifiable design elements was the result of rigid exclusion of dubious examples. Many of the designs, of course, utilized the same basic elements, and only when enough of a design was present to be entirely sure of what it was, was that sherd included in the sample. In addition, many of the sherds were much too small to provide a very good idea of the composition of the designs. Further [191]complicating any comments on cazuela design elements is the fact that sometimes the designs themselves were almost obliterated by smoothing, and in some cases, the original incising had been so lightly done that the designs themselves were all but indistinguishable.

The 465 identifiable rimsherds were classified according to twenty-seven preliminary design categories. Some of these were later combined and the total reduced to nineteen when it became apparent that some of the categories treated originally as separate designs were actually parts of larger design elements. These nineteen designs were further arranged into four groups of essentially similar designs: scrolls, sets of interlocking lines ("guilloches"), nested geometric figures, and miscellaneous geometric designs.

The first category, that of elaborate scrolls, consists of a small two or three line loop scroll on a long stem. This scroll is almost always surrounded by radiating concentric circles, which may or may not also function as the fill-in lines between the repeated scroll motifs. In all cases, the design is repeated all the way around the vessel rims. This scroll design occurs in four different variations. In the first of these, the stem of the scroll is parallel to the rim and the radiating curvilinear lines are only half-circles which become straight lines drawn parallel to the rims and serving as fill-in elements between the scrolls (Plate XXX, *a, d*). The second variation also consists of scrolls parallel to [192]the rims, but part of the fill-in design is a set of nested "V's" instead of the series of parallel lines (Plate XXX, *c, b*). The third variation involves the use of the repeated scroll motif set at an angle to the rim with the areas between the figures filled with only the concentric lines radiating from the loops themselves (Plate XXIX, *a, b, c, d*). The fourth variation is an unadorned scroll with only rudiments of the design present and none of the characteristic radiating lines. This last design occurs but rarely, and in each observed case, the scrolls themselves were inverted and incomplete (Plate XXIX, *e*). The scroll design with its many variations is the most common of the cazuela designs and comprises 61.49 per cent (286 sherds) of the total sample.

The second major category includes a number of variations on a basic design of short wavy line segments (often two or three parallel lines) that interlock around the rim to form a continuous linked design (Plate XXXI). There are five variations on this design present: (1) two-lined units interlocking right over left, (2) three-lined segments which interlock right over left, (3) two-lined segments interlocking left over right (Plate XXX, *a*), (4) three-lined elements which are squared at the point of juncture, and (5) three-lined elements which are separated into linked pairs (Plate XXXI, *b*). This design with all its variations comprises 18.68 per cent (87 sherds) of the total.

The third category is of nested geometric figures [193](Plate XXXII) which are repeated around the rim to form a continuous design. The nested figures include angles, half-squares, diamonds, circles, and zig-zag lines. In most cases, the nested figures are set very close together, giving the effect of a continuous distribution even though the figures themselves are not actually linked. Occasionally the design consists of separate units connected by a narrow double-line which does in fact join all the design elements in a continuous figure. Nested geometric figures form 16.57 per cent (77 sherds) of the total sample.

The last category is a residual one containing several designs that occur only rarely in the sample examined and do not readily fit into any of the other broad groupings. These designs include incised lines criss-crossed over the exterior rim, a herringbone pattern, a rare double-line loop, and paired semi-circular loops. None of these designs is common and together they comprise only 3.24 per cent (15 sherds) of the total sample.

Preference of the potters for these designs was centered definitely on the scroll and variations of the basic scroll design. Apparently the most popular of these variations was also the most stylized and elaborate of them, the scroll in combination with nested "V's." The concentration of over half of the rimsherds in scroll designs, however, should not obscure the fact that many other design elements were used by the potters and that a very wide range of possibilities was open to them. [194]Apparently, experimentation and variation were permissible even to the extent of sometimes doing artistic violence to traditional patterns.

The execution of the designs varies as much as do the designs themselves. The quality of incising ranges all the way from deeply incised, smoothly drawn lines to faint and almost rudimentary scratches. Occasionally the design elements themselves were drawn in with a minimum of detail, producing an effect of carelessness and lack of skill. In almost forty per cent of the sherds of the sample of 465, the designs were smoothed over and in some cases almost entirely obliterated. Occasionally the designs were smoothed and then retraced in spots almost as if the potter were trying to achieve a balance between a suggestion of a design and complete eradication. In some cases, the incised patterns are very crudely done, almost to the point of producing real errors in their execution. The design elements often do not match and are poorly done from the point of view of the most elementary canons of balance and form. The sloppy, often rudimentary character of designs on *Ocmulgee Fields Incised* cazuelas is one of the most frequently cited attributes of this sherd type (Fairbanks 1952: 299, 1958: 55; Kelly 1938: 56) and certainly deserves attention in any kind of critical examination. The very noticeable number of really crudely incised sherds, however, is not sufficient reason to dismiss the whole of *Ocmulgee Fields Incised* ceramics as [195]equally careless. Often the designs are well drawn, carefully executed, and more artistically pleasing than would be expected from an examination of some of the cruder examples.

A small number of *Ocmulgee Fields Incised* sherds were from large bowls with narrow flaring rims set at right angles to the vessel bodies. From the total sample of incised rims, 2.5 per cent (63 sherds) proved to be from this type of vessel rather than from the cazuela form. Of these 63 sherds, only a much smaller number provided any information about design or vessel shape so that comments on this variant of *Ocmulgee Fields Incised* are more provisional than for the much more common cazuela bowl. Ware characteristics for the flaring-rimmed bowls appear from the available sample to be identical to those of the cazuelas, and designs and treatment of the decorated surfaces are quite similar.

In shape, the bowls appear to be deep rounded vessels with steep sides and a narrow flaring rim. Two restored bowls in the Ocmulgee National Monument collections (Plate XXIV, figure 2) show rounded bases whose shape is determined, at least in one case, by actual original basal sherds. One or two of the flaring rims are broad enough and flat enough to be plate rims although no really diagnostic body sherds have shown up in combination with these suspiciously broad, flat rims. In size, the flaring-rimmed bowls range from a very small 26 centimeters in diameter (8.5 cm. high) to a very large 56 [197]centimeters in diameter (24 cm. high). Occasionally, large oblong lugs were placed on either side of the vessel or perhaps at intervals around it, possibly as aids in lifting it. Exactly how common these lugs were on the flaring-rimmed bowls is not known, but at this site they occurred on nine of the total number of flaring rimsherds.

TABLE 2
[196]CAZUELA DESIGN ELEMENTS

| Design | no. | % | flaring rim |
|---|---|---|---|
| Scrolls | | | |
| scroll and nested "V's" | 129 | 27.73 | |
| angled scroll | 93 | 20.00 | 3 |
| scroll and parallel lines | 62 | 13.33 | |
| inverted scroll | 2 | .43 | |
| Interlocking lines | | | |
| two-line (right) | 44 | 9.42 | 1 |
| three-line (right) | 19 | 4.09 | |
| two-line (left) | 17 | 3.66 | 1 |
| squared | 5 | 1.08 | |
| separate pairs | 2 | .43 | |
| Nested geometric figures | | | |
| angles | 28 | 6.02 | 7 |
| half-squares | 19 | 4.09 | |
| diamonds | 17 | 3.66 | |
| zig-zags | 8 | 1.72 | 2 |
| connected circles | 3 | .65 | |
| circles | 2 | .43 | |
| Miscellaneous | | | |
| criss-crossed lines | 7 | 1.51 | 1 |
| herringbone | 5 | 1.08 | 2 |
| paired semi-circles | 2 | .43 | |
| double-line loop | 1 | .22 | |
| Total | 465 | 100.00% | 17 |

The flaring rims are often slightly thickened, but no extrusions or protuberances are present on them. They are almost uniformly rounded with an occasional more "pointed" than rounded lip occurring. A number of the the rims (37.5%) have a notched or pinched strip added just under the lip on the exterior of the vessel. In one case, notches had been placed in the lip itself, apparently all the way around the vessel, as a variation on the added rim strip.

Designs appear on the interior of the flaring rim, and the basal portions of the bowls are almost uniformly plain and smoothed. There is, however, one instance of a flaring rimsherd with a brushed base, indicating that the flaring-rimmed bowls, like the cazuelas, have a brushed base variant. Range in design is more limited for the flaring-rimmed bowls than for their cazuela counterparts. Only seven separate designs appear on the bowls in contrast to the nineteen found on the cazuelas. The popular scroll design occurs only three times on flaring rimsherds and then it appears in its least complex form (the angled scroll). As a whole, preference in design [198]seems to lean heavily toward linear motifs rather than curvilinear ones on the flaring-rimmed bowls. This preference results in a definite association between the linear designs and flaring rims, an association which may in part be a mechanical one. Unless the potter incised her designs upside down, working on the flaring rims would be more difficult than on the more readily accessible cazuela shoulders and hence more condusive to simpler designs.

The third variation of *Ocmulgee Fields Incised* is the incised globular olla or "water jar." In sorting out sherds from these vessels, no difference except for the not always readily discernible one of shape was noticed between them and the remainder of the *Ocmulgee Fields Incised* series. The same range in sherd color, temper, texture, and surface treatment is present in the ollas as in the cazuelas and flaring-rimmed bowls. The sample of sherds for this particular form, however, is very small (49 sherds, representing at most 7 vessels), and a larger one might produce attributes distinguishable enough to justify a separate type for the olla. Because none were obtained here, the olla or "water jar" has been included as a variety of *Ocmugee Fields Incised* and not as a separate type.

The *Ocmulgee Fields Incised* olla is a very narrow-necked jar with a large globular body and a rounded base (Plate XXIII). Some of these vessels were very large, judging from the curvature of the shoulder and the breadth [199]of a few shallow basal sections. However, no exact dimensions can be given since no complete or nearly complete vessels were recovered from the excavations at Ocmulgee National Monument. A very small example of this distinct shape was found at the Woolfolk site in western Georgia, and it is only 23 centimeters high (Plate XXII, figure 1).

The short, narrow necks of the ollas are set at varying angles to the shoulders. Occasionally the angle of the neck to the body is ninety degrees or sometimes even more than ninety degrees. In one case, the neck met the body at an angle of less than ninety degrees, resulting in a slightly flared neck instead of the more common straight ones The necks themselves are quite short and average about 3.3 centimeters in height. The orifices are small, the orifice of the one extant complete neck being 8.7 centimeters in diameter. There are no rim modifications of any kind in the sample examined except for a slight thickening of the lip on one rim. In most cases, the body sherds of these vessels, particularly in the shoulder region, were poorly smoothed in the interiors with coils more commonly visible than in either of the other *Ocmulgee Fields Incised* shapes. This is probably a mechanical feature resulting from less easy access to the vessel interiors.

Designs in all observed cases consist of four "spiral" elements incised on the shoulders of the vessels. These four design elements are connected by a narrow [200]double line that forms one end of each spiral. The spirals themselves are not single line figures but instead consist of two double-line segments which interlock upon themselves to produce the visual effect of a single-line spiral element (Plate XXXIII, figure 2). As a design motif, these "spirals" are actually the familiar interlocked line segments elaborated to an almost unrecognizable degree. The finished design elements range from seven to eleven centimeters in diameter and average about nine. Like the design elements on the cazuelas and the flaring-rimmed bowls, they are often smoothed over, entirely or only in part.

The exclusive association at this site of the connected spiral design with the olla or water jar does not mean that no other designs were ever employed on it. Other sites with a Creek component have produced ollas with the same design (Woolfolk, for example), but other designs do occur on these sites. Fundaberk and Foreman 1957: Pl. 127) illustrate an example with a simple interlocking line around the vessel shoulder. Variations on the four large spirals also occur (see *Arrowpoints* 1931: 23 for an olla with a repeated single-line spiral design). It may well be that the variation in the olla incised designs and in the occurrence of the vessel shape itself is a temporal one, subject to analysis in terms of short time spans in Lower Creek history.

The second most numerous historic ware at Ocmulgee [201]Town is *Walnut Roughened* (Jennings and Fairbanks 1940). This is a characteristically brushed or roughened pottery that appears in one form or another in Creek ceramic sequences until the end of the nineteenth century and the cessation of pottery making. For purposes of this study, 6302 sherds were examined, 5198 body sherds and 1104 rims. Most of these sherds were from the immediate trading house area and from the house sites, but many of them were from the "general" collections with no specific locations noted. *Walnut Roughened,* with its areal and temporal correlatives *Chattahoochee Brushed* and *McIntosh Brushed,* is really critical to an understanding of the development of Lower Creek pottery. Until its origins are fully understood, little progress can be made in clarifying the important issues of the origins of the Lower Creek ceramic sequence as a whole.

Vessel form for *Walnut Roughened* is apparently a globular to elongated wide-mouthed jar with a flaring rim and a rounded base. Judging from the available rimsherds, a majority of the vessels have a slightly constricted collar area although the extant whole or nearly whole vessels in the Ocmulgee collections are globular jars without this characteristic feature (Plates XXV and XXVI). There was no evidence present to indicate any base type other than a distinctly rounded one.

Method of manufacture was by coiling, but only very seldom is a coil fracture observable in any of the sherds. Coil fractures, when they are present, occur [202]usually in rimsherds. Most of the vessels were originally tempered with crushed shell, which ranges from very sparse to very plentiful in individual sherds. Often the shell temper appears on the surfaces of the sherds where it is sometimes leached out, giving them the untidy appearance characteristic of shell tempered wares in this central Georgia area. In addition to shell, grit and other materials occurred in the paste, presumably as temper, in almost one fourth of the total number of sherds. Sherds tempered with both shell and grit comprised most of this group (20% of the total) while entirely grit tempered sherds were much less common (.1% of the total). In each case identified as grit tempered or shell and grit tempered, particles of grit obtruded on the surfaces and were additionally plentiful in the paste. This is in direct contrast to shell tempered sherds, which were exclusively shell tempered and did not have a noticeable inclusion of grit particles in the paste. In addition to grit and shell, occasionally sherds contained limestone or pulverized bone in quantities sufficient enough to describe them as tempering materials. Two sherds of the characteristic brushed ware were sherd tempered but nevertheless seem to fall easily within the description of *Walnut Roughened*. Occasional sherds contain flecks of carbon and flecks of some kind of red substance (red ocher?), much like those more commonly found in the paste of *Kasita Red Filmed*. A single sherd of *Walnut Roughened* was found with a tiny Cornaline d'Allepo seed bead embedded in the paste, [203]probably not intended as tempering. Further miscellaneous materials in the paste of *Walnut Roughened* sherds include pieces of what appears to be charred wood and the burned out holes resulting from an occasional (and probably accidental) inclusion of fibers with the shell temper. Apparently, *Walnut Roughened* is fairly consistently a shell tempered ware although infrequent deviations from this norm indicate that the potters of Ocmulgee Town were not overly particular about what went into the standard recipe for *Walnut Roughened* paste.

Generally *Walnut Roughened* has a compact texture and a hard, even surface. Like the rest of the Ocmulgee Fields ceramic series, it is technically good pottery. Sometimes, however, it may be friable, uneven, and surprisingly soft considering the fact that the majority of the sherds are so compact and hard. Surface color is variable and includes buff to orange, brown, gray, and black with a majority of the sherds being in the buff to brown range. Fire clouding does occur and mottled buff and black or brown and black surfaces are common. Sherd cores are buff, brown, or black and very often contrast in color with one or both surfaces. A clay wash occurs on about eleven percent of the sherds and produces a surface finish that ranges from a light dull brown to a wet-looking shiny brown.

All of the rimsherds that could be identfified as belonging to the historic brushed pottery are slightly to pronouncedly flaring. Even vessels lacking the [204]characteristic collar area have this typical rim form. The lips on these rims are somewhat variable, but a nearly pointed lip is the most common. Only occasionally is the lip well rounded and smoothed. An almost universal feature of these rims is a notched or pinched strip added to the exterior of the vessel just under the lip. This rim strip is very seldom any distance from the lip proper and is usually immediately below it. In a few rare cases (only three observed instances), the same kind of rim embellishment was effected by folding over the lip itself and. pinching it rather than adding an entirely separate rim strip. One vessel had the rim strip replaced by a row of separately applied nodes added just under the lip. Of the total of 1104 rimsherds, only four lacked the pinched rim strip (or the two variations thereon), and only one was observed to have a simple folded lip unadorned by any kind of pinching or notching.

Vessel interiors were sometimes well smoothed with the marks of the smoothing tool still visible in the clay. In slightly over half of the total number of rim sherds, the collar area below the rim was noticeably smoothed or polished, sometimes even to the extent of smoothing over the added rim strips.

Although the area immediately below the pinched rim is most commonly smoothed and plain above the roughened body, a variety of incised and punctated designs do occur there. In some cases, the collar area is zoned from the rest of the body by a row of triangular, circular, or [205]linear punctations, or by small notches encircling the body. Within the the collar area, short parallel lines in groups of two or three appear at intervals all along the collar around the vessel. These groups of lines were perpendicular to the rim and sometimes at a slight angle to it. Occasionally a line of punctations was included between the incised lines, and sometimes a zig-zag line was drawn to connect two of the parallel incised lines. The only variation on the parallel straight-line design for the collar area of *Walnut Roughened* vessels is a single sherd with nested curved lines drawn parallel to the rim. In this case, the sherd is quite small, and it is impossible to determine whether or not the design resembled the straight lines in their distribution.

As far as this distribution is concerned, the incised parallel straight lines are discontinuous in the sense of being placed at rather wide intervals around the collar area. How often or how regularly placed these designs were on the collars of *Walnut Roughened* vessels is not known. The very small number of actually observed designs (243 out of 1104 rimsherds; 22% of the total number of rimsherds) is probably due in part to the discontinuousness of the designs themselves. Only fairly large rimsherds, or very fortunately fractured ones, would include enough of the collar area to show any of the design.

Execution of these incised designs ranges from good to very poor; the incised lines are sometimes wide and very [206]well drawn, but they are also sometimes very faint and narrow. In no case was the incising smoothed over. Smoothing of the collar was consistently done before the vessel was incised.

The only other modifications present on the collars of *Walnut Roughened* vessels are small handles. Thirty-one of these were observed, twenty being strap handles and eleven, loop handles. These were apparently affixed to either side of the vessel although there is no evidence to eliminate the possibility that more than two handles were present on each vessel. The handles themselves are so tiny as to be termed almost vestigial or purely decorative in nature. From the very small number of them noted on *Walnut Roughened* rimsherds, it seems that they were not at all common unless, of course, the same reason for scarcity that was appealed to in the case of the incised collar designs applies here, too.

Below the smoothed collar area, and in a few cases directly below the pinched rim in vessels without the collar area, the vessel bodies were surface-textured by a number of techniques. These include brushing, cob-marking, stippling, and roughening. Brushing is the most common of these sutface treatments and makes up 41.11 per cent (2148) of the total number of body sherds and 69.1 per cent of all of the textured body sherds. The brushing ranges from heavily applied and fairly dense to lightly done and very scantily applied. Brushed sherds occur that have only one or two faint brushed lines across the surface [207]while others occur that have deep brush marks over the entire surface. In most of the observed cases, brushed lines are very irregular with no readily apparent attempts on the part of the potter to align the brush strokes with each other or to take them all in a uniform direction. The brush strokes themselves criss-cross each other over the surface of the vessel body. The brushed lines are usually quite short although an occasional sherd exhibits longer and more regular brushings. One of the complete *Walnut Roughened* vessels in the Ocmulgee National Monument collections (Plate XXV) has a fairly regularly brushed body with most of the brushing parallel to the rim. Occasional fainter brushing, however, appears perpendicular to the rim on this vessel, and the base has some distinct criss-crossing of brushed lines. The deepest and most pronounced brushing occurs on the body proper with only the faintest of brush strokes visible in the usually smoothed neck area. Brushing on all the *Walnut Roughened* sherds seems to have been done with some kind of fibers (or perhaps corn cobs?).

Cob-marked surfaces comprise 12.7 per cent (396 sherds) of the total number of textured body sherds. Most of these are very clearly impressed with an unmistakable corn cob imprint laid in more or less regular rows across the vessel body. Although more neatly and regularly done than brushing, cob-marking, too, exhibits the same crossing over and over-impressing in places, particularly on the bases of vessels. A small number of sherds included [208] with the cob-marked group are so faintly and irregularly applied as to resemble fingernail punctations. Only one sherd had these punctations in rows so irregular as to qualify positively as fingernail punctations, but a few other sherds may be listed as possible examples. An occasional sherd (2% of the decorated body sherds; six sherds in all) was both cob-marked and brushed with no apparent zoning of either decorative style. It is the presence of these sherds with cob-marking blended with brushing that suggests that the same tool used for producing the one surface texture was also responsible for the other.

Stippled sherds comprise five per cent of the decorated body sherds with 154 specimens recorded. The surface finish referred to as "stippled" in this paper describes a surface that appears to have been impressed with a wad of fibers and hence is stamped rather than brushed. An occasional stippled sherd also shows evidence of brushing much like the combination cob-marking/brushed sherds and indicates that perhaps more than one way of brushing pottery was employed at Ocmulgee Town. The same tool used in producing the brushed surfaces could also have been used to produce the stippled ones, the only change being in the way the tool was applied to the surface of the pottery.

The surface treatment described as "roughened" is a catch-all category that includes all sherds whose actual surface treatment cannot be identified. These sherds all [209] have in common a characteristic roughened surface, but the process involved in producing the roughening is unknown. The sherds themselves are not clearly brushed or stippled or cob-marked or any recognizable combination of these techniques. Roughened sherds comprise 12.8 per cent (408 sherds) of the total number of decorated body sherds.

A large number of the sherds with typical *Walnut Roughened* ware characteristics were completely plain (2086; 40.11% of the total number of body sherds). Some of these, certainly, are parts of smoothed collar areas and places on textured vessels where the potter failed to cover the surface evenly. Such a very large percentage of plain sherds, however, indicates the presence of plain vessels having all the traits of the typical brushed or roughened vessels except for the characteristic surface texturing. Further supporting the presence of such plain vessels are certain of the pinched rim-sherds which have enough of the body remaining to indicate that the bodies, too, were plain. These "Walnut Plain" vessels were apparently an important ceramic ware if the large numbers of plain body sherds is an accurate indication of the number of pots present.

One of the most interesting of the minority wares found in the Lower Oreek ceramic series is *Kasita Red Filmed* (Jennings and Fairbanks 1940), a painted ware that is not always red in spite of the name. This ceramic type has as yet no known prehistoric ancestors and may [210]eventually prove to have been stimulated in its origin by certain European—particularly Spanish—forms.

Technically, the best of the *Kasita Red Filmed* pottery is the best of the entire historic series. It is thin, hard, and very dense with smooth hard surfaces. Temper in the finest examples is most often very fine grit although sometimes the paste in these sherds appears to be almost temperless. Occasionally, flecks of black (carbon?) or red (red ocher?) are present in the paste and very infrequently shell is also used for tempering. It should be pointed out, however, that there is some overlap in ware characteristics between some examples of *Kasita Red Filmed* and some examples of *Ocmulgee Fields Incised* and *Ocmulgee Fields Plain*. For this reason, only sherds actually having painted surfaces were included as *Kasita Red Filmed* while any plain parts of the red filmed vessels were included in the category of plain sherds. This prejudices the sample since, lacking whole vessels entirely, it is impossible to determine the extent of the painted designs on pots or to state positively whether or not designs were all-over or limited in their application. *Kasita Red Filmed,* then, may have been less of a minority ware than the 274 sherds from the trading house collections would indicate.

Exclusive of painting, the surface color ranges from light buff to black. Occasionally a buff and black mottled surface occurs, particularly on the exteriors of sherds. The cores tend to be gray, buff, or brown. [211]Sometimes the exteriors of the sherds appear to be highly polished or smoothed.

Vessel shape in most instances consists of a broad-rimmed plate with a solid round base (14 present in the sample of 274 sherds) or slightly less often with a ring foot (11 examples). The ring foot is similar except in height to the lower ones present on modern European and American china. Most of these plates have broad flat rims that flare out from the plate body, which drops away from the rims in a manner more similar to a shallow soup plate or tureen than, strictly speaking, to a plate in the modern sense of the term. Plate rims uniformly have rounded lips in the forty-two rims examined.

A few sherds from definitely non-plate forms indicate that sometimes other shapes were made in this fine red-filmed ware. Two rimsherds have an inward curvature quite unlike the flat plate rims and were apparently parts of fairly deep bowls. These rimsherds have strikingly flat lips in vertical cross-section, a feature that fits in with a deep bowl vessel shape. Another rimsherd, probably also from a deep bowl, has a narrow flaring rim all the way around the orifice at right angles to the perpendicular vessel wall. In addition to these bowl sherds, a tiny loop handle of typically fine paste with a very dark red all-over filming was present in the sample. This may be a cup handle since an occasional European-inspired cup form was made by the Creeks at this site. However, no body sherds from positively red-filmed cups [212]turned up in the collections from the Middle Plateau although a possible red-filmed cup was found at Mound D (see below).

Filming on these vessels is most often a dark red color although white and even black painting occur in design combinations with the red. One color may serve as a background on which another is painted as, for example, black used as a background over which red designs were placed. Sometimes the dark red paint is replaced by maroon or orange, possibly the result of fading of the original color. Usually only the interiors of plates were decorated with red or red in combination with white and/or black. A few cases were found, however, of red filming on the undersides of the plates, sometimes even on the bases. Plate rims were almost uniformly painted solid red at least down to the point of juncture with the body, and in the sample of forty-two rimsherds, only a few carried body designs up into the solidly-painted rim areas. Sometimes, the red rim is the only painted decoration present, and the plate bodies were left completely plain. When the plate bodies were decorated, they were painted with a variety of geometric forms, alternating zones of white and red, solid red paint, or a contrasting body color (principally solid black). The commonest painted designs on the plate bodies are all rather rigid designs of narrow stripes or broad triangles. In some cases, the stripes are simply short rectangles radiating from a central circular design or from a band of color encircling the plate [213]just under the point of juncture of the rim with the plate. Often red and white designs are no more than geometrically zoned areas of contrasting color. In only one instance was a non-geometric design observed: this was simply a pale gray-black wavy line drawn across the white background in a manner that could have been accidental. In five percent of the body sherds present, decorated areas were outlined by incised lines. This was not a consistent feature even on the sherds where it was present, for some decorated areas were zoned with incised lines and others were not even on the same sherd. In summary it should be pointed out that few of the *Kasita Red Filmed* sherds present in he Ocmulgee sample provided very much information on the distribution and character of the red and white painted designs on the original vessels. Other than the obvious fact that most of the designs were geometric in character and fairly simple in composition, little can be said about their possible relations with other designs of the Ocmulgee Fields series or with other painted pottery of the same area.

The last major sherd type to be discussed here is *Ocmulgee Fields Plain,* a category that includes at least two different classes of vessels. The first of these is in all respects a residual category that was established to include undecorated body sherds of *Ocmulgee Fields Incised* cazuelas, ollas, and flaring-rimmed bowls as well as unpainted sherds of *Kasita Red Filmed* vessels. [214]In addition to this purely residual category, there is another which includes a small number of entirely plain vessels and a few special forms that share the *Ocmulgee Fields Incised* ware characteristics but not the surface decoration or the distinctive shape. This latter category is an extremely minor one since it comprises only .3 per cent (76 sherds) of the total number of plain sherds (25,541).

Most of the entirely plain vessels identified from plain rimsherds were from flaring-rimmed bowls identical in profile to the incised flaring-- rimmed bowls included above as *Ocmulgee Fields Incised*. Almost as many plain bowls of this kind were made as were incised ones if the sherd samples are an accurate indication of the actual distribution of flaring-rimmed bowls. In the total sample of flaring-rimmed bowls, there are fifty-two plain rims and sixty-three incised ones. Cazuelas, too, were made without the familiar shoulder incising. A very small number of plain cazuela rimsherds (14 in all) were among the sherds sorted out as *Ocmulgee Fields Plain*.

A few small plain globular vessels in the Ocmulgee collections seem to form a bridge between the shape of some of the *Walnut Roughened* bowls and the hard smooth surfaces and ware characteristics of *Ocmulgee Fields Incised*. These vessels (Plate XXIV, figure 1) have plain, slightly flaring rims (with occasional punctations below the rim) and round globular bodies that are usually associated [215]with *Walnut Roughened* pottery. They do not, however, have any of the other distinctive characteristics of *Walnut Roughened* and, except for the rim form, would be as sherds indistinguishable from others included in *Ocmulgee Fields Plain*. It is impossible to estimate, even roughly, how many of these bowls were present in the large sample of plain sherds.

Another separate category of plain pottery is one of plain vessels whose inspiration was clearly European rather than Lower Creek. These are not common and apparently at this site, at least, had not reached the point of becoming a real part of everyday household equipment. The greatest number of sherds from articles of this kind were from cups or mugs: two handles, three bases, and one rim. An almost whole cup was recovered from a refuse pit near Mound D, north of the trading house site. This cup is ten centimeters in diameter and almost eight centimeters high; its sides slope gently to a slightly flared ring base. The handle is incomplete but apparently is very much the same as the two other handles in the collections. All three are heavy and crudely modeled with circular cross-sections. This particular cup has a smoothed and polished surface pitted in several places by what appear to be holes resulting from the leaching of shell temper. However, the temper is predominantly grit, which is visible on the surface in several areas. The interior of the cup may have once been painted, for very minute trades of red paint are still present on [216]the inside surfaces. It is interesting to speculate on a possible prototype for these cups among the European vessels in use by the Carolinians and presumably brought to the frontier through trade, but it is difficult to see an immediate ancestor for them in the English cups unless the Creeks were singularly poor imitators. Most of the English cups and mugs of that period had the widest part of the vessel at the base. If the Indians were imitating these, their copies reversed the silhouette with the widest part at the mouth and the sides sloping down to a restricted base. The result was a profile exactly opposite to that of the English ceramic mugs. This may, of course, be the result of unfamiliarity on the part of the potters with what was then a scarce trade item.

In addition to the cups, a single example of a vase form was recovered from an erosion channel in privately-owned property west of the National Park Service's boundaries. This vessel has a globular body with a perfectly flat bottom and a long, narrow neck. The neck ends in a flaring rim with a pinched rim strip added on the exterior just under the lip. Certainly all of the elements that went into this vessel, except for the elongated neck, were present in strictly aboriginal pottery of the Ocmulgee Fields series, but their proportions in this combination are unlike anything else present in Creek ceramics. The nearest formal counterpart for this vessel seems not to be within the immediate Lower Creek ceramic tradition but rather within that of the Europeans [217](see Cotter 1958: 182, 183 for similar vessel shapes in European pottery of the same general time period).

Of the minor varieties of the Ocmulgee ceramic series, *Ocmulgee Check Stamped* is the least well represented. Only twenty-two sherds were present to add to the ninety-seven originally used to define the type (Fairbanks 1956b). Almost all, and perhaps all, of the sherds identifiable as historic check stamped pottery were from area IV, area VII to the north of the trading house stockade, and from burial 10, where half of a check stamped vessel was included in the burial. Conceivably all these sherds could have come from the same vessel. The original vessel was a large elongated jar with a rounded base. The rim was slightly flaring and had been folded over and pinched, a fairly uncommon form at Ocmulgee, where the pinched added rimstrip is the rule. Surface decoration consists of a barely visible check stamping that was smoothed and burnished almost to the point of complete obliteration. As Fairbanks (1956b) has pointed out, this type is of interest because of its position on one end of a long tradition of check stamping in the Southeast, but it seems, at least in the context of historic Lower Creek ceramics at this site, to have been little more than a curious and unrepeated survival.

Judging from the gross totals of the historic sherds, the potters at Ocmulgee Town preferred the incised cazuela two to one over the next most popular decorated [219]type, *Walnut Roughened*. The disproportionately large number of sherds typed as *Ocmulgee Fields Plain* probably indicates that more than one type is subsumed under this general heading and something more than just the basal portions of the incised series is involved. type *Walnut Roughened*. An occasional sherd of plain grit-tempered *Walnut Roughened* may have been included, but judging from the tiny percentage of grit temper in *Walnut Roughened* sherds as a whole, this number must have been quite small.

TABLE 3
[218]SHERD TOTALS

| Types | | number | per cent |
|---|---|---|---|
| *Ocmulgee Fields Incised* | | 2,684 | 7.70% |
|     cazuelas | 2572 (7.38%) | | |
|     f.r. bowls | 63 ( .18%) | | |
|     ollas | 49 ( .14%) | | |
| *Walnut Roughened* | | 6,302 | 17.76 |
|     body sherds | 5198 (14.60%) | | |
|     rims | 1104 ( 3.16%) | | |
| *Kasita Red Filmed* | | 274 | .78 |
| *Ocmulgee Fields Plain* | | 25,541 | 73.42 |
| *Ocmulgee Check Stamped* | | 119 | .34 |
| | | 34,920 | 100.00 |

Artifacts / 123

## MISCELLANEOUS ARTIFACTS

Many kinds of aboriginal artifacts besides pottery and projectile points were recovered from the Middle Plateau during the two long series of excavations. For almost all of these, there is no adequate cultural association and no way of determining to which of the many occupations at the site they pertain. Many of them, by a simple process of elimination, fit easier into purely aboriginal contexts rather than into any historic one. In addition, many of them further belong to classes of artifacts that were often quickly replaced by European ones: flint hoes, clay beads, stone axes, and flint knives. It is unfortunate that Ocmulgee Old Fields was occupied for so long by so many different groups of people. Because of this long occupation, replacement of specific aboriginal artifacts by European ones is very difficult to determine.

The only known non-European ornaments to survive [220]the competition with glass beads and copper decorations were several kinds of ornaments made of conch shell. These were unquestionably made and used by the historic peoples since they occur as burial accompaniments along with articles obtained through the Carolinian trade. The most common of these shell ornaments are small barrel-shaped beads cut from conch columellas. These beads average about two centimeters in length with only an occasional really long one (Plate XVIII, figure 2). They were strung and worn as necklaces, sometimes in combination with European glass beads. At least one shell bead was recovered with glass seed beads embedded in the holes, and the shell beads seldom occurred in burials without being accompanied by glass trade beads. Fairbanks (1956b:35) reports the presence of unfinished conch shell beads in the historic burials of two children in the Mound C village area. These unfinished beads consisted of conch columellas that had been grooved in preparation for the manufacture of the small barrel-shaped beads. No similar unfinished beads were found around the trading house or in any of the burials there. The only incomplete shell bead from this area is fully formed one, lacking only the hole.

In addition to the barrel-shaped beads, other shell ornaments include long pendants made of sections of conch columella perforated at one end (Plate XVIII, figure 2, *b*). Recovered specimens range from five to eight centimeters in length although they were originally somewhat longer. They were invariably in a very poor state of preservation [221]when recovered, and because of this poor condition and the obvious erosion that has taken place since, any estimates of original length or diameter are not reliable. Like the other shell ornaments, these were almost always with the burials of infants or children.

Other than these conch columella ornaments, a single circular gorget made from the outer shell of the conch was found. The gorget is perfectly plain with no engraved designs of any kind present on either surface. The only modifications other than the smoothed edges are three holes drilled in the center for suspension (Plate XVIII, figure 2, *a*). The gorget is about ten centimeters in diameter and was found with burial 18.

A number of other artifacts could be tied directly to the historic occupation because they imitated European objects or were made of materials unavailable to the Indians before white contact. Scrapers of rum bottle glass and European inspired ceramics are the most conspicuous examples of this group. In addition to them, pipes made of a soft green stone were shaped in imitation of the white clay pipes brought in by the trade. There is no doubt that these pipes were in fact modeled after European ones. They are small and similar in silhouette and, in addition, often have the tiny protruding spur that is characteristic of so many of the European pipes (Plate XIV, figure 1). Many fragments of bowls and stems of these green stone pipes occurred within the trading house area and in the house sites. The bowls of the pipes are uniformly undecorated [222]although they are carefully formed and finished with a fine smooth surface. The pipe stems are longer and more slender than those on other pipes known to have been made by the historic Creeks (see, for example, the pipe removed from the burial at Kasita, in Willey and Sears 1952: Pl. 1, 8), and occasionally they have distinctly formed mouthpieces. The stems are sometimes grooved longitudinally, and there is one very long stem with an octagon-shaped cross-section. These green stone pipes were evidently made at Ocmulgee since an unfinished pipe stem was among the fragments recovered from the site.

# Plates

Plate I. The trading house.

Plate II. Trading house ditch and refuse pits.

Plate III. View of the trading house ditch and cleared stockade with Mound A in the background.

Plate IV. Burial 1.

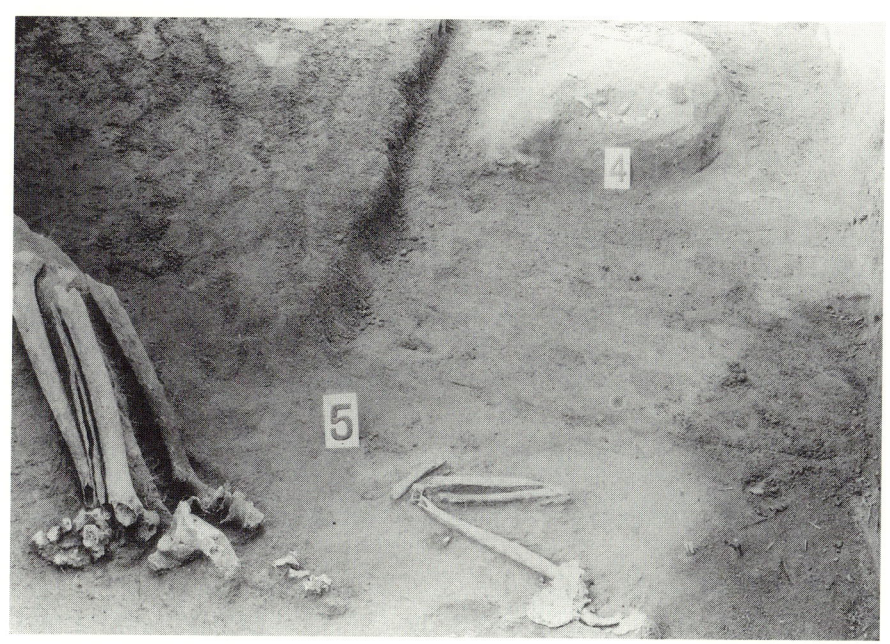

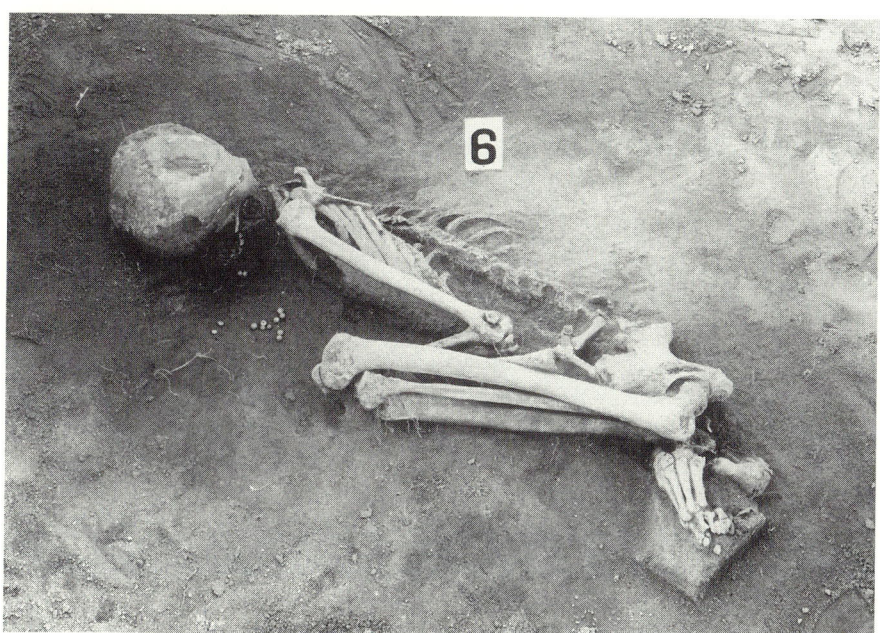

Plate V. Figure 1, burial 5. Figure 2, burial 6.

Plate VI. Profile of the Lower Creek Trading Path and burial 8.

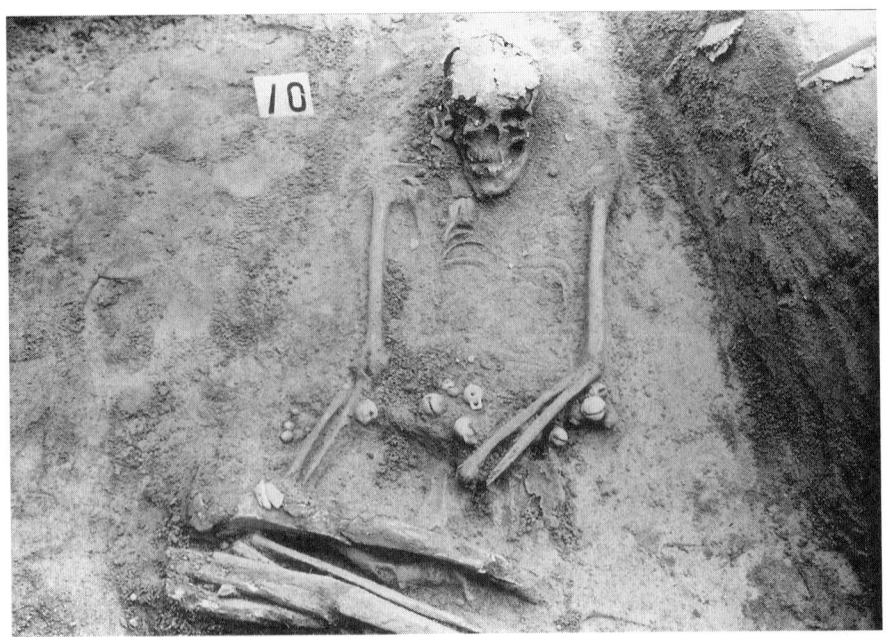

Plate VII. Burial 10.

Plate VIII. Burial 51.

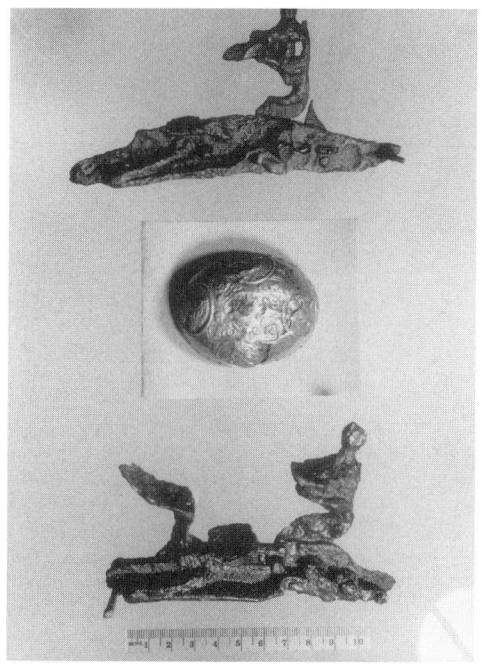

Plate IX. Lock plates with mechanisms. *Center,* ornament for pistol butt.

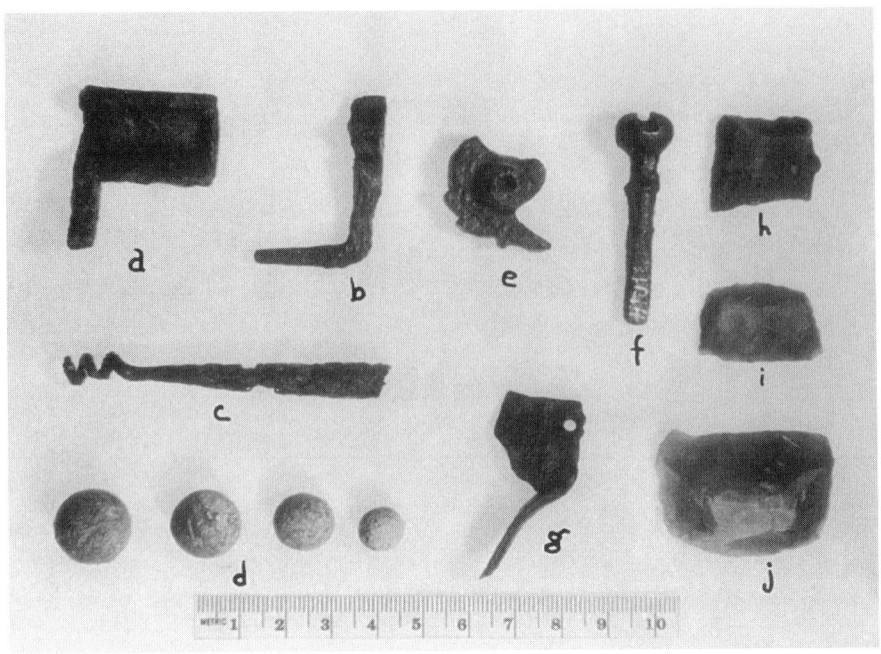

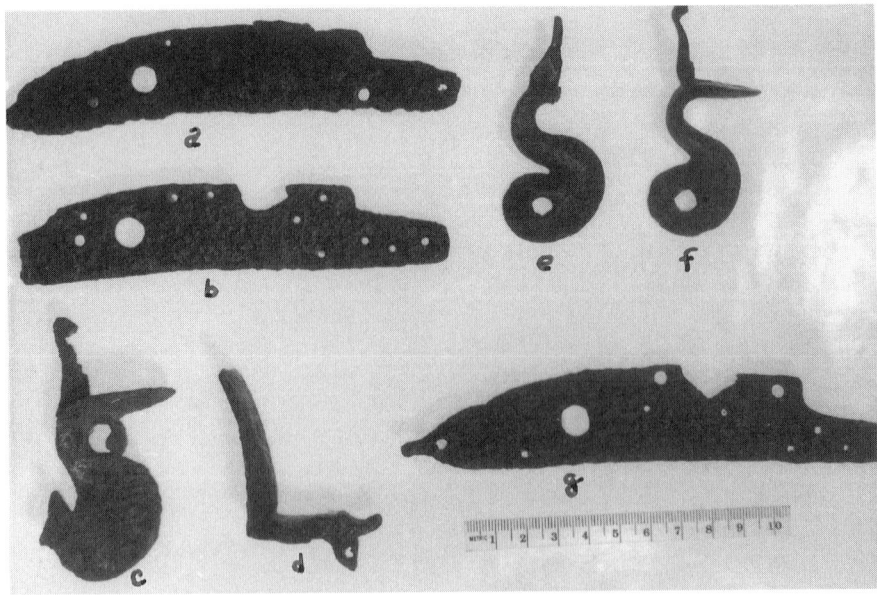

Plate X. Figure 1, gun parts: *a*, pan; *b*, sear; *c*, worm; *d*, musket balls; *e*, tumbler; *f*, flint screw; *g*, trigger; *h–j*, gunflints. Figure 2, gun parts: *a–b*, lock plates; *c*, early cock; *d*, frizzen; *e–f*, cocks; *g*, lock plate.

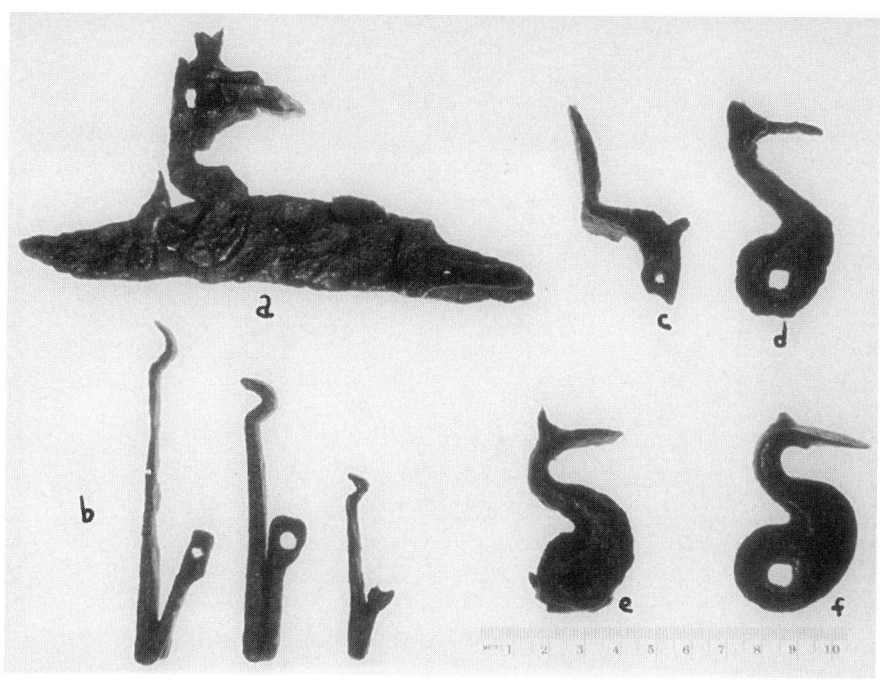

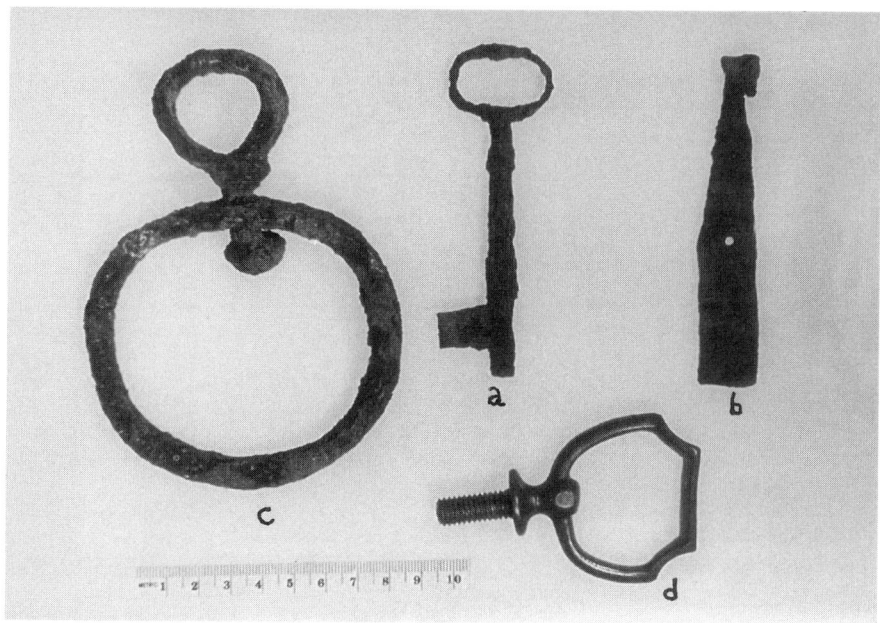

Plate XI. Figure 1, gun parts: *a,* lockplate with cock and mainspring; *b,* mainsprings; *c,* frizzen; *d–f,* cocks. Figure 2, miscellaneous hardware.

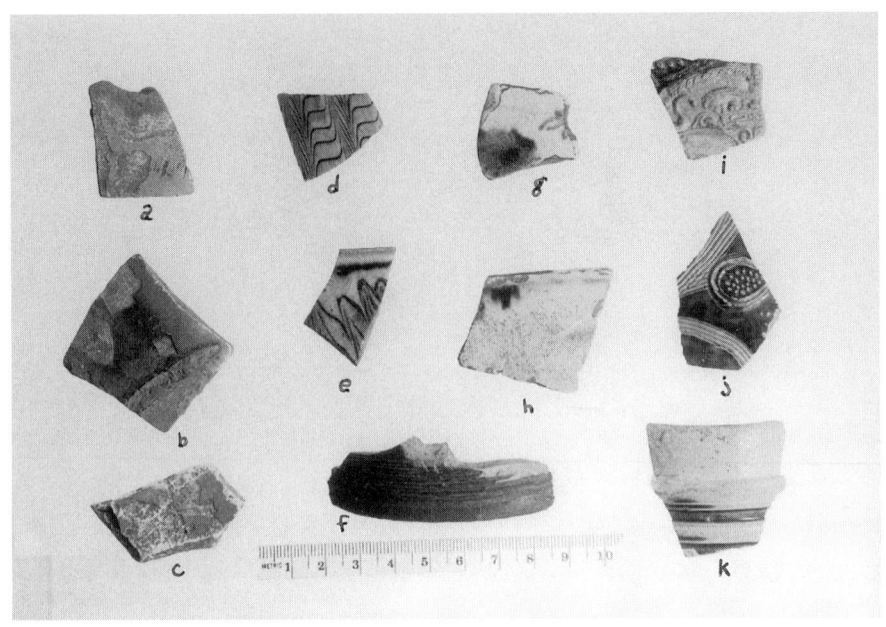
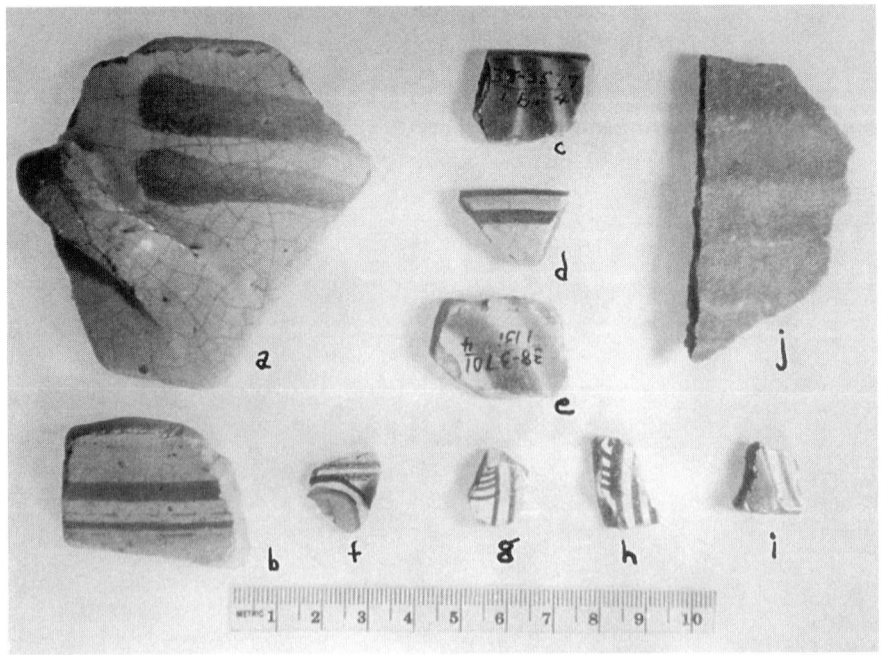

Plate XII. Figure 1, English ceramics. Figure 2, Spanish ceramics: *a–i*, majolica; *j*, olive jar.

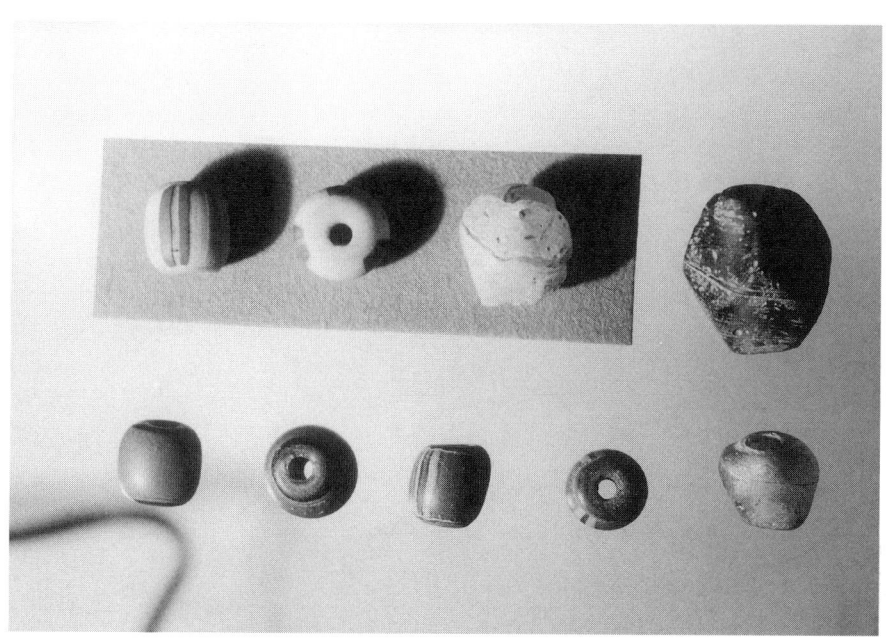

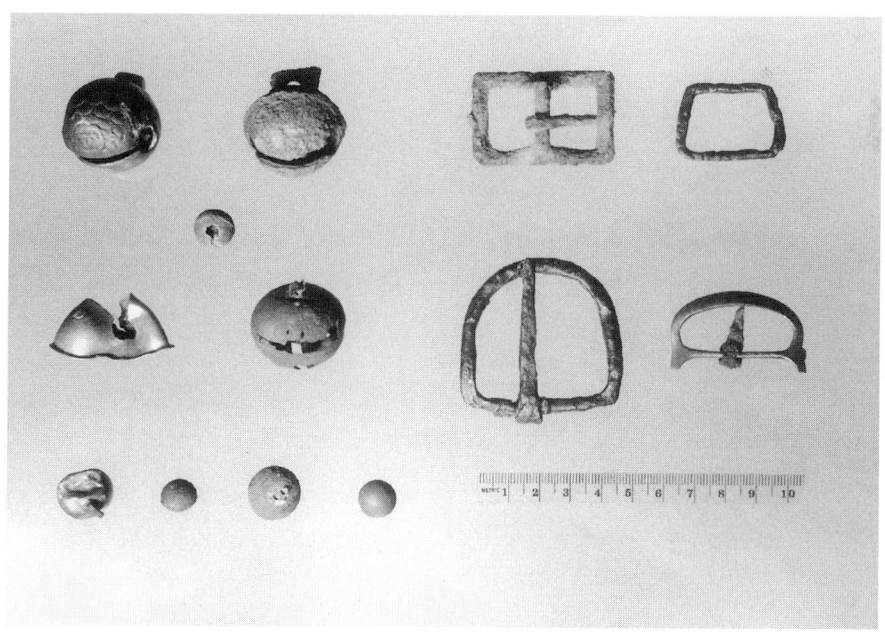

Plate XIII. Figure 1, trade beads. Figure 2, bells, buttons, and buckles.

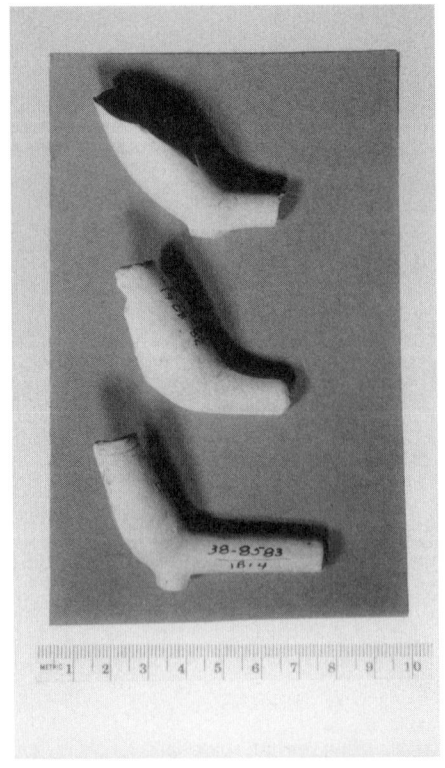

Plate XIV. Figure 1, pipes and scrapers: *a,* clay pipe; *b–f,* stone pipes; *g–i,* glass scrapers; *j,* reworked gunflint. Figure 2, clay pipes.

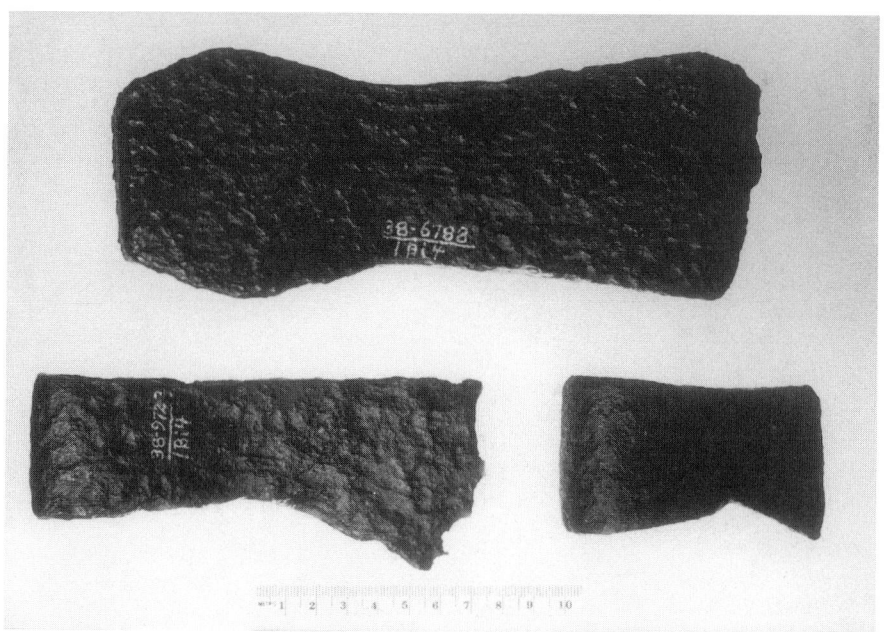

Plate XV. Figure 1, iron objects: *a,* lock plate; *b,* axe; *c,* chisel. Figure 2, axes.

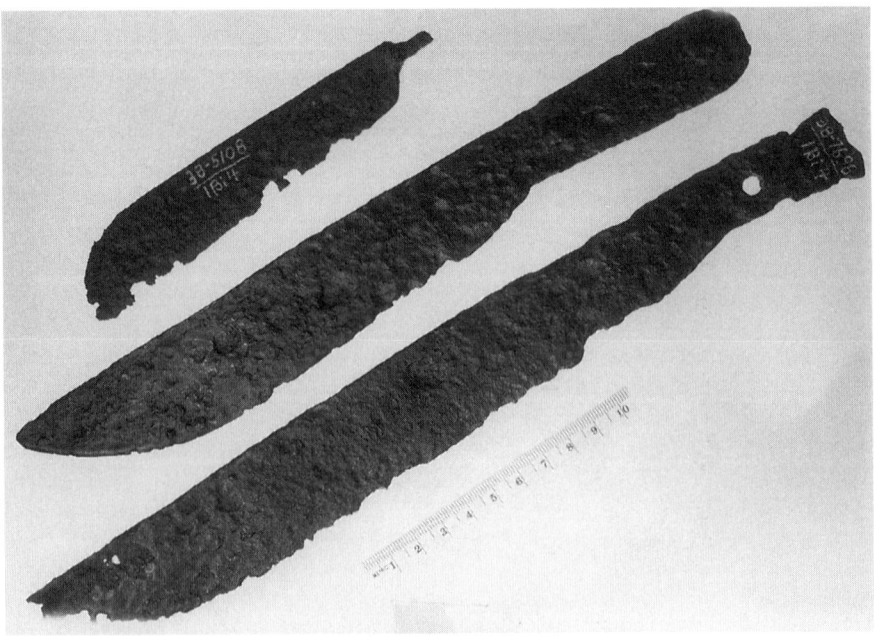

Plate XVI. Figure 1, hoes. Figure 2, knives.

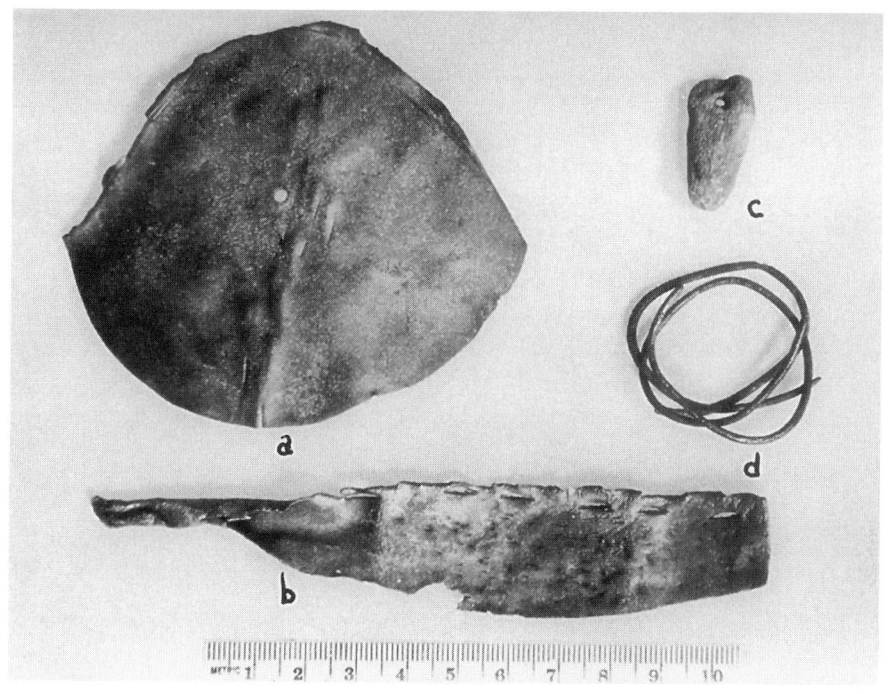

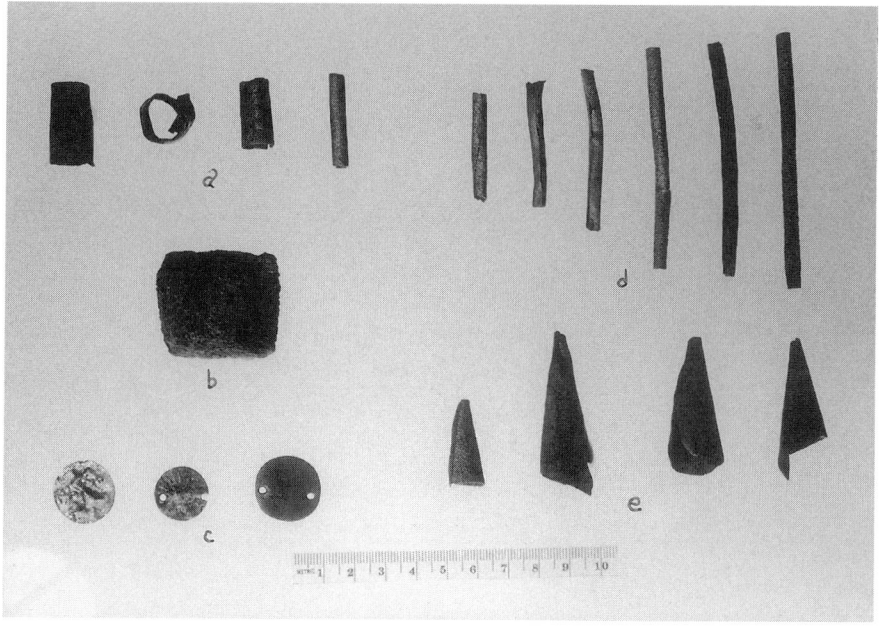

Plate XVII. Figure 1, artifacts of brass and clay: *a*, gorget; *b*, unidentifiable object; *c*, clay pendant; *d*, bracelet. Figure 2, miscellaneous ornaments: *a*, brass tubes; *b*, wire bracelet; *c*, metal disks; *d*, tubes; *e*, tinklers.

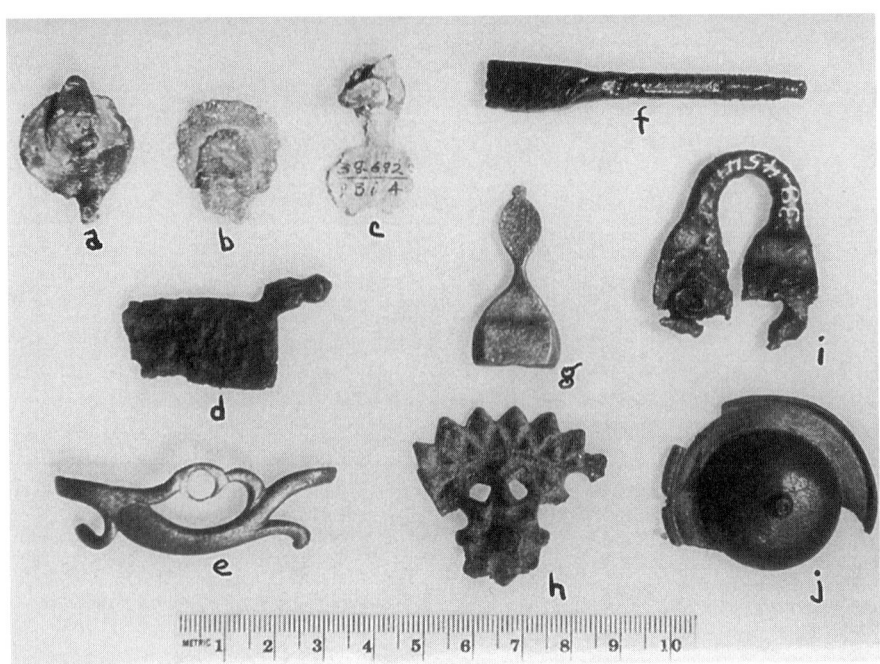

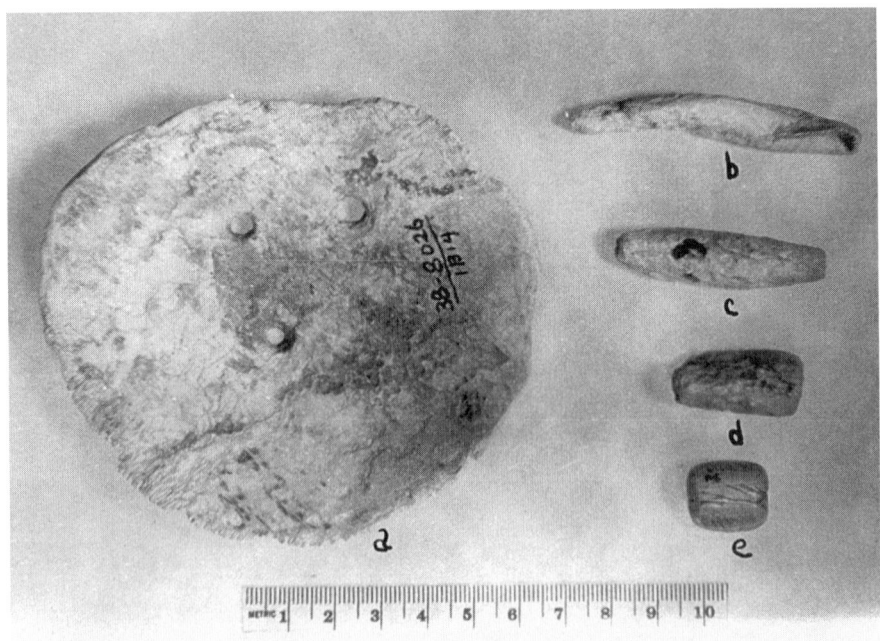

Plate XVIII. Figure 1, miscellaneous artifacts: *a–c*, bale seals; *d*, matchlock pan cover; *e*, gun ornament; *f*, stamp; *g*, gun sight; *h, j*, bridle bosses; *i*, bail. Figure 2, shell gorget and shell beads.

Plate XIX. *Ocmulgee Fields Incised* cazuela (restored).

Plate XX. *Ocmulgee Fields Incised* cazuela (restored).

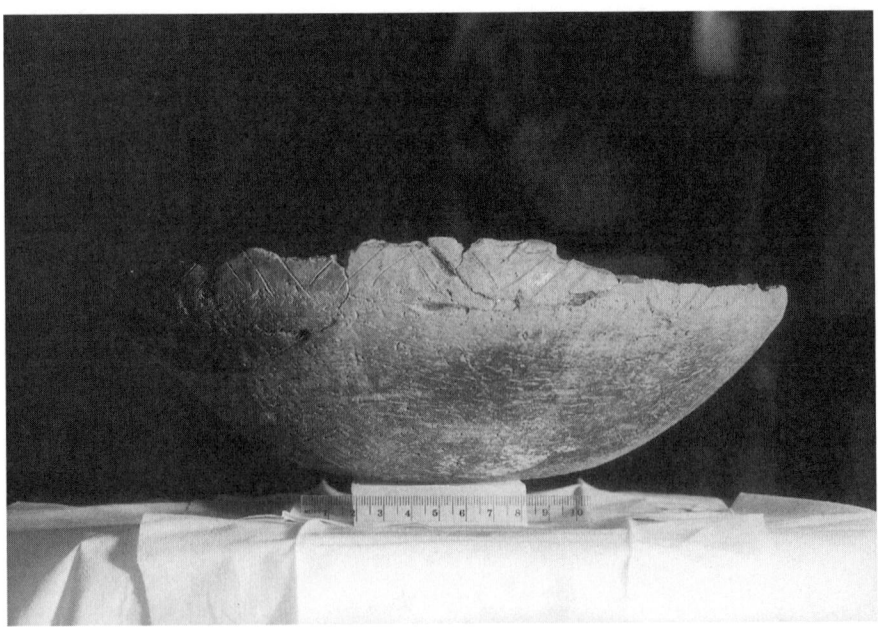

Plate XXI. Figure 1, *Ocmulgee Fields Incised* cazuela. Figure 2, *Ocmulgee Fields Incised* cazuela.

Plate XXII. Figure 1, *Ocmulgee Fields Incised* jar (Woolfolk site). Figure 2, base of historic olla or jar.

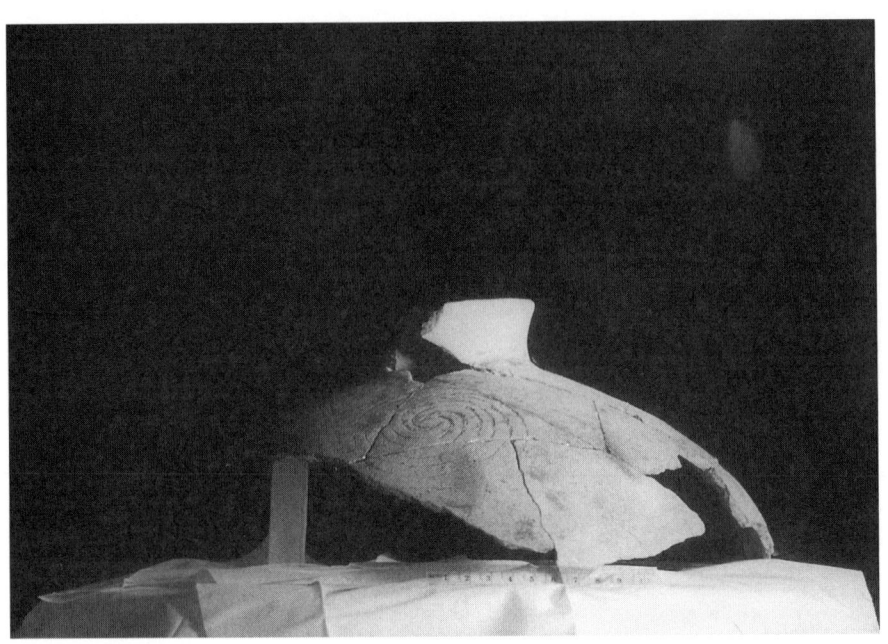

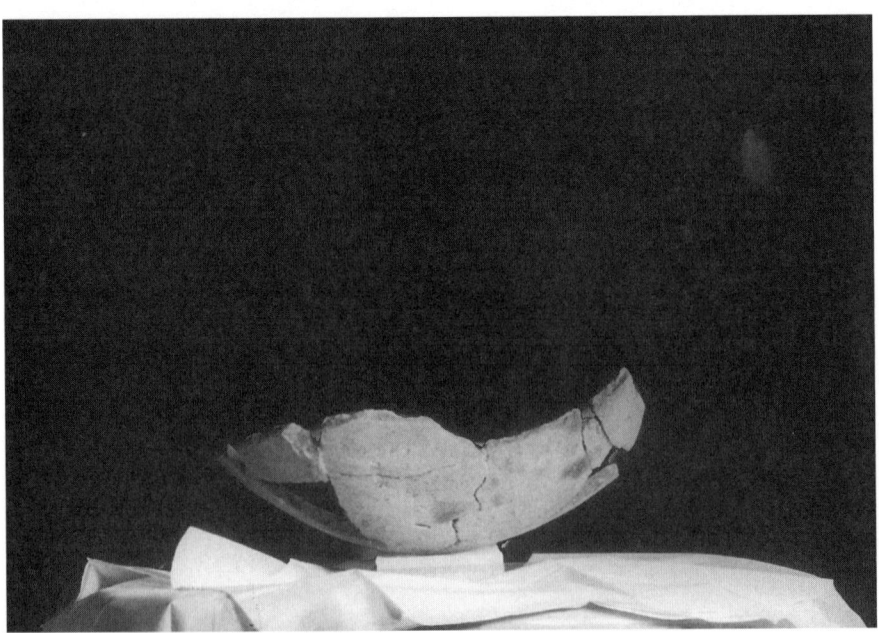

Plate XXIII. *Ocmulgee Fields Incised* jar, upper half and base.

Plate XXIV. Figure 1, plain historic vessel. Figure 2, *Ocmulgee Fields Incised* bowl.

Plate XXV. *Walnut Roughened* bowl.

Plate XXVI. *Walnut Roughened* bowl (restored).

Plate XXVII. Historic vessel of unknown type.

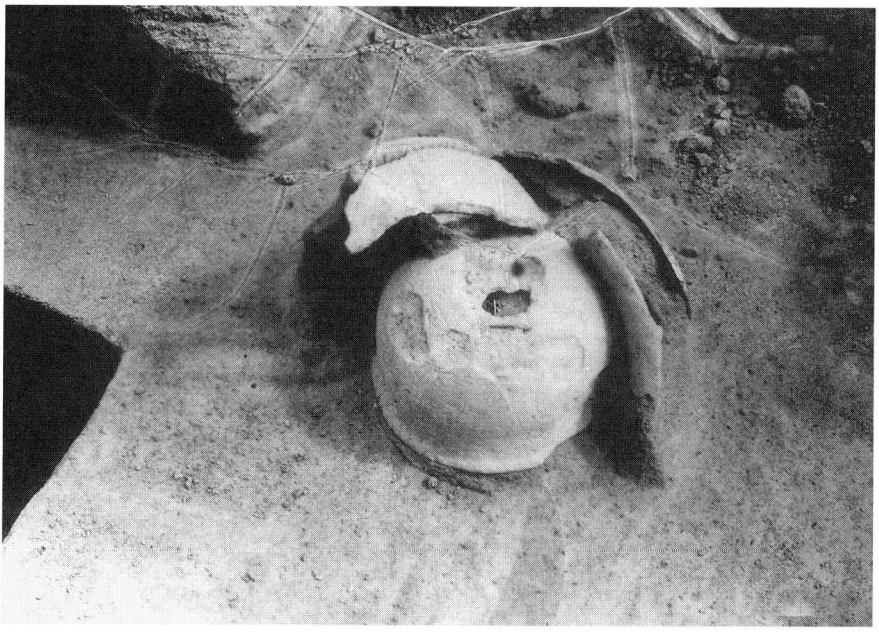

Plate XXVIII. Inverted bowl from house site III.

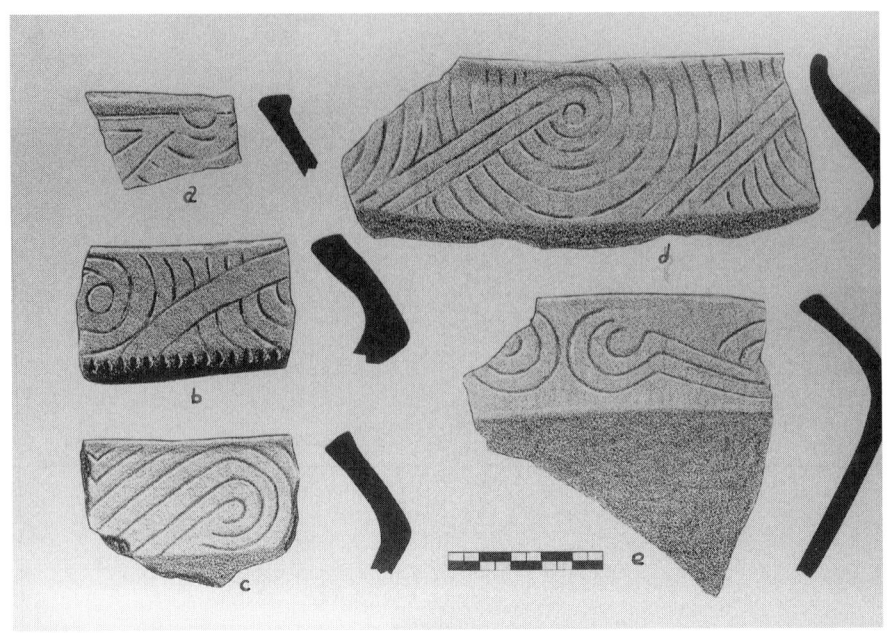

Plate XXIX. *Ocmulgee Fields Incised* scrolls.

Plate XXX. *Ocmulgee Fields Incised* scrolls.

Plate XXXI. *Ocmulgee Fields Incised* linked lines.

Plate XXXII. *Ocmulgee Fields Incised* nested geometric figures.

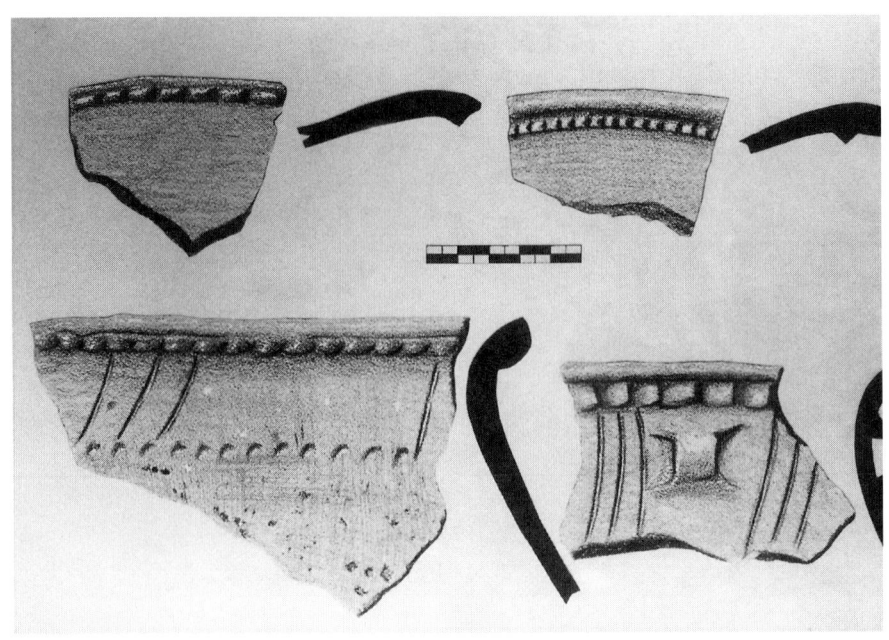
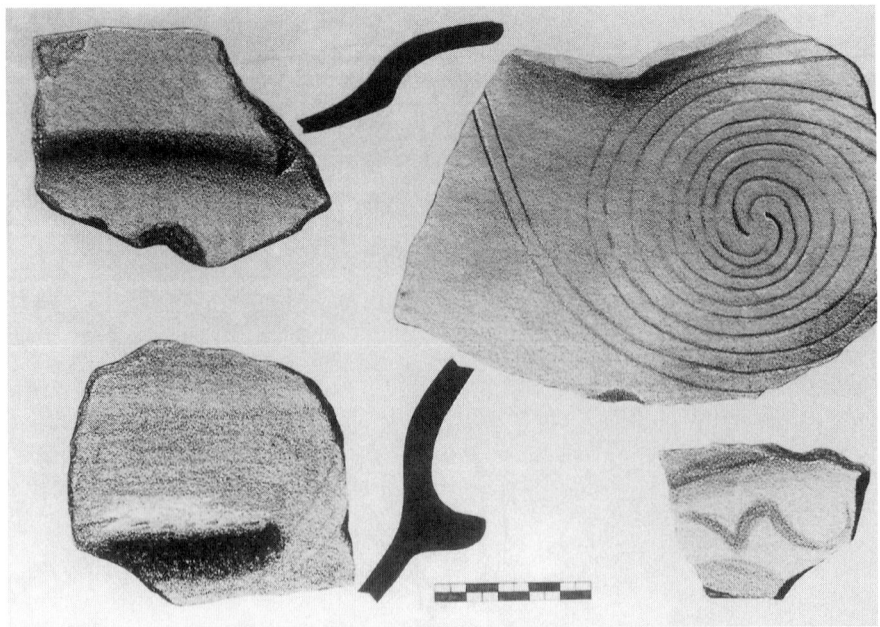

Plate XXXIII. Figure 1, *Walnut Roughened* designs. Figure 2, miscellaneous designs.

# PART TWO
Archaeological and Historical Implications

# 6
# Identification of the Creek Town

[224]There are two lines of evidence bearing on the identification of the specific Lower Creek town that occupied the Macon site during the tenure of the Lower Creeks on the Ocmulgee River. The first of these indicates that the town was Hitchiti Town, the head (and probably mother) town of a number of Hitchiti-speaking settlements. In later years, at least, this group included Hitchiti, Sawokli, Ocmulgee, Oconee, Apalachicola, and perhaps Chiaha (Swanton 1922: 172). The other line of evidence identifies the site at Macon as Ocmulgee Town, one of this group of Hitchiti-speaking peoples, but quite distinct as a town from the separate town of Hitchiti.

Identification of the town as Hitchiti was first made by Swanton (1922: 176) and is usually accepted by most of those who have occasion to mention the site at all. A number of factors led Swanton to make this identification: (1) the Mitchell map of 1755 identifies the site as Hitchiti Old Fields, the presumed former site of the Hitchiti town; (2) Hitchiti, which first appeared under this spelling after the 1690 period, was considered by him to be definitely recorded as one of the Ochese [225]Creek settlements —in other words, it was in the right place at the right time; (3) Swanton had absolutely no evidence of the existence of a town called Ocmulgee before the Yamassee War in 1715 and the retreat to the Chattahoochee River; (4) native tradition, as recorded by Gatschet, supported these facts by asserting that the Hitchiti were the "first to settle at the site of Okmulgi town" (Gatschet 1884: 78), a statement that Swanton understood to mean that Hitchiti Town itself was first located at the conspicuous mound group at Macon.

The most important of this evidence, and the part upon which most of Swanton's other evidence depends, is that obtained from the Mitchell map of 1755, "A Map of the British and French Dominions in North America" (Cummings 1958: Pl. 59; Swanton 1922: Pl. 6). This map locates the Lower Creeks in their post-1715 sites on the Chattahoochee River but cites their former presence on the Ocmulgee and Oconee Rivers: "on these Rivers the lower Creek Indians formerly dwelt, before the war with Carolina in 1715, when they moved to Chattahoochee River." The trading path from Augusta crosses the Ocmulgee River at a point labeled on the map as "Echete Old Town" and the Oconee River at "Ocone Old Town," thus anchoring the identification to the well traced and familiar trade path. "Echete," of course, is simply another spelling of "Hitchiti" and certainly points to the juncture of the Ocmulgee River with the trade path as the former site of the Lower Creek town of Hitchiti. [226]The Mitchell map might be objected to on the basis of its late date, some forty years after the last residence of the Lower Creeks on the Ocmulgee River, but it was itself based upon several other earlier maps and used the Barnwell map of about 1722 as its chief source for the Carolina back country. The Barnwell map has a very respectable reputation for accuracy since it was based on the findings of John Barnwell, touted by contemporary observers as one of the most well informed persons on conditions, and presumably also locations, in the interior (Cummings 1958: 47). It is unfortunate that extant copies of the Barnwell map (Cummings 1958: Pl. 48) are too indistinct to provide any additional information and too blurred to even second the Mitchell map's identification of the Macon site as old Hitchiti Town.

The second line of evidence, which points to the identification of the site as Ocmulgee Town, was supported, at least indirectly, by Crane (1956: 133) although not at all by Swanton. The principal piece of late eighteenth century documentary evidence is that of Hawkins, who included Ocmulgee in his lists of villages belonging to mother towns. Hawkins listed it as the "Ocmulgee Village" and said of it that "there is a few families, the remains of the Ocmulgee people who formerly resided at the Ocmulgee fields on Ocmulgee River" (Hawkins 1916: 173). Swanton, using Hawkins's classification of Ocmulgee as a daughter village of Hitchiti, reconciled this reference with his own hypothesis by supposing that Ocmulgee Town [227]broke off from the Hitchiti town during or immediately upon the exodus from the Ocmulgee-Oconee area and only existed as a separate and independent village after that event (Swanton 1922: 178). Ocmulgee village, then, could reasonably be supposed to have adopted its name from that of the river upon which the Lower Creeks formerly dwelt.

It must be remembered that Swanton did not have any reason to belive that an Ocmulgee Town was in existence prior to 1715. Early maps consulted by him did not show an Ocmulgee among the towns of the Lower Creeks, and he was also handicapped by inaccurate dates for some of the early Creek movements. Information from Spanish sources, however, coupled with more reliable information on the movements of the Lower Creek towns, indicates quite clearly that a town named Ocmulgee did in fact exist among the Lower Creeks before the original removal to the Ocmulgee-Oconee area. Matheos's punitive expedition to eliminate in 1685 Woodward's trade outpost on the Chattahoochee River passed through twelve towns, among them "Ocmulgue" (Bolton 1925: 121). In addition to this recording of the presence of the town on his first trip, Matheos listed "Ocmulgue" as one of the towns that submitted to him during his second trip up the Chattahoochee River later the same year (p. 122). Further supporting evidence for the pre-1715 existence of an Ocmulgee Town comes from Crane. He lists the "Okmulgee" town as one of the signers of a treaty of alliance between Carolina and the Creeks in August of 1705, [228]fully ten years before the Yamassee War (1956: 82). Bishop Calderón in his important listing of the Lower Creek towns in 1675 included among them the town of "Ocmulgui" (Wenhold 1936: 9). All of this material supports the existence of Ocmulgee Town before 1715 and lends more authority to Hawkins' statement that a town named Ocmulgee was the original occupant of the old fields at Macon, Georgia.

Additionally, there is a historic continuity through the eighteenth, nineteenth, and twentieth centuries of referring to the site at Macon as "Ocmulgee Old Fields" or "Old Ocmulgae Fields," never Hitchiti Old Fields or any name that could be interpreted as referring to Hitchiti Town. James Adair specifically cited "*Okmulge,* the old waste town, belonging to the *Muskohge* 150 miles S.W. of Augusta in Georgia" (Williams 1930: 39). Adair further commented on his route through the site as the "tedious Chikkasah war path," known to an earlier generation as the Lower Creek Trading Path, whose traces are part of the archaeological evidence uncovered on the Middle Plateau. This information securely ties Adair's "Okmulge" to the Macon site as early as 1744, when he began his operations among the Chickasaw (p. ix). William Bartram mentioned the area as the "ancient Indian fields, which are called the Oakmulge fields" (Harper 1958: 34) during his travels of the last part of the eighteenth century. Hawkins also referred to the site itself as being the "Ocmulgee fields" (Hawkins 1916: 173, 427). Gatschet [229](1884: 152n.) in his discussion of the lower trade path stated that it "passed Fort Hawkins built upon the Okmulgi old fields, then the site of Macon." Gatschet's other reference to the site (see above), interpreted somewhat differently by Swanton, could also mean that the *site* of the town named Ocmulgee was anciently settled by Hichiti-speaking peoples. In that case, the Hitchiti occupation would have been the Mississippian peoples, a viewpoint certainly compatible with the way the Creeks themselves interpreted the mounds at Macon. Treaties with the Creeks in 1803 and 1806 also identify the site as "Ocmulgee Old Fields" or "Ocmulgee Old Towns"

(Harris 1958: 27) using the familiar "old fields" designation to indicate an area once occupied by a certain town. Thus the extant literature provides a continuous trail of information stretching over the centuries even to the present when the site at Macon is called Ocmulgee National Monument.

Some of the confusion about the identification of the site stems from the fact that the nearby river bears the same name as the Lower Creek town that formerly stood on its banks. Confusing the name of the river with the name of the town has made it easy to overlook statements in the literature that might have provided clues to the identification of the town site. Thus, for example, Colonel Moore's raid into Florida from central Georgia has been considered in his own words to have referred to the Ocmulgee River rather than to Ocmulgee Town (see below) while other references to Ocmulgee have been similarly [230]misinterpreted.

The Ocmulgee River itself received a name fairly late in history and was given that particular name because the Lower Creek Trading Path, the most important route into the area, crossed its banks at a Creek town, or more probably the site of a former Lower Creek town, called Ocmulgee. During most of the early historic period and certainly during the tenure of the Lower Creeks in the Ocmulgee-Oconee area, the river was known to the English as Ochese Creek (Crane 1956: 36; Swanton 1922:32). The earliest mention of the name Ochese Creek in official government records was in 1702 when Colonel Moore mentioned "ye Cussatoes which live on Ocha-Sa Creek . . . " (Salley 1932: 6).

The name Ochese Creek is itself not one of very great antiquity. It appears to have been bestowed on the river as a consequence of newly acquired importance after the Lower Creeks moved there around 1690. Bolton and Ross credit the name as coming from the fact that a group of Yuchis were already settled on the river, and it now "became known to the English as Ocheese (Uchis) Creek" (Bolton and Ross 1925: 54). This interpretation of the term "Ochese" is probably incorrect since as early as the Desoto expedition (Robertson 1933: 77) the term "Achese" occurs in the central Georgia region in a context that seems to be Hitchiti. The names Ochese Creek and Ochese Creek Indians appear occasionally in the official records of early South Carolina after 1702, but the Ocmulgee River [231]by that name does not. Crane has demonstrated that the old name of Ochese Creek is really responsible for the naming of the Creeks themselves since they derived their name from a shortening of the term "Ochese Creek Indians" (Crane 1918).

Evidence from early maps leaves no doubt at all that Ochese Creek and the present-day Ocmulgee River are one and the same. The Nairne map of 1711 includes a reference to the "Ochese" nation in the proper spot even though he does not show the river itself (Cummings 1958: Pl. 45). The Mitchell map, while giving the Ocmulgee River its modern name, still clings to the name Ochese Creek for the whole upper part of the river above the juncture with Tobesofkee Creek, where the "old towns" are located. The Lamhatty account of about 1707 (Bushnell 1908) clearly shows a "Wichise River" as one of the two rivers running through the Lower Creek settlements. Incidentally, Bushnell's identification of these rivers as the Flint and Chattahoochee is in error since by 1707 the towns cited in the Lamhatty acccount were no longer in the Chattahoochee region but east on the Ocmulgee River; apparently Beverley confused the Altamaha River with the Apalachicola, and Bushnell followed suit.

Given the name Ochese Creek, the problem becomes one of demonstrating when Ochese Creek became the Ocmulgee River. If it acquired that name even one year before the Lower Creek removal from central Georgia, then there is [232]no sure way of proving that the river was indeed named after the town. Determining the date upon or near which the river acquired its name involves checking some of the extant maps of the southeastern United States during the early years of exploration and expansion. Many of these maps are not detailed enough to record specific Indian towns or to mention trading houses, but they do provide an interesting developmental sequence for river names. The Le Maire map of 1716, "Carte Nouvelle de la Louisiane" (photocopy in the Clements Library, University of Michigan), shows the "Caouitas" on an unnamed river with no mention of either the Ocmulgee River or the Oconee. De Lisle, "Carte de la Louisiane" of 1718, labels the Ocmulgee River as the "R. des Caouitas" or "R. de May." The Moll map of 1729 (Moll 1736: no. 51) labels neither the Ocmulgee River nor the Oconee with their modern names although the Altamaha, of which the Ocmulgee and Oconee are branches, is properly named. Moll shows the Lower Creek Trading Path crossing the unnamed Ocmulgee River at a town called "Ocounelias" and the similarly unnamed Oconee at a town called "Oconery's." The second of these is evidently Oconee Town, but the first, from its position on the site at Macon, is untranslatable as far as known Lower Creek towns are concerned. Particularly important in this context is the map made by Thomas Nairne as an inset into the Crisp map of 1711 (Cummings 1958: Pl. 45). Nairne of all sources should have been a model of accuracy since he was an Indian agent for the Board of Commissioners of the Indian Trade and was [233]intimately familiar with most of the interior. However, he shows the Ochese Creek settlements entirely on the Oconee River (called "Okuny" on the map) and illustrates no separate branch of the Altamaha that could even be considered as the future Ocmulgee River. Apparently Nairne mistook both the Ocmulgee and Oconee for

156 / Part Two. Archaeological and Historical Implications

a single river, which he labeled as the Okuny. As late as 1733, the Popple map of that year fails to name the Ocmulgee River (Swanton 1922: Pl. 4).

Such later maps of the Southeast as the Wright map of 1735 (Cummings 1958: Pl. 60), the Mitchell map of 1755 (Pl. 59), the DeBrahm map of 1766 (Pl. 61), the 1764 map of the Southern Indian District (Hulbert 1908: no. 41), and the Purcell map of around 1770 (Swanton 1922: Pl. 7) do show a river labeled the Ocmulgee and certainly some of them were based on maps nearer in time to the critical year of 1715. They seem to indicate overwhelmingly, however, that information about the back country was very incomplete during the period immediately following the Yamassee War and that the Ocmulgee River must have received its name well after that event. This, coupled with the fact that the Spanish sources indicate the existence of an Ocmulgee town on the Chattahoochee River before 1690 (Bolton 1925) and give the town name a clear priority in time, seems to provide sufficient information to completely eliminate the possibility that the town was named for the river rather than vice versa.

Since the river name was bestowed so late, apparently [234]well after the Creeks left the Ocmulgee River area, there can be no question but that its source was Carolinian even if the word itself was Indian. The problem remains to demonstrate that the Carolinians named the river for the abandoned Indian town situated at the juncture of the Lower Creek Trading Path with the river. The best supporting evidence comes from the nearby Oconee River; this river bears the name of the Lower Creek town on the trading path at the point where that path crossed the river. Like Ocmulgee, the town of Oconee has a clear priority in time over the Oconee River, but unlike Ocmulgee Town, Oconee has good documentation as far as its location between 1685 and 1715 is concerned (Hawkins 1848: 68). For travelers along the Lower Creek Trading Path, the fords across the Oconee and Ocmulgee Rivers bore the names of the towns that had once been there (hence the Moll map's "Oconery's" and "Ocounelias"). Eventually these names were transferred to the rivers themselves, and old names, like Ochese Creek and Kasita River, fell into disuse.

Information on the late dating of the Ocmulgee River's name makes possible a different interpretation of Moore's often cited narrative of his 1703 raid on the Apalachee. His brief mention of Ocmulgee must now be interpreted as referring to the people or town called the Ocmulgee rather than to the river as has previously been assumed (Kelly 1938: 55; Pope 1956: 52): "may it please your honour [the governor of South Carolina] to accept of this short narrative of what I, with the army under my [235]command, have been doing since my departure from the Ockomulgee, on the 19th of December" (Swanton 1922: 121). Further on in his narrative, Moore used

Identification of the Creek Town / 157

the same grammatical form in referring to another town, "I sent to the cassique of *the* Ibitachka" and "we have left *the* Apalatchia but that one town" (my italics). In the first statement, the interposition of the definite article is the way modern speakers of English would refer to a river, that is, *the* Ocmulgee. Other examples of similar construction in Moore's literary style indicate that he used the definite article in referring to groups of people or towns, as *the* Ocmulgee. Coupled with the knowledge that Moore could not have been referring to the river at all, it seems that he was unquestionably mentioning Ocmulgee Town and not the Ocmulgee River. Thus, Moore's raid to ravage and destroy the Apalachee missions and towns can be defiinitely related to the Macon site, and the call to arms of a thousand Lower Creeks and fifty Carolinians can be given a solid location in space as well as in time.

One further subject should be considered in this context—the problem of specific historic references to the trading house and its occupants. As early as 1938, an attempt was made to track down citations in the historical literature that might refer, directly or indirectly, to the trading house itself (Friedlander 1938). In spite of considerable effort, no information was obtained, perhaps because of inability to correctly identify the Indian town name and confusion of the town and the river name. The [236]trading house remained until the present as "an historical foundling" (Kelly 1939) and "Ocmulgee's trading post riddle" (Kelly and Friedlander 1939). Critical to answering the whole question is determining exactly when during the 1690 to 1715 period the trading house was in use. Specific dates of one particular year or another have not been forthcoming from any of the trade materials recovered in and around the remains of the stockade during archaeological work there. Kelly, however, has recorded a brass scale weight stamped with the date 1712 (Kelly 1938: 55; 1939: 332) which was found by an early visitor to the site. This scale weight, consonant with the commercial nature of the establishment, has long since disappeared, but it seems a usable date indicator. The date of mean distribution of English pipestems is 1709.9 or 1710, a date in close agreement with that on the scale weight.

Further supporting this general time period is the only entry in the *Journals of the Commissioners of the Indian Trade* that mentions the trader at Ocmulgee: "upon reading a letter of James Lucas who complains against Captain Musgrove detayning two Slaves unjustly from him dated at Oakmulgoes, July the 12th, 1710; Ordered that the Agent give the said Lucas notice that he appear before the Commissioners who will hear his Case att his coming to Town" (McDowell 1955: 6). This entry indicates that Lucas, complaining against Captain Musgrove, was in fact a resident in the back country since his case could not be judged until he put in an appearance in Charles

[237]Town. It also indicates that Lucas composed his letter specifically at Ocmulgee Town, where he was most probably the resident trader. At that time, trading with the Indians was the only reason for any individual to actually live within an Indian town, and the entry in the journals clearly places Lucas as a participant in the slave trade. Unfortunately, Lucas must have settled out of court with Captain John Musgrove, for no other entries in the brief trade journals mention him. This single reference, cryptic as it is, nevertheless is sufficient to provide Ocmulgee's trading house not only with a tenant but also with a date for its occupation and a record of at least one of the many things that happened there.

Information from other government records supplies some additional information on Lucas and Musgrove as well as on several others operating in the vicinity of Ochese Creek. John Musgrove was an Indian trader of long and somewhat unsavory reputation. He was among the traders called to Charles Town to testify on Spanish and/or French aggression in 1703 (Salley 1934: 97), but there is no indication of where he was trading in those early years. By 1706, Musgrove again appeared in the government records, this time because of action taken against him for his many misdeeds among the Indians (Salley 1939). By 1710 he was trading with Tomolla or Tumella King (McDowell 1955: 5, 24), a Yamasee chief (Salley 1934: 36), and it is probable that he was principally concerned in the Yamassee trade during most of his career.

[238]James Lucas also appeared in the records by virtue of his misdeeds among the Indians. In 1706 he and two other traders, John Pight and Anthony Probat (or Probert), were the subject of Commons House of Assembly action because of their unscrupulous behavior among the Indians (Salley 1939: 24). These three men, cited as partners in the Indian trade, were accused of acting in concert with some unidentified Indians in order to enslave twenty Indians from the Yamassee town of Illcombee (p. 33). Their action was considered all the more reprehensible by the Commons House since it took place *after* direct government order to these three men to cease slave-taking among the free Illcombee. Who the other Indians concerned in this slave raiding were is not known, but judging from Pight and Lucas's trade locations, they were very surely Lower Creeks. John Pight was the trader at Kasita (McDowell 1955: 26), and his partner James Lucas, according to the brief mention in the trade journals, was the trader at Ocmulgee Town. No information is yet available on the location of Anthony Probat, the third trader mentioned in the partnership of Pight, Lucas, and Probat.

Further investigation into the matter of the unfortunate Illcombee Indians brought another trader, James Child, into the affair. When the Commons House of Assembly finally ordered the Attorney General to prosecute the

## Identification of the Creek Town / 159

guilty men, Child and Probat, Musgrove and Pight were the traders indicted. James Lucas appears to have escaped prosecution of any kind.

[239]Other traders mentioned for the Lower Creeks during their 1690–1715 residence on the Ocmulgee River include a number agitating for military action against the French and Spanish during 1702 and 1703. In 1703 the elusive trader and border intriger "Captain Antonio" Dodsworth was in Charles Town to be examined before the Commons House although there is no record that he ever put in an appearance before the House (Salley 1934: 97). Dodsworth may have been the trader at Coweta, for the records state that he and his Indian followers built some kind of fort at Coweta in preparation for conflict with the Spanish (Bolton and Ross 1925: 58). He and his followers led their expeditionary force south from the town of Achito, however, and not Coweta (Bolton 1925: 126), and there is no mention of the name of the trader or traders at Achito.

Other traders in the Ochese Creek settlements with Dodsworth were Francis Williams and Samuel Veals, both of whom wrote insistent letters to Charles Town about the imminent danger of French and/or Spanish attacks on the Ochese Creek towns (Salley 1934: 97). Three other traders of the same time period, but not known positively to have been trading on Ochese Creek, were Thomas Walsh, William Steen (Salley 1934: 97). and Robert Mackoone (Rivers 1856: 456). These men were lumped with Dodsworth in the records, but no really definite information is available on their locations in the Indian towns.

# 7
# The Lower Creeks and Their Neighbors

[240]For a number of years, attempts have been made to reconcile the succession of archaeological cultures in Georgia and Alabama, particularly as it is expressed in ceramic traditions, with the various modern Indian groups that lived in those two states at the time of European contact. The two main, and also conflicting, points of view on this matter involve the specific historic Indian groups that are or are thought to be the genetic descendants of the as yet poorly defined culture known as Lamar (Fairbanks 1952; Sears 1952, 1956). The most recent of these two schools of thought, represented primarily by William H. Sears, suggests strongly that Creek culture developed in the Coosa–Tallapoosa area and only later, as late as the 1685–1690 movement of the Lower Creek towns from the Chattahoochee River to the Ocmulgee–Oconee drainage, spread into what is now the state of Georgia (Willey and Sears 1952; Sears 1955). Lamar, or certain parts of it, can then be equated with prehistoric Cherokee cultures (Sears 1955: 143). The traditional view, stated most recently by Charles H. Fairbanks (1952; 1958), is that at least some of the Lamar sites in Georgia are [241]prehistoric Creek and that the Creeks are indigenous enough to Georgia to have shared in the general Lamar tradition.

Sears bases his arguments primarily on what he feels to be the close similarity between Cherokee ceramics (Sears 1952; Caldwell 1955) and some of the Lamar materials as well as on a denial that Creek pottery is "Lamar-style" (Sears 1955: 146). He also supports his arguments by stating that the only known locations for the Creeks in Georgia are the Chattahoochee River Valley and the upper Ocmulgee–Oconee drainage (1955: 145) where they moved in the late seventeenth century. Hence, the Creeks, because their movement into what is now Georgia was so late, could not have been responsible for the prehistoric Lamar or Lamar-like materials of Georgia and/or Florida. Fairbanks bases his arguments on similarity of culture content as he sees it between modern Creek culture and some of pre-

## Lower Creeks and Their Neighbors / 161

historic Lamar (Fairbanks 1952) and specifically upon a close resemblance between Creek and some of the Lamar pottery (Fairbanks 1958).

Both of these points of view agree on the fact that the peoples later known as Creeks or Muscogees are intrusive into the more ancient cultural tradition of Georgia, but they differ sharply in the matter of time. Sears maintains that original Creek entry into central Georgia proper was an event of the late seventeenth century and no earlier (Willey and Sears 1952: 11) while Fairbanks supports the traditional view that Muskhogean-speaking peoples—[242]specifically the Creeks—entered the Southeast with the first appearance of Mississippian cultures and remained there to contribute genetically and culturally to the mainstream of Georgia prehistory (Fairbanks 1952: 295).

One of the major unrecognized problems in this controversy is the lack on either side of a real definition of the term "Creek" and an additional lack of any attempts to decide how extensive the genetic relationships of the Creeks actually are or who is to be admitted as being Creek. It is possible in historic times to isolate the large group of towns known then as Lower Creeks, but it is very difficult to decide what correspondence this group has to any indigenous political or social or linguistic entities. A case can even be made for considering much of the political organization of the historic period as a result of white contact rather than reflecting prehistoric units of government. In early historic times, the processes that produced the confederacies and the fairly clean lines of division between the Creeks and, say, the Apalachees were already at work; and the incredible effects of European contact were already driving the natives westward and creating a shatter belt whose original components are sometimes incapable of identification. The complex composition of the original Lower Creeks, as so named by the Carolinians (see below), in addition to the common Southeastern practice of adopting and sheltering whole towns of quite foreign peoples are telling clues to the looseness or lack of any tribal political structure [243]in aboriginal times and even to the lack of any clear-cut "tribal" consciousness as would later emerge for them from the pressures placed upon them by English and American colonists.

The Lower Creeks felt themselves peoples "of one fire" with many other groups, and determining the extent of this common feeling, insofar as it coincides with common culture, is a major project in understanding the derivation of the towns later called Creek and in understanding their archaeology. A term other than "Creek" seems to be required for this broader group, a term that will not only include the Ochese Creeks proper and the Lower Chattahoochee Valley Creeks (meaning those towns that failed to join in the eastward movement in the late seventeenth century) but will also recognize the at present somewhat nebulous Hitchiti sub-stratum, whose membership is a decidedly important factor among all the recognizable groups that emerged as Lower Creeks in historic times. This whole problem is no matter of simply splitting hairs; it is one of critical importance to any understanding of cultural development in the far Southeast. It is an easy matter to isolate a few towns using wholly arbitrary criteria and propose to trace their ancestry, but it is quite another matter to isolate in the historic Southeast meaningful groupings that exhibit common cultural characteristics, some of which can be the basis of an archaeological attack on origins and development. The complexity of this problem is well reflected in [244]Swanton's scholarly study *The Early History of the Creek Indians and Their Neighbors* (1922). Not even Swanton, with his extensive fund of knowledge on early Creek history, was able to clearly divide the dozens of groups and towns he was working with into mutually exclusive categories of "Creeks" and "neighbors." The lines between them are often so hazy in clearly historic times that attempts to enforce them rigidly in the prehistoric past are almost impossible.

Fairbanks and Sears, both attempting to trace the ancestry of certain Creek towns, never really face this problem. Fairbanks limits himself to the specific towns of Kasita, Coweta, Ocmulgee, and Oconee in his early discussion of the origins of the Creeks (Fairbanks 1952) and apparently treats as "Creeks" only the towns that emerged from the 1690–1715 residence of a particular group of towns on the Ocmulgee River. It is not clear from his discussions whether he would include such groups as the Apalachicola or any of the towns associated with the Apalachee or whether his criteria for including a town as "Creek" are linguistic, cultural, political, or simply spatial.

Sears's usage is even less clear since his use of the terms "Upper" and "Lower" Creek is quite different from the traditional usage of the Carolinians or that employed by Swanton (1922). In most aspects it seems closest to the old classification of William Bartram (Harper 1958). In his discussions, Sears includes Kasita [245]as an Upper Creek town (Willey and Sears 1952: 11), which means in his terminology a Muskogee-speaking town, and with Kasita he includes only Hitchiti, Ocmulgee, and Oconee as being "Creeks" (Willey and Sears 1952: 12). Elsewhere Sears admits Coweta as a Creek town in addition to these four (Sears 1955: 148). Specifically excluded from this group are "the various units of Hitchiti-speaking 'Lower Creeks' such as Apalachicola, Apalachee, and Yamassee" (Sears 1955: 145). Exactly why certain groups should be excluded as Creeks while others are included is never quite clear. It cannot be on the basis of language in spite of the label "Hitchiti-speaking" since three of the towns that Sears is willing to call

Creek (Hitchiti, Ocmulgee, and Oconee) are, like the excluded Apalachicola, Hitchiti speakers. The Yamassee and Apalachee, while classified as Muskogean by Swanton (1922), were not included by him among the Hitchiti and cannot be excluded for that reason. Cultural or even political differences cannot be the basis of Sears's selection since Apalachicola, at least, shares most of the traits, ceramic and otherwise, found at Kasita and Ocmulgee (Caldwell 1948, 1952). Apalachicola was very closely associated with the loosely-defined Creek sphere long before the removal to the Ocmulgee River area and enjoyed the reputation of having shared with Kasita and Coweta the position of "lead town" among the Creeks at an earlier date (Swanton 1922: 129–130). To the Spanish, at least, all the towns in the area north of the Apalachee were simply called Apalachicola, including [246]the Indians residing on Ochese Creek (Boyd, Smith, and Griffin 1951: 8). It is therefore difficult to see why Oconee, Ocmulgee, and Hitchiti should be treated as "culturally close relatives" (Sears 1955: 146) of the "upper, Muskogee-speaking" (p. 146) Creeks (meaning Kasita and Coweta) while the rest of the culturally close relatives are entirely ignored. Sears's final conclusion from this selective choice of towns is that " . . . it is likely that the inhabitants of Coweta, Kasita, and the Ocmulgee and Oconee moved in from some such area . . . in Alabama known . . . as the 'Upper Creek' area with Coosa at its center" (Sears 1955: 148). This involves the curious picture of Kasita and Coweta bringing their Hitchiti-speaking towns, bound to them by as yet unknown ties, down into the Chattahoochee River Valley to develop Creek culture in an area where peoples of Creek culture already resided.

The many problems involved in setting useful limits to any "Creek" culture sphere are only incidental to the realization that there is such a thing, an area where as yet the political alignments and foreign alliances of the contact period had not developed and an area where archaeologically there is some hope of tracing roots into the prehistoric past. Any student working in this area must realize that the few towns named as Creeks by the English or any arbitrary selection of towns from this group do not constitute the whole of the cultural tradition. They are part of it, and their relationships [247]to the many other groups defined by the English or Spanish—Apalachee, Yamassee, Guale, Apalachicola—must be considered before any sweeping stantements about origins or lack of them can be made.

At the present time, judging from available historic sources, the extent of any proposed Lower Creek or Lower Creek–allied culture area appears to be from the lower part of the Chattahoochee River Valley across the lower part of Georgia, following the fall line, all the way to the borders of South Carolina. This is the area where Desoto found towns and villages with Mus-

164 / Part Two. Archaeological and Historical Implications

khogean names, some of which are still recognizable among Apalachee, Yamassee, and Creeks (Swanton 1922; Robertson 1933; Bourne 1904). This is also the area where archaeological assemblages—Apalachee, Georgia Coastal, and others—share a cultural tradition loosely defined as a kind of Lamar (Willey and Sears 1952: 12). It is also, incidentally, the land that the Creeks claim as a traditional home both in folklore (Hawkins 1848: 19, 23) and in official government treaties (Rivers 1856: 37). The position of the Lower Creeks (including the Ochese Creeks and the Chattahoochee River Valley Creeks) seems to be more within this milieu rather than within that of the Coosa-Tallapoosa Creeks as Sears has maintained for at least some of the towns.

The composition of the Ochese Creeks proper provides an excellent cross-section of the towns that were [248]later the core of the Creek Confederacy and illustrates the fact that these eleven or so towns were not a neat, homogenous whole set off by linguistic or cultural differences from towns south and southwest of them. Their composition, and more importantly, their original geographic positions at the time of European contact are the principal evidences for the former wide spread in Georgia of the towns that were later known as Creeks. In general, the names of the eleven or so towns that comprised the Ochese Creeks have been difficult to determine with complete and unquestionable accuracy. All of them are by no means equally well documented, and in some cases documentation is so scanty as to be almost non-existant. However, the towns appear to have been Sawokli, Oconee, Ocmulgee, Kolomi, Taskigi, Atasi, Hitchiti (Achito), Coweta, Kasita, Westo, at least one Yamassee town, and perhaps one of Yuchi. Other possibilities include Tukabachee, Tallapoosa, and Kealedji.

The principal documentation for the existence of these towns immediately *prior* to the Ochese Creek movement of around 1685 are the lists made by the Bishop of Cuba (Wenhold 1936: 9) and those made by the Spanish commander Matheos when he went up the Chattahoochee River to reprimand the Apalachicola for their trade with the English (see Chapter I above) in 1685. Matheos passed through Sabacola el Grande, Jalipasle, Ocone, Apalachicola, Achito, Ocute, Osuchi, Ocmulgee, Casista, Colone, Caveta, and Tasquiqui (Bolton 1925: 121). Matheos's list, of course, is [249]probably not a complete census and includes only those towns he actually passed through on his journey. These towns were those from which the exodus to the Ocmulgee River occurred, and by 1709 the English noted that "about one hundred and fifty miles westward are settled on ochasee River eleven Towns of Indians consisting of six hundred men amongst whom are several family's of the aforesaid Appatalchy's . . . " (Salley 1947: 208).

Boyd (1953) is certainly in error in assuming the Spanish sources he quotes are referring to numbers of towns left on the Chattahoochee River after 1690. These important sources are undoubtedly referring to the Ocmulgee River region, which was to the Spanish an integral part of the provice of Apalachicola. Because of confusion of the Spanish province of Apalachicola with the river of the same name, Boyd has suggested that the movement to the Ocmulgee River area was confined solely to the towns actually burned out by the Spaniards—Coweta, Kasita, Taskigi, and Kolomi (Boyd 1953: 459). There is sufficient evidence from English sources, however, to indicate that many more of the Chattahoochee River Valley towns were involved in the move than just these four.

Of the towns that did move, Oconee is probably the best documented during its stay in the Oconee-Ocmulgee drainage area. Hawkins (1848: 65) noted its location on the Oconee River and stated that the town gave its name to the river. The Moll map of 1729 cites it by the name of "Ocounelias" while the Lamhatty account (Bushnell 1908) [250]listed it under an even less recognizable version of the name. The Mitchell map pinpoints "Oconee Old Town" at the point of juncture of the Oconee River and the Lower Creek Trading Path.

Sabacola el Grande, under its more common name of Sawokli, was also among the emigrants. The Moll map shows Sawokli among the towns in the Ocmulgee River area, and it appears in several Spanish sources (Boyd 1953). Swanton probably used the Moll map as his source for locating Sawokli on the Ocmulgee River (1922: 142), but he seems to have been somewhat dissatisfied with the placement of the town on the river at this time.

Kasita and Coweta are clearly documented for their stay on the Ocmulgiee River between 1690 and 1715. Kasita was the one town cited by Colonel Moore in his message to the Commons House of Assembly in 1702 (Salley 1932: 6). Several maps additionally provide information by citing one or both of these important towns in the Ocmulgee area: the Delisle map of 1718 (Cummings 1958: Pl. 47), the Moll map (Moll 1736: no. 51). the Mitchell map (Cummings 1958: Pl. 59), the Popple map (Swanton 1922: Pl. 4), and others. Kasita and Coweta were for such a long time the political "lead" towns of the area, and for this reason are especially important to locate exactly.

Kolomi is listed on both the Moll map of 1729 and the Popple map of 1733 in the Ocmulgee River area. Taskigi, under the spelling "Tascage," appears on the Popple map as one of the Ocmulgee River towns. Ocmulgee was also one of [251]the towns of this group (see Chapter 6).

Achito, listed among the Chattahoochee River towns by the Spanish, was probably Hitchiti, which under that spelling has only the questionable authority of the Mitchell map for any place among the towns that moved

166 / Part Two. Archaeological and Historical Implications

to the Ocmulgee River. As Achito, however, it was the Ocmulgee River town from which Anthony Dodsworth led his forces south to meet the Spanish (Bolton 1925: 126; Boyd 1953: 469), and as Ahachito it appears among the Lower Creeks as early as 1675 although its exact geographical position is uncertain (Wenhold 1936: 9).

Of the list of towns provided by Matheos, only four have no known references for any locations in the Ocmulgee-Oconee area during the years between 1690 and 1715. These four—Ocute, Jalipasle, Osuchi, and Apalachicola—could have been known by other versions of their names or other spellings and perhaps are actually present in such unidentified towns as "Chehams" (from the Moll map of 1729). Some of them (although not Apalachicola) did, however, remain in the Chattahoochee Valley region during the period in which the majority of the towns moved eastward. In the Bishop of Cuba's list of towns (Wenhold 1936), four others are present which have no known location in the Ocmulgee-Oconee area between 1690 and 1715. These towns—Chicahuti, Ilipi, Tascusa, and Cuchiguali—presumably also remained on the Chattahoochee River when the others removed to the Ocmulgee.

If the Carolinians' count of the Ochese Creek [252]settlements is correct, the eight towns from Matheos's list and the corresponding seven from Bishop Calderón's list that can be said to have positively removed to the Ocmulgee River were joined there by three or four others. One of these towns was Atasi, cited as "Attasi" by Boyd (1953: 459) and "Addasles" on the Moll map (Moll 1736: no. 51). This town appeared on neither Matheos's list nor that of the Bishop of Cuba, but it was nevertheless one of those to move to the Ocmulgee region, presumably from the Chattahoochee River Valley. Another of the towns was a Westo town, for the Westo were planning as of the summer of 1694 to settle a town or towns among the Coweta, Kasita, and Taskigi (Salley 1907c: 12). A Westo town does in fact appear on the Moll map of 1729 among the Ochese Creek towns. Swanton cites the presence of a Yamassee village on Ochese Creek (Swanton 1922: Pl. 1), and some Yamassees, at least, lived among the "Cowetaws and Kussetaws" around 1685 (Salley 1929: 8). It is not clear from the available records exactly where this living together occurred, for the date is borderline enough to have referred to the Chattahoochee River Valley settlements as well as to the ones on Ochese Creek. If Swanton's identification of the Westo with the Yuchi is not correct, and it seems much less secure than Swanton has maintained, then another of the Ochese Creek towns was Yuchi (Boyd 1953: 469).

Another of the towns may have been Tukabachee, if Swanton's information on it is reliable (Swanton 1922: 180), [253]or Kealedji, if the very scanty evidence available on this town will support its formation so early. There is also the bare possibility that one or more Tallapoosa towns lived on Ochese Creek for a time. A statement in the government records mentions gifts to be given to the Indians to "persuade ye Talabooses if possible to Remove to the Cussitaw River . . . " (Salley 1934: 32). Whether or not this gambit succeeded is not mentioned in subsequent government records, but an indirect reference to the Tallapoosas indicates that it may have failed. In 1703, John Howell, trader to Tallapoosa, was recorded as having written a letter to the Ochese Creek traders (Salley 1934: 96) implying that he was not one of their number and was far enough away from them to have to correspond with them by letter.

Eliminating such questionables as Tallapoosa, Kealedji, and Tukabachee and ignoring for the time being the Yamassee, Westo and/or Yuchi, the remaining towns of the Ochese Creek group are Sawokli, Oconee, Ocmulgee, Kolomi, Taskigi, Atasi, Achito (Hitchiti), Coweta, and Kasita. These towns not only provide some idea of the complexity of the cultural and linguistic composition of the Lower Creeks but also provide rough boundaries of their settlement in the Southeast. Sears's blanket statement that the only known location for the Creeks in Georgia was in the Chattahoochee River Valley—even using only the towns he is willing to admit as Creeks—needs some revision in view of the historic data available on the locations [254] of these towns prior to Matheos's and Calderón's listing of them on the Chattahoochee River in the last part of the seventeenth century.

Sawokli, classified by Swanton as Hitchiti-speaking (1922: 11), is listed by him as being near or upon the Gulf Coast at the time of earliest continuous Spanish contact in the area. His evidence for this location is primarily from Spanish sources, and as Sabacola this town figures prominently in the mission records until the eastward movement of the towns in 1685–1690. From what little is known of the customs of the people of Sawokli, they resembled the towns referred to as Creeks by Sears—Kasita, Coweta, Ocmulgee, and Oconee.

Oconee, also classified by Swanton as Hitchiti (Swanton 1922:11), is mentioned in Matheos's list as a Chattahoochee River Valley town and appears in Spanish records as early as 1602, but not then on the Chattahoochee River (p. 179). There seem to have been at least three separate settlements of the Oconee, and Swanton, at least, considers them all to be late divisions of the same group (1922: 179–180). One of these three Oconee groups was in Guale on an island and enjoyed the status of a Spanish mission during the mission period in that area (Serrano y Sanz 1912: 132). The second was the well-known mission of San Francisco de Oconi (Boyd, Smith, and Griffin 1951) in the Apalachee country while the third was the familiar Lower Creek town of Oconee (Hawkins 1848: 65). The fact that Oconee's immediately direct ancestors or descendants [255]or collaterals are connected with Guale and Apalachee rather than with peoples of Alabama makes it difficult to assume that these people were such late migrants into the Georgia area.

Ocmulgee is also one of the Hitchiti-speaking towns (Swanton 1922: 11), but there is presently no known location for it prior to Matheos's and the Bishop of Cuba's listing of it among the Chattahoochee River towns. If Swanton's derivation of Ocmulgee as a daughter town of Hitchiti is correct, even though his dating of such a split is in error, then Ocmulgee may not have been a sufficiently ancient town to have been in existence at the time of Desoto. Swanton's information for the relationship between Ocmulgee and Hitchiti, however, seems to have been derived from Hawkins in the nineteenth century.

Kolomi, classified as a Muskhogean-speaking town by Swanton, has no presently known earlier location than the valley of the Chattahoochee River. Both the Calderón list and the one made by Matheos place Kolomi in the same position between Coweta and Kasita on the Chattahoochee River. Kolomi under that spelling does not appear at all in the Desoto narratives (Swanton 1939).

Taskigi seems to have been originally, in position at least, an Upper Creek town although Swanton is unable to firmly classify it either linguistically or historically (Swanton 1922: 207–211). It was apparently a refuge village among the Lower Creeks, the main body of Taskigi [256]having been absorbed by the Cherokee (Swanton 1922: 209). Taskigi appears in north Georgia in the Pardo narrative near or very close by some unidentifiable but rugged mountains (Smith 1857: 18).

Atasi, like Oconee, has ancient roots in the Guale area. Swanton (1922: 265) cites Spanish sources that place this town within the northern limits of Guale during the Spanish mission period there. Swanton does not mention the linguistic affiliation of this town, but he does include it among the "Muskogee." Atasi does not appear on either of the available town lists nor does it occur in any of the Desoto expedition reports (Swanton 1939).

Hitchiti, if its identification with Achito is correct, appears under that spelling only after the Lower Creeks left the Ocmulgee River area to retreat to the Chattahoochee River after the Yamassee War. If Swanton's identification of Hitchiti with Ocute is accurate, then it was known by the name of Ocute up until the movement to the Ocmulgee River and presumably remained where it was on the Chattahoochee River when the other towns moved.

Ocute, which still existed as a recognizable town as late as 1685, points out another line of evidence for the early presence of Creek and Creek-related towns across the very early historic Southeast. Although the arguments over the exact route of Desoto's expedition through the Southeast have not been completely resolved to everyone's satisfaction (Swanton 1939), there is no doubt that he did in fact find a town called Ocute somewhere [257]within the lower half of what is now the state of Georgia. Ocute and other Lower Creek towns occur across Georgia in the Desoto chronicles (Bourne 1904; Robertson 1933; Swanton 1939) and provide additional data for the widespread presence in the Southeast of some of the components of what later emerged as the Lower Creeks.

In historic times, the core of Lower Creek culture was, of course, the two towns of Kasita and Coweta, although they seem to have shared this preeminent position in somewhat earlier times with the town of Apalachicola. It becomes critical, then, to discover their earliest geographical positions in order to add to the information on the range in space of the future Ochese Creek towns. Tracing the earliest known sites of Kasita and Coweta involves following references through both English and Spanish sources from the earliest contacts of these groups with the Indians.

The first English references to towns identifiable as Coweta and Kasita come from the correspondence to and from Carolina in the earliest years of settlement. During these years, contacts were just beginning to be made with the Indians, and trade alliances with them were being sought. At this time also, information was being more or less systematically gathered on the resources of the back country, the locations and actions of the Spanish, and the possibilities for economic exploitation of Carolina by the proprietors, who then had a monopoly on any forthcoming trade with the interior. The work of gathering [258]this information was performed by the able agent of the proprietors, Henry Woodward, and is chronicled in the Shaftesbury Papers (Cheves 1897).

Woodward's first venture into the interior was in 1670 when he discovered "Chufytachyqj," described by him as "the fruitfull Provence where ye Emperour resides" (Woodward to Yeamans in Cheves 1897: 186). This famous trip was to the northwest of the English settlements on the coast: "it lys West & by Northe nearest from us 14 days trauell after ye Indian manner of marchinge" (Cheves 1897: 186–187). This would place Chufytachyqj in the headwaters of the Savannah River in northwest Georgia or in southern South Carolina. Woodward established peaceful relationships with the "Emperour" of Chufytachyqj to the extent that around September 10, 1670, some of the Emperor's people were in the English settlement with Woodward (p. 201); and in February of the following year, the Emperor himself was in Charles Town with a hundred of his warriors to gape at the English and vice versa (pp. 201, 388). The Emperor delayed in coming to the English settlement and excused himself for not returning immediately to Charles Town with Woodward after the latter's first trip to Chufytachyqj because "he heard in his way that ye Spaniard had defeated us [the English]" (p. 201). Much to the delight of the English, the Emperor further stated that "his friendship with us is very considerable against the Westoes if ever they intend to Molest us he hath often defeated them and is ever their Master . . ." (p. 201).

[259]Woodward's trip to the country of Chufytachyqj revealed two facts of primary importance to the Lords Proprietors. One of these had to do with the possible existence of silver mines there (Cheves 1897: 327), a discovery so important that Woodward wished to go to England himself and inform the proper authorities personally (p. 220). The other discovery that Woodward made had to do with the Spanish settlements in Florida: "Mr. Woodward when he was up in the Emperor of Tatikequias country had then discovered that it bordered upon the Spaniards . . . " (pp. 201, 327). The lands of the Emperor of Chufytachyqj also bordered in some manner on Virginia since the Indians reported people living to the north of them "who ride upon greate deer as they term it putting things across in their mouths" (p. 201). These "greate deer" can only mean men on horseback, apparently from the nearest northern white settlement in Virginia. Incidentally, Bartram gives "echolucco," the great deer, as the Creek word for horse (Harper 1958: 136). Thomas Woodward also lists the same term in use among the Creeks in the nineteenth century (Woodward 1936: 21).

The opening up of peaceful relationships with the Emperor of Chufytachyqj and his people was a tremendous diplomatic coup for Henry Woodward and a matter of extreme importance to the struggling colony at Charles Town. Pursuing his explorations still further, Woodward made a second trip in the interior in 1671, this time reaching the borders of Virginia (Cheves 1897: 338). This trip, [260]apparently against the wishes of at least some people in Charles Town, resulted in no new discoveries and in no new and enthusiastic reports back to England to the Lords Proprietors.

In 1674, Woodward journeyed to the Westo nation, seeking further alliances for Carolina. Of this journey, he said: "eight daies journey from the towne the River hath its first falls West N. West, where it divides it selfe into three branches, amongst which dividing branches inhabit the Cowatoe and Chorakae Indians with whom they are at continual warrs" (Salley 1953: 133). This mention of the "Cowatoe" Indians locates one recognizable Lower Creek town, Coweta, on one of the three branches of the Savannah River—the Broad, the Savannah proper, and the Rocky—in the same general area where Woodward had previously reported the Emperor of Chufytachyqj to have lived. Also in his Westo narrative, Woodward mentioned the

## Lower Creeks and Their Neighbors / 171

Cussetaws, who were reported by him as ready to "come down and fight the Westoes" (Salley 1953: 134). This important narrative places two recognizable Lower Creek towns, Kasita and Coweta, in northeast Georgia near the Savannah River and somewhat north of the Westo settlements. Both of these two towns were characterized by Woodward as being unfriendly and at war with the Westo.

In the same year as Woodward's Westo journey some of the Lords Proprietors tried to have established a plantation at their own private expense on the Edisto River on a place called by them "Loch Island." This proposed [261]plantation never materialized "no doubt from the fact that the settlement on Loch Island would have been too weak an interposition between the unfriendly tribes of Westoes and Cussatoes and the colonists on Ashley River . . . " (Rivers 1856: 121). Evidently the Cussatoes were close enough to represent a possible threat to the colony, something that would hardly be expected if these people were not in fact at least as close to Charles Town as were the Westo.

It seems clear from information in the Shaftesbury Papers (Cheves 1897) that Kasita or Cussitaw is a simplification or a clarification of the "fruitfull province of Chufytachyqj," which appears so prominently in correspondence to and from Carolina until after the visit of the Emperor to Charles Town in 1671. Perhaps as a consequence of that visit and a closer relationship between Chufytachyqj and Charles Town that developed because of the opening of trade between them, such a simplification or a clarification of the name occurred. Certainly, the Carolinians were never quite sure of either the pronounciation or the spelling of Chufytachyqj even when they had Henry Woodward's example to guide them. The town of Chufytachyqj appears in the Shaftesbury Papers in a variety of spellings, all of them unmistakably from the context referring to Chufytachyqj and all of them in the space of the two years following the discovery of the town by Woodward and the memorable visit of the Emperor to Charles Town. These spellings include: Cotachico (John Locke in Cheves 1897: 338), Cotachicach (Mathews to Ashley in Cheves 1897: 334), Tatchequiha (Owen [262]to Ashley in Cheves 1897: 201), Chufytachyque (Locke in Cheves 1897: 249), and Tatikequias (Ashley to Saile in Cheves 1897: 188). Cheves also cites "Cusitachique" as another variant (1897: 188), although he omits his source for this spelling. Rivers, in many respects a less reliable source, cites yet another variant of the name, "Cutisichiqui" (Rivers 1856: 17), again with no source indicated.

After 1672, Chufytachyqj and its Emperor abruptly disappear from the correspondence, and the people called Cussitaws and their "Emperor" are substituted. The use of Cussitaw for Chufytachyqj is plainly detailed in the correspondence preserved in the Shaftesbury Papers (Cheves 1897). By 1674, Woodward was referring to the "Cuss-i-taws" (Salley 1953: 134), and Shaftesbury was following his lead. In 1674 in a directive to Woodward for the purpose of establishing trade with the Indians, Shaftesbury stated, "you are to consider whether it be best to make a peace with the Westoes or Cussitaws which are a more powerful nation said to have pearle and silver and by whose Assistance the Westoes may be rooted out, but noe peace is to be made with either of them without including our Neighbour Indians who are at amity with us" (Cheves 1897: 446). This directive to Woodward summarizes all the information known about Chufytachyqj at that time. First, Shaftesbury attributes more actual military strength to the Cussitaws than to the Westoes on the basis of the words of the Emperor when he visited Charles Town: "he hath ever defeated them [the Westo] (Cheves 1897: 201). Then Shaftesbury notes that the [263]Cussitaws may be of aid in stamping out the Westo, using information supplied to him in a letter from William Owen in 1670. This letter cites the Emperor of Chufytachyqj as being ever an enemy of the Westo and "ever their Master" (Cheves 1897: 201). Finally, Shaftesbury mentions the all important silver mines, which were the most important discovery of Woodward's first trip to the land of Chufytachyqj.

By 1677, a general order was issued for opening trade with both the Westoes and the "Cussatoes" (Rivers 1856: 389), and Henry Woodward was given official credit for discovering both of them. It is sufficient to point out that Woodward made only two trips resulting in important discoveries of new Indian nations—one to Chufytachyqj and the other to the Westoes. The correspondence of 1674 and later discussed these trips, only the references were to the Cussitaws and the Westoes rather than to Chufytachyqj and the Westoes. In some way, after 1672, the familiar name of Chufytachyqj became abbreviated to the Lower Creek town name of Cussitaw or Kasita, and it is by this name that the town is known throughout the rest of English contact. This abbreviation is difficult to understand, but can be blamed on the unfamiliarity of the newly-arrived English with the local languages and perhaps on the use of an Indian interpreter. Woodward on his earliest trip used the Casique of Kiawah, the town near the English settlement on Ashley River, as his interpreter (Cheves 1897: 191).

[264]Tracing the history of the Cussitaws or Kasita Town after the Carolinians' first pleasant relationships with it is very important to an understanding of the whole problem of Lower Creek origins. In spite of Shaftesbury's hope that the Cussitaws would help the English eliminate the Westo towns and in spite of the Emperor's warlike words in reference to the Westo (Cheves 1897: 201), the Cussitaws and their neighbors were conspicuous by

their absence during the Westo War of 1680 when the Savannahs came to the assistance of Carolina and helped to destroy the Westo. The problem then becomes one of determining the positions of the Cussitaws and their allied towns during the Westo War. Information on the locations of these towns is present in records kept by the Spanish concerning the military activities and missions in Apalachee. When the Spanish sent friars to Sabacola in 1679 to establish a mission, they were ordered to leave the area by the "Gran Casique or Emperor of the Cavetas," who had not been consulted about the establishment of the mission (Bolton and Ross 1925: 46). From this information, it is certain that the Creek towns had moved to the Chattahoochee River Valley, where the Apalachicola, at least, were in some kind of contact with the Spanish in Apalachee. Perhaps the inroads of the Spanish were the cause of the Lower Creek concentration on the Chattahoochee River or perhaps the towns moved in anticipation of the Westo War. Certainly, in spite of the warlike words of the Emperor and the hopes of Shaftesbury, the Cussitaw did [265]not aid the Carolinians against the Westo and even later sheltered the remnants of the scattered Westo towns.

Whatever caused the exodus of the Creeks from the headwaters of the Savannah River, it is certain that by the time of the Westo War and probably some years before, they were lined up on the Chattahoochee River. Woodward was among them again in 1685 rebuilding the aborted trade that the Lords Proprietors had commenced in 1677. The immediate success of Woodward's mission and the fact that he directly began trade in skins and the construction of a trading house among the Lower Creek towns indicates that he was among old friends, not among newly contacted towns with whom alliances had to be carefully established. By this time, too, the chief of Kasita had been replaced as "leader" of the towns by the head chief of Coweta, significantly the lead "red" or war town of the Lower Creeks. This replacement points to the personal leadership of individuals as a critical factor in mobilizing the towns that later solidified into the Lower Creeks and probably also to the death of the chief of Kasita, the Emperor of Chufytachyqj, whose prestige and "power" did not outlive him. Kasita, however, remained a powerful town, refusing to submit to the Spanish in 1685 and joining in the movement back east to the Ocmulgee River.

From the historic records, sometimes admittedly scanty, a skeletal network of locations for the towns that became the Ochese Creeks emerges. Coweta and Kasita were from the time of Desoto to prior to the Westo War [266]located in the headwaters of the Savannah, between that river and the Oconee. Towns such as Atasi and Oconee were near enough to the coast to have been within Guale. Sawokli was far enough south to be counted within the Spanish sphere of influence. The whole picture in historic times is one of displacement of these towns westward, a fate shared by most of the groups that survived the impact of European contact, and the rapid development of a stronger political union than can be inferred from the sketchy comments of the Desoto chroniclers or interpolated from the first few years of correspondence between Carolina and England.

In addition to the Ochese Creeks, those towns that have been termed Lower Chattahoochee Valley Creeks for want of a better way of differentiating them require some comment since they are unequivocally one part of what was known after 1715 as the Lower Creeks. Apalachicola, the most important of these towns, has no positively known location prior to Calderón's 1675 comments and Matheos's listing of it in 1685. The Lower Chattahoochee River Valley may or may not have been Apalachicola's original homeland. Like the other Creeks, it, too, may have been displaced westward. The Spaniards' truly catholic description of the whole hinterland as "Apalachicola" (Boyd 1953) leaves little room for very specific locations prior to (or even after) 1675. Apalachicola, at least in any recognizable variant of the name does not appear at all in the records of the Desoto [267]expedition (Swanton 1939).

If Swanton's location of Ocute is accurate (1922: Pl. 1) and the association of Ocute with Apalachicola persisted from prehistoric times, then both towns may have shared a south-central Georgia locale. The location of Ocute seems to be very reliable since it is based on consistent mention in the Desoto records from southern Georgia and on the comment by Matheos that places the town in the midst of the Lower Creeks on the Chattahoochee River in 1685. After 1690, the town of Apalachicola itself also moved from the Chattahoochee River Valley, for just prior to the Yamasee War, it appears on the Savannah River as Palachicolas Town (Swanton 1922: 129). In moving closer to the English settlements after 1690, Apalachicola of all the Lower Creeks towns seems to have moved the closest.

This whole interpretation of the position of the Lower Creeks at the beginning of European contact, while compatible with English sources and the earliest Spanish sources, is at variance with certain of the Spanish records particularly as regards the time of contact of specific Lower Creek towns with the Apalachee missions. The comments made by the Bishop of Cuba during his pastoral visit to Florida in 1675 are a case in point. Bishop Calderón, describing the various sections of his extensive see in a letter to the Queen of Spain, made some remarks that can be assumed sufficient to locate all of the Lower Creek towns, including Kasita and Coweta at a time that [268]is almost too early to fit with the English sources, on the Apalachicola River (and by extension, the Chattahoochee River). This important

Lower Creeks and Their Neighbors / 175

document deserves to be quoted in part so that its bearing on the important issue of Creek locations may be assessed:

> At 2 leagues from the afore-mentioned village of San Luis, on the northern frontier, is the river Agna which divides the provinces of Apalache and Apalachicoli, and at a distance of 12, on the bank of another large and copious river which takes its name from that province and runs through it from north to south, is a heathen village called formerly Santa Cruz de Sabacola el Menor . . . especially as the 13 Apalachicolan villages which are on the bank of the river of that name, 30 leagues to the north, have offered to do likewise. These are: Chicahûti, Sabacôla, Ocôni, Apalachicôli, Ilapi, Tascûsa, Usachi, Ocmûlgui, Ahachîto, Cazîthto, Colômme, Cabita, Cuchiguâli. (Wenhold 1936: 9)

The critical part of this comment is the identification of the various rivers. If the "large and copious river" is the same river as that upon which the thirteen Apalachicolan towns were located, then it is inescapable that all these towns were on the northern part of the Apalachicola River, that is, the Chattahoochee. Interpretation of this part of the bishop's letter is aided by the fact that Santa Cruz de Sabacola el Menor may be located exactly in the fork of the Flint and Chattahoochee Rivers (Boyd 1958). The river Agna, known only a very few years later to the Spanish as the Amarillo River (Leonard 1939: 266), was undoubtedly the present-day Ochlocknee, a river north of Tallahassee and about two "leagues" distant from the site of San Luis. The large and copious river, which Calderón named the Apalachicola, was surely one of [269]the two northern branches of that river. This places a number of Lower Creek towns as early as 1675 in a position occupied by them until the eastward removal to the Ocmulgee. There seems no reason to doubt the accuracy of the bishop's list or his placement of the towns since both are very similar to the list and placement of Matheos, both in the towns listed and in the order of their listing.

The fact that this list is so early seems hardly to leave enough time for the "Cussitaws" and "Cowatoes" that Woodward found on the Upper Savannah in 1674 to have made their move in order to be recorded the next year by the Spaniards. A little longer than one year is involved since the English did not adopt the same calendar as the Spanish until the eighteenth century. The date for the Calderón manuscript seems to be completely reliable except for one contradiction as far as dates are concerned. This involves the establishment of the mission of Santa Cruz de Sabacola el Menor, which Calderón avers was in existence in 1675, but which other contemporary documents assert was not founded until after 1678 or 1679 (Bolton 1925). Given the 1675 date of the Calderón letter, it requires either fast movement on the part of Coweta and Kasita or a movement by them on the heels of a general westward attrition which had been slowly occurring over many years and culminated in the removal of Kasita and Coweta only in the late seventeenth century. Some evidence for a gradual movement is provided by the town locations in the Desoto chronicles and subsequent listing of the same towns in areas [270]farther west than their original sixteenth century locations. One of the towns showing westward removal is Ocute, which is shown in central Georgia in the records of the Desoto expedition and then appears in the Matheos list on the Chattahoochee River. The Creek town of Hilibi, which at the time of Desoto was only twelve leagues from Chufytachyqj, is another evidence of westward movement since it later shows up in Calderón's list in the midst of the Lower Creek towns just north of Apalachicola on the Chattahoochee. Additional information from the Desoto narratives indicates that the area around Chufytachyqj was being abandoned at that time and the population during the period of first contact with the Spanish was less than it had formerly been (Swanton 1939: 171).

From the list of Lower Creek towns compiled by Matheos and Calderón and from other data in historic records, it is of interest to note that the towns which did become the Lower Creeks included, in addition to minor extraneous elements, two separate major linguistic groups. Both sections of the Lower Creeks—the Ochese Creek towns and those left on the Chattahoochee River after 1690—contained towns speaking what European observers considered to be mutually unintelligible languages. These were, of course, the related languages of Hitchiti and Muskogee, which are both classed as sub-groups of the Eastern division of Muskhogean by Haas (1941: 54, 55) and as separate groups in the (respectively) southern and northern divisions of Muskhogean by Swanton (1922: 11). Culturally, at any [271]rate, there seems to be little or no difference between the Hitchiti-speakers and the Muskogee-speakers in historic times except for the single one of language. Archaeologically, using Kasita (Willey and Sears 1952) and Ocmulgee as representatives of the two language divisions, they are almost identical from as early as the seventeenth century until much later.

Swanton has commented on the significance of this linguistic division and places an emphasis upon it that, if warranted, has some interesting implications as far as the interpretation of Lower Creek archaeology is concerned. Swanton believed, apparently on the basis of origin myths as well as on distributional data, that the Hitchiti components of the Creeks were among the first inhabitants of Georgia and that an amalgamation of these people and the intruding Muskogee produced the cultural grouping later labeled as Lower Creeks. He commented that "the Creek Confederation owed, if not its origin, at least its complexity to union between the true Muskogee and several mutually related tribes in southern Georgia which called themselves Atcik-hata but are usually known to ethnologists as Hitchiti or Hitchiti-related people from the name of their most prominent tribe" (Harper 1958: 346, 347). Elsewhere and much earlier he stated that "at one time the Hitchiti were probably the most important tribe in southern Georgia and their language the prevailing speech in that region from the Chattahoochee River to the [272]Atlantic Ocean" (Swanton 1922: 173).

The time of this early Hitchiti dominance in Georgia as well as the time of the Muskogee entrada are critical in attempting to use any of Swanton's hypotheses. Surely, if the culture of the two groups was a shared one in historic times, then their union must have occurred at an extremely early date; yet, if their union was indeed early, then the retention of both Muskogee and Hitchiti as viable languages is difficult to explain. Swanton, easily the most knowledgable source available on Creek history and ethnology, was able to have it both ways. In 1922 he said that " . . . the true Muskogee entered at such an early period that we cannot say we have historical knowledge of a time when the Hitchiti were its sole inhabitants" (1922: 173). In 1958, in a series of notes appended to the Harper edition of Bartram's *Travels*, he stated that "the Muskogee and the Hitchiti were still at war when Desoto passed through their country in 1540" (Harper 1958: 346), implying that the Muskogee were still essentially newcomers. The union of Hitchiti-speakers and the presumably invading Muskogee is a tempting background against which to project the Hitchiti origin myth (Swanton 1922: 173) and the general outlines of Georgia archaeology (Fairbanks 1952: 294), but the scarcity of data on the Hitchiti themselves as well as appreciable gaps in archaeological knowledge make any such projection premature.

# 8
# The Origins of Lower Creek Ceramics

[273]Combining historic information on the Lower Creeks with data from the areas of their supposed prehistoric residence is anything but a simple exercise in archaeological correlation. Tracing the roots of Lower Creek ceramics into the prehistoric past has always foundered on the total lack of demonstrably pre-contact sites bearing pottery recognizable as Lower Creek and on the total lack of any clear evolutionary sequence leading gradually from prehistoric ceramics to the historic ones. This situation suggests either that Lower Creek ceramics as they are now known are a strictly historic development of a rather abrupt nature within the state of Georgia or that the Lower Creeks migrated into Georgia in historic times from an as yet undetermined homeland bearing this ceramic tradition already developed. Selecting the better of these two possibilities must be done using what data are presently available, and only when clearly prehistoric Lower Creek sites are excavated can a final choice be made between them or a more reasonable hypothesis devised.

Fairbanks, although admitting that more than one ceramic tradition is involved in historic Creek pottery [274](1958: 53), is committed to its derivation from the widespread and widely divergent Lamar culture (1952; 1956a; 1956b; 1958; 1962). The mechanisms involved in this alteration of Lamar to Ocmulgee Fields are essentially cultural ones: the breakdown of many of the old patterns of life under the direct and indirect pressures of acculturation and the loss or modification of others through the substitution of trade artifacts for native-made goods. Alterations in the economic basis of the society must have been the critical factors in these changes, causing as they did the introduction of European economic systems in the persons of English traders and in the institution of a cash (or credit) market. Fairbanks's comparison of Lamar and Creek social and religious institutions, such as can be reconstructed for the one and interpreted from modern accounts for the other, shows striking instances of correspondence; and if such

# Origins of Lower Creek Ceramics / 179

comparisons were done more extensively for the Creeks and for other historic groups in the Southeast, they might prove exceptionally fruitful in understanding both historic and prehistoric interrelationships (Fairbanks 1952).

The most important of Fairbanks's evidence, as far as archaeological attacks on the problem are concerned, is the ceramic sequence he proposes from the Lamar series to specific types within the Ocmulgee Fields series (Fairbanks 1958). His derivation of *Ocmulgee Fields Incised* from *Lamar Bold Incised* (or something very close to it) is particularly convincing and is the most secure [275]of the Lamar to Ocmulgee Fields comparisons. The occurrence of *Ocmulgee Fields Incised* cazuelas with brushed bases (Plaate XXI, figure 2) and flaring rimmed bowls with similarly brushed bases (see Chapter V) supports his arguments for the substitution of brushing for complicated stamping on the incised vessels in the historic period, at least as far as distribution on analogous vessel forms is concerned. The rare incidence of *Ocmulgee Fields Incised* rimsherds with typical Lamar lips lends additional support to the derivation and removes one objection that Fairbanks himself raised to it (1958: 55). He also noted the absence of any feature in Ocmulgee Fields that is similar to the frequent Lamar circular or annular punctations at the base of incised shoulders on cazuelas (1958: 55). Present evidence from Ocmulgee Town indicates that such punctations do in fact occur, but they occur very rarely and never in the typical Lamar form.

The major problem in Fairbanks's Lamar to Ocmulgee Fields sequence is that of demonstrating a convincing ancestor for *Walnut Roughened* and also incidentally for *Chattahoochee Brushed* (Bullen 1950), its descendant by only a very few generations. Fairbanks has made a case for the independent development of *Walnut Roughened* from *Lamar Complicated Stamped* but not as convincing a case as he has for his derivation of *Ocmulgee Fields Incised* from *Lamar Bold Incised* (1958). His argument is strongest when demonstrating the many shared traits of *Walnut Roughened* and the Lamar pottery and weakest when neglecting to [276]handle the many areal correlatives of the brushed ware, some of which certainly had a development entirely independent of any stamped tradition. The best summary to date of the many problems involved in determining the ancestry of historic brushed ware in the Southeast is Goggin (1953), who points out that Natchez, Chickasaw, and even possibly Yuchi, all possessed some variety of brushed pottery in historic times.

Establishing a clear-cut progression of any specific Lamar types into *Walnut Roughened* or other Creek and Seminole brushed wares involves accepting the substitution of brushed surfaces and brushing as a finishing technique in the place of complicated stamping. Fairbanks (1952: 299) is inclined to treat surface malleation and hence complicated stamping as both a decorative device and a technical process in the manufacture of pottery. He therefore has less trouble than Goggin (1953) or Sears (Willey and Sears 1952: 12) in seeing complicated stamping as the ancestor of brushing and regards the process of transition from the one to the other as the result of "the simplification of the traditional potters' tools" (Fairbanks 1956b: 4). Something of this sort may be in progress in at least one Lamar site. Sears has described a collection of 162 Lamar sherds from the Wilbanks site (1958: 177) with a "deliberately roughened" surface although he was unable to determine the techniques used in the roughening process. Goggin (1953) finds too much of an aesthetic difference between stamping and brushing to [277]derive one from the other. However, there is this to be said for *Walnut Roughened* as a stamp substitute: stippling (as defined in this paper) and cob-marking, both minority types as of 1700, *are* in fact stamps although considerably less sophisticated than the carved paddle-stamps of Lamar. Cob-marking and other miscellaneous roughening techniques were much more common in the earliest Lower Creek towns (of a time period equivalent to that represented by Ocmulgee Town). By the post–Yamassee War period and later (as represented by Kasita), these other techniques were less frequently employed, and brushing became by far the dominant form of decoration. The general picture of the evolution of surface treatments seems to be one of progressive loss through time of techniques that are more closely related to stamping.

Fairbanks's derivation of *Walnut Roughened* may also be criticized for its failure to handle adequately the emergence of brushed wares in historic assemblages across the Southeast and the possible relationships of these brushed wares to the historic Creek type. It seems too much of a coincidence that all of these brushed types should have become so prominent in historic times, most of them, incidentally, without any known ancestor. Although brushing occurs occasionally in *some* Southeastern assemblages, the only good candidate as an ancestor for the historic brushed pottery is the prehistoric type *Plaquemine Brushed,* which does occur late on some Natchez sites (Goggin 1953). *Plaquemine Brushed,* however, judging from [278]published illustrations (Ford 1951: Pl. 21), shares little more than the identification of a surface finish with the historic brushed wares of the east; certainly, it has none of the other formal attributes associated with *Walnut Roughened* or *Chattahoochee Brushed.* It requires too much manuevering at this stage of information to transport *Plaquemine Brushed* east to become a convincing ancestor. The intermediate steps in such a diffusion require the introduction of a single trait—brushing—into an already established ceramic tradition and suggest, at least, that brushing as an attribute is capable of diffusing all by itself. Until more is known about the occurrence of brushing as a ceramic attribute in the prehistoric Southeast, there is no known possibility for a brushed ancestor of *Walnut Roughened* in the right place at the right time.

Other problems in seeking to derive the historic brushed pottery of the Lower Creeks from *Lamar Complicated Stamped* involve vessel shape and some minor decorative additions. The elongated jar form, common to both Lamar and Ocmulgee Fields, is not the only vessel form known for *Walnut Roughened*. At Ocmulgee, several round-bottomed, almost globular bowls (Plates XXV, XXVI) were found and seem to represent a consistent minority vessel shape within *Walnut Roughened*. This vessel form is found in Cherokee ceramics (Caldwell 1955) but does not occur in this exact shape in *Lamar Complicated Stamped* or in any other Lamar type from the site near Macon. The closest equivalent is [279]a more elongated vessel (Jennings and Fairbanks 1939), which may, however, be similar enough to be considered analogous. Although strap or loop handles occur only rarely in Lamar ceramics (Fairbanks 1952: 298), they appear on *Walnut Roughened* vessels but apparently are not known as yet on *Chattahoochee Brushed* (Bullen 1950) or on the still later Seminole brushed types (Goggin 1953). Strap handles do, however, occur on the imported Lamar of St. Augustine (from Guale) in Florida (Smith 1948: 316). Incising on the smoothed neck areas of elongated jars is very rare in Lamar (Jennings and Fairbanks 1939), appearing occasionally on *Irene Incised* jars in what may not be a truly similar situation (Caldwell and McCann 1948: 48). Thus incising, a fairly typical *Walnut Roughened* trait, has almost no roots in *Lamar Complicated Stamped*.

The formidable task of eventually finding a sure ancestor for *Walnut Roughened,* the earliest of the historic Creek brushed wares, must involve finding answers for all of the objections raised above if the solution is based upon a *Lamar Complicated Stamped* to *Walnut Roughened* sequence. If the solution is based, however, on a non-Lamar and presumably non-Georgia origin for *Walnut Roughened,* then it must be prepared to account for the many shared traits of *Walnut Roughened* with the Lamar series. These include rim treatment, the elongated jar form, and the slightly flaring rim. In addition, the shared attributes include the association of *Walnut Roughened* with the more clearly Lamar form, *Ocmulgee Fields* [280]*Incised*. This association is an important one, for the Ocmulgee Fields pottery forms a unit whose members are usually all represented on sites identifiable as Lower Creek. When looking for the ancestors of this unit, it is necessary to consider the total pattern and to avoid the error of treating one attribute (in this case, brushing) as separate and independent. When the total morphological pattern of the ceramic series of one group is compared to other patterns, it is to be expected, short of miracles of independent invention, that related se-

182 / Part Two. Archaeological and Historical Implications

ries of pottery will resemble each other more closely than unrelated series. If the Ocmulgee Fields series is indeed a descendant of Lamar or a Lamar variant, it might be expected that it would share more traits in common with other descendants of Lamar than with non-related ceramic traditions. The pottery of the Apalachee Indians, considered to be in historic times "a kind of Lamar" (Willey and Sears 1952: 12) by most observers (Smith 1948), is a case in point.

The close relationship between Apalachee pottery and that from Ocmulgee Old Fields has been recognized ever since the beginning of extensive archaeological work in the northwest Florida area (Willey 1949). The closeness of this relationship becomes more apparent when the Ocmulgee Fields ceramic series is compared type for type with that of the Apalachee. Apalachee pottery, defined for the Leon-Jefferson period in Florida (Smith 1948), is well known, thanks to excavation and documentation [281]of Spanish mission sites in the northwestern part of the state (Boyd, Smith, and Griffin 1951; Smith 1956). The major ceramic types include *Mission Red Filmed, Leon Check Stamped, Aucilla Incised, Miller Plain,* and *Jefferson Ware* (Boyd, Smith, and Griffin 1951) in addition to Spanish pottery and a certain number of minor aboriginal wares (including some supposed Lower Creek imports) whose status in the total assemblage is unknown.

*Mission Red Filmed* and *Kasita Red Filmed,* although differing in some details, are directly corresponding types. Smith, probably on the basis of the early type description of *Kasita Red Filmed* (Jennings and Fairbanks 1940), sees more difference in vessel shape than the evidence actually warrants (Smith 1956: 126). *Kasita Red Filmed* does indeed have a plate form while no sherds demonstrably from red-filmed cazuelas were recovered at all from Ocmulgee Town or from Kasita (Willey and Sears 1952: 7). What little can be determined about designs on the two red-filmed wares indicates that they are generally similar, and zoning and incising on the vessel interiors seem to be the same. Both of these two types are so very much alike that Smith in one place (1956: 126) tentatively derived *Mission Red Filmed* from *Kasita Red Filmed,* probably via the Oconee.

*Leon Check Stamped* (Boyd, Smith, and Griffin 1951: 170–171) is similar to the minority type at Ocmulgee, *Ocmulgee Check Stamped.* Both types share many features in common including occasional sherd temper and a surface [282]treatment after stamping that all but obliterated the check design. Smith described the form of *Leon Check Stamped* as a large globular vessel with an outflaring rim (Boyd, Smith, and Griffin 1951: 170) as opposed to Fairbanks's deep jar with slightly flaring rim for *Ocmulgee Check Stamped* (Fairbanks 1956b: 1). Dimensions of checks as well as such things as method of manufacture and surface color agree very closely in both types. The only really disparate note in the comparison is rim treatment. The rims of *Leon Check Stamped* vessels are thickened and folded with an occasional line of punctations around the lip while the single extant example of an *Ocmulgee Check Stamped* jar has a folded, pinched rim.

*Aucilla Incised* (Boyd, Smith, and Griffin 1951: 172–173) is certainly an areal correlative of *Ocmulgee Fields Incised,* sharing vessel form and even several specific forms of decoration with it. *Ocmulgee Fields Incised,* however, does not share the occasional punctated background of some of the *Aucilla Incised* rimsherds. As far as ware characteristics are concerned, both types are generally similar.

*Miller Plain* (Boyd, Smith, and Griffin 1951: 165–166) has specific similarities with both *Ocmulgee Fields Plain* and *Ocmulgee Fields Incised*. The resemblances extend not only to ware characteristics and the cazuela shape but also to minority forms present in both Georgia and Florida. *Miller Plain* includes a water bottle shape similar to the incised olla present in Ocmulgee Fields and [283]has a shallow bowl with lugs similar to the one present in Ocmulgee Fields. Both, incidentally, include a number of possibly European-influenced forms, although in the case of *Miller Plain* the inspiration for such forms was certainly Spanish rather than English.

The last Leon-Jefferson pottery category is Jefferson ware, which includes both a large number of plain sherds and a comparatively small number of complicated stamped sherds. This complicated stamped pottery is a minority ware, comprising eleven per cent of total aboriginal sherds at San Luis and only nine per cent at San Francisco de Oconi. While it is quite variable as far as specific complicated stamped motifs are concerned, the complicated stamped pottery is more Lamar than Floridian in its origins (Smith 1956: 126). Vessel form for Jefferson ware is also variable but for the complicated stamped pottery is an elongated, flaring-rimmed, globular jar with or without a pinched, folded lip. As a whole, rim treatment in Jefferson ware is a variation on the common Southeastern theme of punctating below or pinching a folded lip.

Compared type for type, the ceramics of Ocmulgee Fields and Leon-Jefferson agree remarkably in analogous, closely related forms except for the presence of a complicated stamped ware and the lack of a brushed ware in the Florida series. This provides some support for Fairbanks's contention that brushing is simply a substitution for [284]stamping. According to his reasoning, this substitution occurred in the Georgia series with complicated stamping being retained in the closely similar Florida area. At any rate, it is difficult to understand the closeness of these two ceramic series unless they do indeed share a common ancestor or at least share in the same pool of ceramic traits. Granting this closeness of relationship makes it more and more difficult to look outside the indigenous Southeastern ceramic tradition for ancestors of even such problem types as *Walnut Roughened* and *Chattahoochee Brushed*.

One other point deserves to be mentioned for the light it may throw on the historic relationships of the Apalachee and the Lower Creeks and perhaps on the prehistoric relationships of both groups as well. Significantly, one of the excavated Apalachee towns is San Francisco de Oconi (Boyd, Smith, and Griffin 1951). The Oconi of this mission, believed by both Smith (1956: 126) and Swanton (1922: 179–180) to be a section of the same people who formed the Lower Creek town of Oconee, were manifestly more similar ceramically to the Apalachee group of which they were then a part than to the Lower Creek group from which they presumably were derived. Fairbanks, however, has pointed out that linguistically the name Oconi or Oconee could have occurred independently in both Apalachee and Hitchiti although, like Swanton and Smith, he inclines to an identification of the Oconee of Georgia with the Oconi of Florida and places the movement of the former at a "relatively early date, 1659 or earlier" (Fairbanks 1956c: [285]80). The exact date at which the several Oconee groups went their separate ways is unfortunately impossible to determine short of clairvoyance, but it seems to have occurred before the differentiation of a presumed common ceramic substratum into the more fragmented cultures of historic times. If Fairbanks is correct in his derivation of Ocmulgee Fields ceramics, then the gathering of native satellites around differing Spanish and English centers of influence might well have been the moving force in the separation of Oconi from Oconee and the significant factor in determining the direction of their separate ceramic evolutions.

Fairbanks's derivation of historic Lower Creek pottery from Lamar has the advantage that no other hypothesis, *Walnut Roughened* notwithstanding, fits the available data as well. It is unfortunate, however, that Lamar and its many areal and temporal affiliates are so poorly integrated into some kind of broad pattern. A synthesis of all the elements comprising Lamar and a careful analysis of them might make it possible to tie Ocmulgee Fields closer to one section of it than to another. Lamar, as it is known today, is liable to mean a number of different things, depending on who is using the concept. By Lamar in this paper is meant a ceramic and cultural assemblage resembling the Lamar of central Georgia, specifically as defined at the type site at Macon and at similar sites in the surrounding area (Fairbanks 1952: Kelly 1938; Jennings and Fairbanks 1939). This does not [286]mean, however, that Lamar as defined from central Georgia is the totality of Lamar or even that it surely represents an average or a typical Lamar assemblage. What it does mean is that central Georgia Lamar is at least well-defined cerami-

## Origins of Lower Creek Ceramics / 185

cally and is well enough known to be used as a basis for comparison and discussion. Other Lamar cultures are identified here as Lamar of Guale or Lamar of north Florida, using additional geographical or cultural terms where these are applicable. Determining the many variations present in Lamar and its cultural correlatives in all directions is beyond the scope of this paper although such a study is unfortunately long overdue. Any understanding of a possible alteration of complicated stamping to brushing in the Creek ceramic tradition as proposed by Fairbanks is hampered by not knowing what part of the widespread Lamar tradition, in its broadest sense, provided the ceramic genes for Ocmulgee Fields and where to look for evidence of such a presumably abrupt mutation.

The principal opposition to a Lamar ancestor for Lower Creek ceramics has been raised by Sears, whose arguments for a non-Lamar but somehow Lamar-related origin for Creek ceramics have clearly pointed out the weaknesses of the Lamar to Ocmulgee Fields sequence (Sears 1955). Sears's data, both historical and archaeological, support a more central role for the Cherokee in the major stream of cultural development in Georgia than is usually allotted to them by ethnologists and archaeologists (Swanton 1922). [287]His conclusions as to the position of the Lower Creeks in this cultural development, necessarily a provisional one based on the available data, point to a likelihood that their ceramic homeland is the "Upper Creek" area of Alabama (Sears 1955: 148) rather than in Georgia at all.

Part of Sears's argument is based on the information he has on the locations of Creek (meaning the towns of Kasita, Coweta, Hitchiti, Oconee, and Ocmulgee) and the Cherokee towns at the time of earliest historic contact. For the Lower Creeks, at least, his data are not adequate enough to eliminate entirely locations well within Georgia for some of the towns that became Lower Creeks in historic times (see Chapter VII). His information on the location of the Cherokee towns in the upper Savannah River drainage, on the Hiwassee River, and on the eastern Tennessee River seems substantially correct although I am unable to find any justification from historic sources for Cherokee occupation in the Etowah River drainage as early as he would place them there. It is true, as he points out (1955: 145), that there are few written records from this area at an early date, but such as they are, they do not support a southern extension of the Cherokee towns into the Etowah drainage until late times. In reverse temporal order, some of these sources are: the Purcell map, the Mitchell map, the Moll map, the Crisp map, and the Pardo narrative. By 1770, the Purcell map of that year (Swanton 1922: Pl. 7) locates the Cherokee in the headwaters of the Savannah and on the eastern branches of the [288]Tennessee while the Mitchell map of 1755 (Cummings 1958: Pl. 59) agrees, placing the Cherokee villages on the Tennessee River and on the Savannah a good distance above the confluence of that river with the Broad. The somewhat earlier Popple map of 1733 places the Cherokee essentially where the Purcell map does except that it places them farther north, entirely on the Tennessee River (Swanton 1922: Pl. 4). The still earlier Moll map of 1729 (Cummings 1958: Pl. 50) indicates that the main body of Cherokee was located on the Tennessee River (thirty villages) while a smaller group was on the headwaters of the Savannah River (ten villages). The less reliable Nairne insert into the Crisp map of 1711 (Cummings 1958: Pl. 45) places the Cherokee villages entirely on the Tennessee River. Still earlier, Henry Woodward placed the Cherokee villages in the upper headwaters of the Savannah River in 1674 (Salley 1953: 133), and the earliest French map of the area is credited by Crane as placing the Cherokee in the upper headwaters of the Tennessee River by 1688 (Crane 1956: 40). Swanton, although not primarily concerned with the early history of the Cherokee, identified the Tali of Desoto with the Cherokee and found their location on the Tennessee River to have remained essentially unchanged from Desoto's visit in the sixteenth century to the description of Tali by Daniel Coxe a century and a half later (Swanton 1922: 212–213). In the interval after Desoto and before Coxe, there are few historic comments from the general area. One [289]of the most important of these is the record of the Pardo expedition of 1566–1567, which moved up the Savannah River into Tennessee and only there encountered anything identifiable as Cherokee (Smith 1857). After the period of Coxe's description, the Cherokee moved south as the Melish map of 1814 indicates (Swanton 1922: Pl. 8) and the subsequent history of the Cherokees describes. Evidently there is still much to be said of the movements of the Cherokee in prehistoric times, but the earliest written records, unfortunately scanty, do not yet admit of an extension of the Cherokee villages as far south as the Etowah drainage unless it was before 1540 and the beginnings of these written records.

If archaeological data can support the Cherokee affiliation of early occupations at Etowah (Sears 1955), then combining what is presently known of both Creek and Cherokee early history must require a fast enough exodus of the Cherokee to allow the Lower Creeks to settle across north Georgia as far as Cofitachiqui by the time of the Desoto entrada and to remain there until the Carolinians discovered Chufytachyqj in what was substantially the same geographical position. In any case, these Lower Creeks, if they were in north Georgia long before 1540 or made a hasty entrance only a few years before that date, must have left archaeological materials of a non–Ocmulgee Fields type throughout the area up until the settlement of Charles Town in 1670. Since there are no known Ocmulgee Fields [290]sites without the ubiquitous English or Spanish trade goods, it seems impossible to escape the conclusions that some of the Lamar materials must indeed be Lower Creek. The only way to effectively eliminate Lower Creek claims to a share in the Lamar tradition is to demonstrate some non-Lamar ceramic assemblages within Georgia in the areas known to have been occupied by some Lower Creek towns prior to 1680 (the date of the Westo War), a non-Lamar assemblage that can serve equally well as Lamar as an ancestor for Ocmulgee Fields.

Sears has attempted to show that comparisons between Lamar pottery and that from Ocmulgee Fields sites are fruitless since Ocmulgee Fields is "not Lamar-style pottery" (Sears 1955: 146). His emphasis on the lack of a clear-cut derivation of the brushed surface technique of *Walnut Roughened* is well taken and cannot be satisfactorily answered at this stage of information. His willingness to allow only the rim treatment of Ocmulgee Fields ceramics as being Lamar is, however, something less than generous. The combination of traits that appears in the Ocmulgee Fields series—vessel shape, style of incising, surface treatment, basic design elements, distribution of incising, and rim treatment—forms a constellation whose Lamar affinities are striking. There is little doubt that Ocmulgee Fields shares heavily in the same ceramic tradition as Lamar, but whether this relationship is directly ancestral or collateral remains to be determined.

If Lamar of Georgia does eventually prove to have [291] large increments of non-Muskhogean populations, it seems unnecessary to have to import the Cherokee into Georgia at an as yet undetermined archaeological period to make them responsible for it. Cherokee position from historic records is apparently too peripheral to have been responsible for ceramic development at least in post-1500 Georgia; and Cherokee ceramics, from what little information is presently available (Caldwell 1955; Caldwell 1950; Kneberg 1952), seem likewise too peripheral to be an end product of the central moving source in much of the ceramic development of the proto-historic period. It is unnecessary to go that far afield when Muskhogean-speaking peoples still possessed as recognizable a Lamar ceramic tradition as did the Cherokee well into historic times: the Guale, the Yamassee, and the Apalachee (Smith 1948). Incidentally, one of the Guale mission towns of the sixteenth century was Oconi, the third division of the Oconee proper. There is unfortunately no archaeological evidence to indicate whether this Oconi town was similar ceramically to the main Lower Creek Oconee or to the Guale sphere of which it was a member.

Sears's recommended origin place for Creek ceramics (meaning those of Kasita, Coweta, Oconee, Ocmulgee, and Hitchiti) points to the relationships of the Lower Creeks with their Creek cousins of Alabama. Before compar-

188 / Part Two. Archaeological and Historical Implications

ing this group with the Lower Creeks, it is important that the data available from sites other than Ocmulgee Town be presented in order to determine the amount of variation in Lower Creek artifact assemblages and assess some of the [292]changes that have occurred over time. Other Lower Creek sites that have been excavated or at least tested include Kasita, Oconee, Big Sandy, Abercrombie, and Apalachicola.

The Kasita site (Willey and Sears 1952) near Columbus, Georgia, dates very roughly between 1716 and 1830 and most probably nearer to the last part of the range than to the beginning of it. Pottery from the site includes the three types *Ocmulgee Fields Incised, Kasita Red Filmed,* and *Chattahoochee Brushed* as well as two unnamed plain wares. Since this site is later than Ocmulgee Town, some interesting—and presumed temporal—changes have occurred in the pottery. The most striking of these is the complete dropping of any shell tempering. The grit-tempering of *Chattahoochee Brushed* has replaced the shell tempering of *Walnut Roughened,* and no shell temper occurs even rarely in either *Kasita Red Filmed* or *Ocmulgee Fields Incised*. This loss of shell tempering seems to be a characteristic of the later sites since all the other known Lower Creek sites of the 1690–1715 time range (in addition to Ocmulgee) have shell tempered pottery on them (Oconee, Big Sandy, and Apalachicola). *Kasita Red Filmed* vessels, about as common at Kasita as at Ocmulgee (1.0% as opposed to 0.78%), seem to have been more often in an "open to slightly compressed" bowl form (Willey and Sears 1952: 7) rather than in the more familiar soup plate shape found at Ocmulgee. Whether or not this reflects a trend away from Spanish-influenced plate forms is impossible to determine on the basis of present evidence. Sears and [293]Willey describe a "coarse plain" ware from Kasita that includes what are probably plain rims and bases from *Chattahoochee Brushed* jars. This category may also include an actual "plain" variant of *Chattahoochee Brushed* which was foreshadowed in the occasionally "plain" *Walnut Roughened* vessels from Ocmulgee Town. *Chattahoochee Brushed,* at least as represented by the sherds from this site, seems to have lost much of the variety of surface texturing found on *Walnut Roughened* sherds. Surface treatment is almost exclusively brushing with only an occasional use of cob-marking or stippling. The rimsherds from Kasita, presumably from *Chattahoochee Brushed* vessels, all have appliquéed pinched rim strips added to them. These strips are sometimes at a distance of two inches below the rims and contrast strongly in this respect with similar rimsherds from *Walnut Roughened* vessels, which usually have added rim strips immediately below the rims. The Kasita site, situated in time after Ocmulgee Town, provides an important link in the history of Lower Creek ceramics, one of the few ceramic sequences whose changes in time are actually observable over very short spans of known duration.

The Ennis site (Fairbanks 1940), located near Rock Landing in the vicinity of Milledgeville, Georgia, was the site of Oconee between 1690 and 1715. Like Ocmulgee, Oconee is a multi-component site, the historic occupation being only one of many. Gordon R. Willey's collection from the site, now in the collections of [294]Ocmulgee National Monument, included no historic trade materials, but there is no question, judging from Benjamin Hawkins's exact location of the site (Hawkins 1916), that it was the place where Oconee was situated until the Yamassee War. The historic pottery from the site is closer to that from Ocmulgee than it is to the Kasita material as would be expected from a town of a 1690–1715 time range.

The Big Sandy site (1 Bt 1) in Butts County, Georgia, was one of the Lower Creek towns located on the Ocmulgee-Oconee drainage between 1690 and 1715 although it has not as yet been positively identified as to town name. The pottery from the site is similar to that from Ocmulgee and Oconee with only a few special characteristics to distinguish it. As a whole, the *Ocmulgee Fields Incised* series is similar to the collection at Macon with many of the same design elements employed. Some unique ones, chiefly linear designs, include the paired parallel lines more often associated with *Walnut Roughened* at Ocmulgee. Incised cazuelas tend to have sandier, more granular pastes with thicker rims than their Ocmulgee Town counterparts. Plain cazuelas and plain flat-bottomed bowls occur as do European-influenced forms (cups?); plain bowls with the familiar added pinched rim strip are also present. Interestingly enough, the Big Sandy site has both *Walnut Roughened* and *Chattahoochee Brushed* pottery on it with the former appreciably more plentiful than the latter. The predominant surface treatment for both of these types is [295]not brushing but cob-marking or "finger-nail" punctating or a combination of both. An occasional sherd of this material seems to be limestone tempered rather than shell or ordinary grit.

The Lower Creek town at the Abercrombie Mound, Russell County, Alabama, was located directly across the Chattahoochee River from the Kasita site near Columbus, Georgia (Fairbanks 1955). This site has no known town identification at present, but it could have been Coweta, which was at one time located directly across the Chattahoochee River from Kasita (Swanton 1922: Pl. 2). No dates are available for the occupation at the Abercrombie Mound since the trade goods from the historic component are as yet undated. An identification of this site as Coweta, of course, can be valid only if the site is proved to be late enough in time. Fairbanks, on stylistic grounds, places Abercrombie as ancestral to the 1690–1715 Ocmulgee Town materials and hence datable from the period just prior to the movement of the Lower Creeks east to the Ocmulgee and Oconee Rivers. The fact that the pottery, or at least a good portion of it, is shell tempered (including most of the *Ocmulgee Fields Plain* and the *Ocmulgee Fields Incised*) tends to support this early dating of the site as does the presence of *Walnut Roughened* sherds. *Chattahoochee Brushed* pottery is, however, also represented in the collection from the site. Fairbanks's major basis for considering the Abercrombie Mound site so early, the quality of the incising on [296]*Ocmulgee Fields Incised* vessels, is not entirely convincing since the sherds of this type that he illustrates can easily be duplicated in the collections at Macon. If this is indeed an early Lower Creek site, then it must be only a few years prior to the Ocmulgee movement because of the presence of trade goods. English trade materials were not generally available to these people until after the opening of the trade with the Lower Creeks in 1677. It is difficult to see a site so close in time to Ocmulgee Town so much closer to a possible Lamar antecedent as far as pottery is concerned unless, as Fairbanks has suggested, the development of the Ocmulgee Fields ceramic culture was a very rapid one hard on the heels of the English trade. If, on the other hand, the historic component at the Abercrombie Mound does prove to be a later site, post–Yamassee War, then the progressive loss of shell temper through time, as proposed above, is likely to be an invalid observation. Abercrombie, of course, could be both a later Creek site and an earlier one; the "old fields" along the Chattahoochee were sometimes abandoned and then re-occupied several times by the same towns.

The site of Apalachicola Town on the Savannah River (Caldwell 1948, 1952) shows striking similarities to the Ocmulgee Town materials, a condition that would be expected on the basis of their closeness in time. After the Yamassee War, Apalachicola moved to the fork of the Flint and Chattahoochee Rivers from the Savannah, where it was known as "Palachicolas," and remained in that vicinity [297]for many years (Boyd 1958). Caldwell has observed (1948: 324) that the *Walnut Roughened* sherds from Apalachicola (during the Savannah River period) seemed to have been scratched or incised rather than brushed in the usual manner. The single available illustration of this material, however, shows a cob-marked surface (Caldwell 1952: Pl. 176, F). Otherwise, the pottery was cited by Caldwell as "similar to the historic Hitchiti complex of central Georgia" (p. 321), meaning that from the Lower Creek site at Macon.

Judging from these sites, the pottery of the Lower Creeks is remarkably uniform for sites of the 1690–1715 range (Ocmulgee, Oconee, Big Sandy, and Apalachicola) and for sites both possibly before that time (the historic component at the Abercrombie Mound) and surely after (Kasita). There is, then, a distinguishable body of internally consistent ceramic material that

## Origins of Lower Creek Ceramics / 191

can be labeled Lower Creek and compared as a whole with the Upper Creek pottery of Alabama. The site for which most information is currently available is the Upper Creek site of Childersburg (DeJarnette and Hansen 1960). This site, as the authors have demonstrated, cannot be identified with the Coosa of Desoto and is evidently not pre–eighteenth century. It is, however, very probably the Upper Creek town of Coosa, a descendent of Desoto's Coosa although not necessarily a lineal one. The Melish map of 1814 (Swanton 1922: Pl. 8) shows "Cosee Old Town" just where the Childersburg site is, and the Purcell map of 1770 (Swanton 1922: Pl. 7) shows Coosa in what seems [298]to be the same geographical position. In addition, David Taitt, traveling through the country of the Upper Creeks in 1772, identified what is evidently the same site as Coosa Old Fields (Mereness 1916: 534), the former location of the Upper Creek town of Coosa.

Ceramically, the Childersburg complex is separable into two groups, the McKee Island series and the Childersburg series (DeJarnette and Hansen 1960: 39). Both of these have specific resemblances to Ocmulgee Fields pottery. The McKee Island series, originally defined by Heimlich (1952), includes an incised ware, *McKee Island Incised*. This incised type shares with *Ocmulgee Fields Incised* both the cazuela (DeJarnette and Hansen 1960: Pl. 6) and the large flaring-rimmed bowl (Heimlich 1952: Pl. 6, D) but not the globular jar with the paired strap handles or any of the other apparently straight-sided bowl types (DeJarnette and Hansen 1960: Pl. 3). Designs on these incised vessels are very similar to the Ocmulgee Fields design elements, but they seem to be somewhat more restricted in range. *McKee Island Brushed* occurs as cazuela bowls as well as several kinds of globular jars. The characteristic rim treatment of *Walnut Roughened* appears to be lacking entirely on *McKee Island Brushed* rimsherds (DeJarnette and Hansen 1960: Pl. 7; Heimlich 1952: Pl. 7) while the surface treatment is exclusively brushing as opposed to the multi-roughening techniques employed on the corresponding Ocmulgee Fields type. *McKee Island Brushed* is occasionally combined with incising to produce a brushed [299]jar with a characteristic *McKee Island Incised* rim (Heimlich 1952: Pl. 6, H). The typical parallel-line incising of some *Walnut Roughened* vessels or the vestigal handles are not illustrated for *McKee Island Brushed,* which, when it is incised, resembles the incised ware of its series rather than having a distinctive incised decoration of its own. Both *McKee Island Incised* and *McKee Island Brushed* are shell-tempered and have a similar compact paste and hard surface. As a whole, they contrast most strongly with their corresponding Ocmulgee Fields types in differing vessel shapes, dissimilar rim treatments, and a much stronger commitment to shell temper. They are most similar in such features as the presence of identical incised designs, the occurrence of the cazuela form, and the presence of brushing as a surface treatment.

Plain ware of the McKee Island series is also shell tempered and, according to both Heimlich (1952) and Dejarnette and Hansen (1960), is reminiscent in paste and surface finish of prehistoric wares from the same area. *McKee Island Plain* is characterized by flattened globular jars with paired strap handles as well as by a number of other vessel forms: shallow wide-mouthed jars, flattened jars with high necks and narrow orifices, and several kinds of bowls with incurving rims (apparently only seldom with what can be described as a sharp cazuela shoulder). Many of the plain vessels have an "incised, beaded, or notched" rim strip (Heimlich 1952: 27) encircling the exterior of the vessel just below the lip. Like some of [300]the pottery of the Ocmulgee Fields series, many of these plain bowls have horizontal lugs, sometimes as many as six, affixed to them. One of the McKee Island types, *McKee Island Cord Marked* (Heimlich 1952: 27–28), was not represented at all at the Childersburg site, but it can be definitely associated with the McKee Island ceramic complex on the basis of instances of cord-marking in combination with the typical McKee Island incising on the same vessel (p. 27). Unknown as yet for the McKee Island series are any types corresponding to *Kasita Red Filmed* or the minority ware *Ocmulgee Check Stamped*.

The Childersburg series includes as yet only two named types, *Childersburg Plain* and *Childersburg Incised*. Both of these types are similar to the corresponding McKee Island types except for a change to sand temper in place of the shell temper of the McKee Island series. This separation of types on the basis of the single attribute of change in temper may be justified by a comment of David Taitt's when he visited Coosa Old Town in 1772. He remarked then that the old fields were being settled by some people from Tallassiehatchie, pointing to a second and apparently minor reoccupation of the site in the last quarter of the eighteenth century (Mereness 1916: 534). These later occupants may have been the makers of the Childersburg ceramic series.

In addition to the Childersburg site, the McKee Island pottery series is represented by five sites in the Guntersville Basin (Webb and Wilder 1951). These sites [301]provided the basis for the original type descriptions (Heimlich 1952), but little in the way of identification of town or even of people has been made to date. Webb and Wilder placed all these sites within "Gunterlands V" (Webb and Wilder 1951:269), which is a period beginning with the first introduction of trade goods and ending with the final removal of the Indians from the area. Unfortunately, none of the trade materials that are illustrated from these five sites is particularly diagnostic nor is it known whether or not all of the trade goods are even English. Presumably, most of the sites are Upper Creek, but nothing really can be said as yet about their historic identification.

If the small sample of published Upper Creek pottery truly represents the whole ceramic complex, then what can be said about the closeness of relationship between the pottery of the Upper Creeks and that of the Lower Creeks is less than would be expected on the basis of their common culture and language. Instead of sharing a common pottery with this common culture, the two divisions of the Creeks seem to have separable pottery traditions, which, although certainly closely related, are sufficiently different to require some explanation. The Upper Creek ceramic series is thought to have clear ties to the prehistoric pottery in its own area (Heimlich 1952: 27) but shares with Ocmulgee Fields a lack of any known prehistoric ancestor for its brushed ware. If Upper Creek pottery is in fact an *in situ* development from indigenous Alabama precursors, then it is difficult to consider other Creeks, of the same [302]culture and the same language, sharing for any length of time in what is a long tradition of complicated stamping within the entirely separate South Appalachian province, a tradition that seems to have gone much its own way for many centuries. It is important in this context, however, to note that besides brushing, the major shared traits in the pottery of the two Creek cultural groups—the cazuela bowl form, the closely similar designs, and the style of incising—are elements for which Heimlich (1952: 50) is unable to find any ancestors in the Alabama region. She considers them to represent a diffusion out of central Georgia and specifically from Lamar and Ocmulgee Fields into the Upper Creek area of Alabama.

As information now stands, it appears that the pottery of the Lower Creeks has as close relationships with historic pottery to the south and east of it as it has with the pottery of the Upper Creeks, whose most specific Lower Creek ceramic traits are thought to be the result of Georgian influence rather than vice versa. Perhaps this situation reflects the genetic composition of the Lower Creeks and points to the considerable contributions of the Hitchiti element to what eventually emerged as the Lower Creeks. In any case, Lower Creek pottery with its clear ties to both south (Apalachee) and north (Upper Creek) is morphologically what could be expected, given its intermediate geographical position.

# 9

# Conclusions

[303]The Lower Creek town and Carolinian trading house at Ocmulgee National Monument are together representative of an important juncture both in English colonial history and in Creek archaeology. The establishment of Charles Town and the first attempts at English colonization in Carolina stood for a while on a precarious footing. The spread of the Indian trade and its implications for control of the Indian nations provided real support to European settlement and smoothed the way for European successes in dominating the Indians. Projected against this background, the trading house with its sometimes sordid and petty tale of slavetaking, oppression, and general skulduggery, can be seen as a somewhat soiled but nonetheless efficient instrument of empire. Ocmulgee Town has provided the only known archaeological record of the physical plant of these once numerous trading houses in Georgia although more are undoubtedly present in the old fields of other Lower Creek towns along the Oconee and Ocmulgee Rivers.

It has been particularly significant at this site that definite dates have been established for it and that the twenty-five or thirty year time span has been clearly [304]outlined in terms of the site's occupation and its abandonment. Since the site was never reoccupied by the Lower Creeks, its position as a pure site of the 1690–1715 period gives it special archaeological importance and makes of it a short-time yardstick for comparison with other longer occupied sites. Historical records, while establishing these facts, have also provided information on the trading house and its probable occupant as well as documentation for the town itself. Documentation is unusually complete and not only indicates the specific time period involved but also permits specific identification of the town by name. Such precise identification opens the way to an eventual study of changes that took place over short periods of time in the artifact assemblage of these particular people, once the other locations of Ocmulgee Town on the Chattahoochee River are definitely established and the sites themselves excavated. Considering the numbers of maps and other historic materials that are available from post–Yamassee War times, such a study—almost in terms of years—is not beyond the limits of possibility.

Having exact dates for the site has also provided dates for numbers of English trade goods whose temporal provenience is otherwise unknown. Except for certain datable trade pieces (such as guns, pipes, ceramics, and coins), the collection from the site includes a large number of everyday artifacts of types frequently found on colonial period sites but generally undated. These artifacts, [305]because of a lack of antique value or of actual stamped dates or hallmarks, tend to receive less attention from historians and others responsible for providing dates for European artifacts. Ocmulgee Town has provided certain of them with a definite range in time and added somewhat to the body of information available. Eventually, if a series of well-dated sites can be obtained, the range in time of certain types of fairly common artifacts may be more accurately known and used to date other sites. The use of trade materials is a useful means of dating historic archaeological sites; but until archaeologists can command a broader knowledge of the ranges in time, particularly of the common everyday European artifacts, the usefulness of the technique will remain limited.

The very large sample of aboriginal Lower Creek ceramics that was recovered during the excavation of Ocmulgee Town has produced during this study a broader comparative base than has ever before been available for any Lower Creek town. The sherd types, first defined shortly after the excavations, have been re-examined and redefined on the basis of this larger body of information. The presentation of these data should provide a better point of departure for studies of both pre-contact and post–Yamassee War developments for the Lower Creeks. Particularly important in this context are attempts that have been made to trace the ancestors of the Lower Creeks through tracing the ancestry of their pottery. To date, there is no final answer to this pressing problem, the [306]origins of brushed ware and the proposed loss of complicated stamping being the most difficult aspects to resolve. As yet, however, no convincing alternative to the Lamar to Ocmulgee Fields evolution has been presented and, because of the current status, or lack of it, of Lamar, none seems justified at this time.

More critical to an understanding of the whole problem is the necessity for locating and excavating sites earlier than Ocmulgee Town, sites that date back to the start of European contact and before. Presumably somewhere in this sequence lies the origin of Lower Creek brushed pottery and of such exotics as *Kasita Red Filmed* and the answer to the Lamar to Ocmulgee Fields problem. On sites of this period, postulated trends from shell temper to grit temper in pottery and the progressive loss of a variety of surface texturing for *Walnut Roughened* should have their beginnings.

As far as specific artifacts are concerned, the Lower Creeks had by 1690 replaced almost entirely their aboriginal artifact inventory. The one outstanding exception was pottery, and it, too, was affected by the presence of the Europeans. Exotic shapes modeled after European examples appeared beside the older ceramic wares. Only a few other artifacts survived the competition with trade goods: projectile points, conch shell ornaments, and a few stone pipes. Of these, the pipes show direct influence from English kaolin pipes.

The pattern of life that existed in the Southeast [307]during the early colonial history of that region is a uniquely interesting one, based as it was upon the interaction of comparatively untouched aboriginals with the outposts of a strikingly different civilization. The successive events of this contact resulted eventually in the displacement or destruction of the native peoples and in an alteration of their lifeway, both accidental as a result of the trade and deliberate, as the comments of Benjamin Hawkins bear witness (1916, 1848). In what must have seemed a bewilderingly short time after contact, changes were accomplished in native life that transformed the Southeast of Desoto, still living in a distinctive Mississippian pattern of life, into the Southeast of the deerskin trade and the flintlock musket.

The Lower Creeks, as important participants in this transformation, were at once the losers and the gainers, but they managed to maintain much of their aboriginal culture in the face of constant European assault well beyond their final expulsion from Georgia. Following their losses and assessing their gains in the earliest years of contact is a very difficult task because of the scarcity of historic records and an equally appalling lack of archaeological information. Because of this, the site at Macon is very important: it is a well-dated, well-documented site of a critically early period and was sufficiently excavated to produce an extraordinarily large sample of cultural materials.

# Appendix I
## Catalogue Numbers of Illustrated Artifacts

All catalogue numbers, unless otherwise indicated, have the subscript 1 Bi 4, which is the site number designation for the Middle Plateau, Ocmulgee National Monument.

*Plate IX*—top, 38–8027; center, 58–3; bottom, 58–3.

*Plate X*—fig. 1: a, 38–9349; b, 38–6762; c, 38–6847; e, 38–7176; f, 41–255; g, 38–7143. Fig. 2: a, 41–257; b, 38–6797; c, 53–9; d, 38–7073; e, 38–9469; f, 38–6938; g, 38–9396.

*Plate XI*—fig. 1: a, 38–8027; b, 38–7016, 38–9463, 38–8180; c, 38–8216; d, 38–9434; e, 38–5671; f, 38–7805. Fig. 2: a, 38–6840; b, 38–4344; c, 38–4268; d, 38–7130.

*Plate XII*—fig. 1: a, 38–4261; b, 38–4183; c, 38–5505; d, 38–5082; e, 38–5082; f, 9315; g, 38–4528; h, 38–4077; i, 38–5049; j, 38–8658; k, 38–4560. Fig. 2: a, 38–7250; b, 38–4314; c, 38–3577; d, 38–5125; e, 38–3701; f, 38–4106; g, 38–3764; h, 38–8711; i, 38–3906; j, 38–8654.

*Plate XIII*—fig. 2: top, 38–10703, 38–9352, 38–7181, 38–7764, 39–8669; center, 38–8167, 38–7436, 38–5075, 38–8575; bottom, 38–10702, 38–9477, 38–9476, 38–9477.

*Plate XIV*—fig. 1: a, 38–12950; b, 38–6759; c, 38–8777; d, 38–6315; e, 38–6230; f, 38–8300; g, 38–8965; h, 38–7821; i, 38–8914; j, 38–6617. Fig. 2: top, 38–7267; center, 38–8261; bottom, 38–8583.

*Plate XV*—fig. 1: a, 38–9585; b, 38–9189; c, 38–8618. Fig. 2: top, 38–6788; lower left, 38–9722; lower right, no number.

*Plate XVI*—fig. 1: left, 38–6934; right, 38–7180. Fig. 2: top, 38–5108; center, 38–8165; bottom, 38–7696.

*Plate XVII*—fig. 1: a, 38–8026; b, 8623; c, 38–8086; d, 38–8623. Fig. 2: a, 38–3572, 38–9405, 38–8471, 38–9603; b, 38–8912; c, 38–8687, 38–8616, 38–7977; d, 38–8897, 38–9427, 38–9409, 38–9518, 38–9457, 38–9318; e, 38–7942, 38–8641, 38–9440, 38–8973.

*Plate XVIII*—fig. 1: a, 38-5184; b, 38-5124; c, 38-6821; d, 38-7857; e, 38-8778; f, 38-7187; g, 38-7119; h, 38-4816; i, 38-4541; j, 38-9215. Fig. 2: a, 38-8026; b, 38-8529; c, 38-8106; d, 38-8997; e, 38-6981.

*Plate XIX*—38-7163.

*Plate XX*—38-11613.

*Plate XXI*—fig. 1: 38-7435. Fig. 2: 38-7190A.

*Plate XXII*—fig. 1: 39-23400/2 Me 2. Fig. 2: 38-9566.

*Plate XXIII*—38-7251, 38-4312, 38-10206, 38-10212, 38-7241, 38-4319.

*Plate XXIV*—fig. 1: 38-7839/1 Bi 3. Fig. 2: 40-45/1 Bi 1.

*Plate XXV*—38-7621.

[311]*Plate XXVI*—38-8309.

*Plate XXVII*—38-6839.

*Plate XXVIII*—38-7621.

# Appendix II
## Pottery Types

These pottery—or more accurately, sherd—types were first defined by Jesse D. Jennings and Charles H. Fairbanks (1939, 1940) from preliminary examinations of materials at Ocmulgee National Monument. They are repeated here since some revisions were necessary and also because the original sources, in the *Newsletter of the Southeastern Archaeological Conference,* are no longer easily accessible.

*Walnut Roughened*
Definition: originally by Jennings and Fairbanks (1940); revised by Mason using sample of 6302 sherds.
Paste:
  *method of manufacture*—coiling: coil fractures uncommon and present usually only in rimsherds.
  *temper*—predominantly coarse shell; both grit and shell occur in 25% of the sherds; solely grit-tempered sherds almost unknown.
  *texture*—compact; fine paste.
  *hardness*—2.0–2–5.
  *color*—surface color usually buff to brown; cores buff, brown, or black; fire clouding present.
Surface Finish:
  *modifications*—interior and rim smoothed; exterior brushed, cob-marked, stippled, or "roughened." Distribution variable.
  *filming*—clay wash present on about 11% of sherds.
Decoration:
  *technique*—sharp-line incising, occasionally in combination with punctations.
  *design*—groups of two or three parallel lines set at an angle to the rim; incised band sometimes zoned from body by punctations or notches.
  *distribution*—smoothed collar area between lip and brushed body.

Form:
>    *rim*—flaring, slightly constricted neck.
>    *lip*—pointed to well-rounded.
>    *body*—globular or elongated globular jars
>    *base*—rounded, never flattened or conoidal.
>    *thickness*—4–6 mm.; base, 5–9 mm.
>    *appendages*—notched or pinched strip just below the lip; small strap or loop handles.

Geographical Range: known only for Lower Creek sites in central Georgia and for some Lower Creek sites in the Chattahoochee River area.

[314]Chronological Position: at Ocmulgee Town, range in time is from 1690 to 1715.

*Ocmulgee Fields Incised*

Definition: originally by Jennings and Fairbanks (1939); revised by Mason using sample of 2572 rimsherds.

Paste:
>    *method of manufacture*—coiling.
>    *temper*—grit, occasionally shell; fine to medium; abundant to very scarce.
>    *texture*—fine, sometimes ranging into coarse.
>    *hardness*—4.0–2.5.
>    *color*—buff-orange, gray or black; surfaces often mottled; fire clouding very common; cores dark brown or black.

Surface Finish:
>    *modifications*—surfaces smoothed; marks from smoothing tool present. Occasionally, bases of vessels are brushed.

Decoration:
>    *technique*—incising, some punctations or notches.
>    *design*—scrolls, interlocking lines, nested geometric figures, and other linear and curvilinear motifs. Execution ranges from very poor, careless, and incomplete to well-drawn and well-executed. Designs often [315]smoothed over after incising. Notches or punctations are rarely present on cazuela shoulders.
>    *distribution*—in rim area of cazuela bowls, interior surfaces of flaring-rimmed bowls, shoulders of globular ollas.

Form:
>    *rim*—carinated on cazuela bowls; some horizontal flaring rims; olla rims are almost vertical.
>    *lip*—cazuela lips thickened often with pronounced extrusions; some simple rounded or flattened lips. Flaring rims are thickened and rounded; olla lips are rounded, seldom thickened.

Appendix II. Pottery Types / 201

> *body*—small cazuela bowls; shallow flaring-rimmed bowls; globular ollas with narrow orifices.
> *base*—rounded on all three variations; some cazuelas, however, have flat bottoms.
> *thickness*—3–7mm.
> *appendages*—notched or pinched rim strip added to the underside of flaring rims just below the lip; lugs added to bodies of flaring-rimmed bowls.

Geographical Range: known for Lower Creek sites in Georgia and Alabama.
[316]Chronological Position: from at least 1690 into the nineteenth century.

*Kasita Red Filmed*

Definition: originally by Jennings and Fairbanks (1940); revised by Mason using sample of 274 sherds.

Paste:
> *method of manufacture*—coiling
> *temper*—very fine grit, occasionally shell; flecks of black or red present in the paste. Temper is scarce to very scarce.
> *texture*—compact and very fine.
> *hardness*—2.5
> *color*—light buff to black; some exteriors mottled; cores gray to brown.

Surface Finish:
> *modifications*—surfaces smoothed; some look polished.
> *filming*—red, black, and/or white paint.

Decoration:
> *technique*—painting in blocked out zones or within incised areas.
> *design*—always geometric (narrow stripes, broad triangles, alternating zones of color); no complete designs present.
> *distribution*—on interiors of vessels, only occasionally on exteriors. Rims [317]commonly painted solid red down to the juncture of the rim with the body; major design area is on flat plate bodies.

Form:
> *rim*—nearly horizontal and flaring.
> *lip*—uniformly rounded.
> *body*—soup-plate; only very occasionally other forms (perhaps cups or small deep bowls).
> *base*—ring foot or solid ring base.
> *thickness*—5 mm.

Geographical Range: Lower Creek sites in Georgia and in Alabama.
Chronological Position: from at least 1690 through at least the first part of the eighteenth century.

# References Cited

Berry, Brewton, Carl Chapman, and John Mack
   1944    Archaeological remains of the Osage. *American Antiquity* 10: 1–11.
Bolton, Herbert E.
   1925    Spanish resistance to the Carolina traders in Western Georgia. *Georgia Historical Quarterly* 9: 115–130.
Bolton, Herbert E., and Mary Ross
   1925    *The debatable land*. Berkeley, University of California Press.
Bourne, Edward Gaylord, ed.
   1904    *Narratives of the career of Hernando De Soto*. Vol. 2. New York, A. S. Barnes and Co.
Boyd, Mark F.
   1953    Further consideration of the Apalachee missions. *The Americas* 9: 459–479.
   1958    Historic sites in and adjacent to the Jim Woodruff Reservoir, Florida-Georgia. River Basin Survey Paper 13. *Bureau of American Ethnology Bulletin* 169: 195–314.
Boyd, Mark F., Hale G. Smith, and John W. Griffin
   1951    *Here they once stood*. Gainesville, University of Florida Press.
Brannon, Peter A.
   1935    *The Southern Indian trade*. Montgomery, Paragon Press.
Bullen, Ripley P.
   1950    An archaeological survey of the Chattahoochee River in Florida. *Journal of the Washington Academy of Sciences* 40: 101–125.
Bushnell, David I.
   1908    The account of Lamhatty. *American Anthropologist* 10: 568–574.
Caldwell, Joseph R.
   1948    Palachicolas Town, Hampton County, South Carolina. *Journal of the Washington Academy of Sciences* 38: 321–324.
   1950    A preliminary report on the excavations in the Allatoona Reservoir. *Early Georgia* 1: 5–21.
   1952    The archaeology of eastern Georgia and South Carolina. In *Archaeology*

*of the Eastern United States,* James B. Griffin, ed. Chicago, University of Chicago Press.

1955   Cherokee pottery from northern Georgia. *American Antiquity* 20: 277–280.

Caldwell, Joseph R., and Catherine McCann

1948   *Irene Mound site.* Athens, University of Georgia Press.

Carroll, B. R., ed.

1836   *Historical collections of South Carolina.* 2 vols. New York, Harper and Brothers.

Catlin, George

1913   *North American Indians.* 2 vols. Philadelphia, Leary, Stuart, and Company.

[321]Chalkey, John F.

1955   A critique and a rebuttal of the paper "dating stem fragments" by J. C. Harrington. *Quarterly Bulletin of the Archaeological Society of Virginia* 9.

Cheves, Langdon, ed.

1897   *The Shaftesbury Papers and other records.* Collections of the South Carolina Historical Society 5.

Cotter, John

1958   *Archaeological excavations at Jamestown. Virginia.* National Park Service Research Series 4.

Cotter, John, and J. Paul Hudson

1957   *New discoveries at Jamestown.* Washington, Government Printing Office.

Courtenay, William A.

1907   *The genesis of South Carolina 1552–1670.* Columbia, The State Company.

Crane, Verner W.

1918   The origin of the name of the Creek Indians. *Mississippi Valley Historical Review* 5: 339–342.

1956   *The southern frontier.* Ann Arbor, University of Michigan Press.

Cruikshank, Helen Gere

1957   *John and William Bartram's America.* New York, Devin-Adair Company.

Cummings, William P.,

1958   *The Southeast in early maps.* Princeton, Princeton University Press.

[322]DeJarnette, David L., and Asael T. Hansen

1960   *The archaeology of the Childersburg site, Alabama.* Florida State University, Department of Anthropology Notes in Anthropology 6.

Director of the Bureau of the Mint

1912   *Catalogue of coins, tokens, and medals in the numismatic collections of the mint of the United States at Philadelphia, Pennsylvania.* Washington, Government Printing Office.

Fairbanks, Charles H.

1940   Archaeological site report on the Ennis site. Unpublished manuscript on file, Ocmulgee National Monument.

1952   Creek and pre-Creek. In *Archaeology of the Eastern United States,* James B. Griffin, ed. Chicago, University of Chicago Press.

1955 The Abercrombie Mound, Russell County, Alabama. *Early Georgia* 2: 13–19.

1956a *Archaeology of the funeral mound, Ocmulgee National Monument.* National Park Service Research Series 3.

1956b An historic check stamped pottery. In *Prehistoric Pottery of the Eastern United States,* James B. Griffin, ed. Museum of Anthropology, University of Michigan, Ann Arbor.

1956c Ethnohistorical report of the Florida Indians. Unpublished manuscript on file, Florida State University, Department of Anthropology.

1958 Some problems of the origin of Creek pottery. *The Florida Anthropologist* 11: 53–64.

1962 Report of excavations at Horseshoe Bend National Battlefield Park. *Florida Anthropologist* 25: 41–56.

Ferguson, Alice L.

1940 An ossuary near Piscataway Creek. *American Antiquity* 4: 4–13.

Ford, James A.

1951 Greenhouse: a Troyville-Coles Creek period site in Avoyelles Parish, Louisiana. *Anthropological Papers of the Museum of Natural History* 44: pt. 1.

Friedlander, Louis

1938 Final report regarding research on the trading post at Ocmulgee National Monument. Unpublished manuscript on file, Ocmulgee National Monument.

Fundaberk, Emma L.

1958 *Southeastern Indians life portraits.* Luverne, Alabama, published by the author.

Fundaberk, Emma L., and Mary Foreman

1957 *Sun circles and human hands.* Luverne, Alabama, published by Emma L. Fundaberk.

Gatschet, Albert S.

1884 A migration legend of the Creek Indians. In Brinton's *Library of Aboriginal American Literature* I, no. 4.

Goggin, John M.

1949 A Florida Indian trading post, circa 1763–1784. *Southern Indian Studies* 1: 35–38.

1951 Fort Pupo: a Spanish frontier outpost. *Florida Historical Quarterly* 30: 139–192.

1953 Seminole pottery. In *Prehistoric Pottery of the Eastern United States,* James B. Griffin, ed. Museum of Anthropology, University of Michigan, Ann Arbor.

Goggin, John M., Mary Godwin, Earl Hester, David Prange, and Robert Spangenberg

1949 An historic Indian burial, Alachua County, Florida. *The Florida Anthropologist* 2: 10–25.

Greenman, Emerson F.
- 1951 *Old Birch Island cemetery and the early historic trade route.* Occasional Contributions from the Museum of Anthropology of the University of Michigan 11.

Haas, Mary
- 1941 The classification of the Muskhogean languages. In *Language, Culture, and Personality,* Leslie Spier, A. Irving Hallowell, and Stanley S, Newman, eds. Menasha, Wisconsin, Sapir Memorial Publication Fund.

Harper, Francis, ed.
- 1958 *The travels of William Bartram.* New Haven, Yale University Press.

Harrington, J. C.
- 1954 Dating stem fragments of seventeenth century clay tobacco pipes. *Quarterly Bulletin of the Archaeological Society of Virginia* 9.

[325] Harris, Walter A.
- 1958 *Here the Creeks sat down.* Macon, J. W. Burke Company.

Hawkins, Benjamin
- 1848 A sketch of the Creek country in the years 1798 and 1799. Collections of the Georgia Historical Society 3, pt. 1.
- 1916 *Letters of Benjamin Hawkins.* Collections of the Georgia Historical Society 9.

Heimlich, Marion Dunlevy
- 1952 *Guntersville Basin pottery.* Geological Survey of Alabama Museum Paper 23.

Hodge, Frederick W., ed.
- 1907 *Handbook of American Indians north of Mexico.* Part 1. Bureau of American Ethnology Bulletin 30.

Hulbert, Archer Butler
- 1908 *The crown collection of photographs of American maps.* Vol. 5. Cleveland, The A. H. Clark Company.

Hume, Ivor Noel
- 1958 Williamsburg—textbook of eighteenth century colonial archaeology. *Bulletin of the Eastern States Archaeological Federation* 17: 16.

Irwin, Carol
- 1959 Dating English pipestems. *The Florida Anthropologist* 12: 71–72.

Jennings, Jesse D., and Charles H. Fairbanks
- 1939 Pottery type descriptions. *Southeastern Archaeological Conference Newsletter* 1.
- 1940 Pottery type descriptions. *Southeastern Archaeological Conference Newsletter* 2.

[326] Kelly, Arthur R.
- 1938 *A preliminary report on archaeological explorations at Macon, Georgia.* Bureau of American Ethnology Anthropological Papers 1.
- 1939 The Macon trading post, an historical foundling. *American Antiquity* 4: 328–333.

Kelly, Arthur R., and Louis Friedlander
- 1939 Ocmulgee's trading post riddle. *The Regional Review* 2: 3–12. Richmond, The National Park Service.

Klingberg, Frank J., ed.
  1956  *The Carolina chronicle of Dr. Francis Le Jau 1706–1717*. University of California Publications in History 53.

Kneberg, Madeline
  1952  The Tennessee area. In *Archaeology of the Eastern United States*, James B. Griffin, ed. Chicago, University of Chicago Press.

Kunkel, Peter H.
  1960  *Fort Loudoun archaeology: a summary of the structural problem*. Tennessee Archaeological Society Miscellaneous Paper 6.

Kurjack, Edward B.
  1961  Clay pipes at the Childersburg site in Alabama. *The Florida Anthropologist* 14: 21–22.

Lawson, John
  1860  *The history of Carolina*. Raleigh, Strother and Marcom Company.

Laxon, D. D.
  1959  Excavations in Dade County during 1957. *The Florida Anthropologist* 12: 1–8.

Leonard, Irving A.
  1939  *The Spanish approach to Pensacola, 1689–1693*. Quivira Society Publications 9.

MacNeish, Richard S.
  1952  The archaeology of the northeastern United States. In *Archaeology of the Eastern United States*. James B. Griffin, ed. Chicago, University of Chicago Press.

Mason, Ronald J.
  1958  Archaeological exploration at the site of the casting house, Hopewell National Historic Site. Unpublished manuscript on file, National Park Service.

Mattison, Ray H.
  1946  The Creek trading house—from Colerain to Ft. Hawkins. *Georgia Historical Quarterly* 30: 176–183.

McCrady, Edward
  1897  *The history of South Carolina under the proprietory government 1670–1719*. New York.

McDowell, William L., ed.
  1955  *Journals of the commissioners of the Indian trade, September 20, 1710–August 29, 1718*. Columbia, South Carolina Archives Department.
  1958  *Documents relating to Indian affairs, May 21, 1750–August 7, 1754*. Columbia, South Carolina Archives Department.

Mereness, Newton D.
  1916  *Travels in the American colonies*. New York, The Macmillan Company.

Moll, H.
  1736  *Atlas Minor*. London.

Morse, Dan F.
   1960    Memorandum on recent excavations at the Lingerfelt site. Unpublished manuscript on file, Georgia Historical Commission.

Nunez, Theron A., Jr.
   1958    Creek nativism and the Creek war of 1813–1814. *Ethnohistory* 5, nos. 1, 2, 3.

Okie, Howard P.
   1936    *Old silver and old Sheffield plate.* New York, Doubleday, Doran, and Company.

Omwake, H. Geiger
   1956    Date-bore correlations in English white kaolin pipe stems, yes or no? *Quarterly Bulletin of the Archaeological Society of Virginia* 11.

Oswald, Adrian
   1951    English clay tobacco pipes. *The Archaeological Newsletter* 3.

Peterson, Harold L.
   1956    *Arms and armor in colonial America.* Harrisburg, The Stackpole Company.

Pope, G. D., Jr.
   1956    *Ocmulgee National Monument, Georgia.* National Park Service Historical Handbook Series 24.

Pratt, Peter P.
   1961    *Oneida Iroquois glass trade bead sequence 1585–1745.* Syracuse, The Onondaga Printing Company.

Quimby, George I.
   1960    *Indian life in the upper Great Lakes.* Chicago, University of Chicago Press.

Rivers, William James
   1856    *A sketch of the history of South Carolina to the close of the proprietory government.* Charleston, McCarter and Company.

Robertson, James A., ed.
   1933    *True relation of the hardships suffered by Governor Hernando de Soto and certain Portuguese gentlemen during the discovery of the province of Florida by a gentleman of Elvas.* Vol. 2. Publications of the Florida State Historical Society 11.

Rouse, Irving
   1951    *Survey of Indian River Archaeology, Florida.* Yale University Publications in Anthropology 44.

Salley, A. S., ed.
   1907a  *Journal of the Grand Council of South Carolina, August 25, 1671–June 24, 1680.* Columbia, The Historical Commission of South Carolina.
   1907b  *Journal of the Grand Council of South Carolina, April 11, 1692–September 26, 1692.* Columbia, The Historical Commission of South Carolina.
   1907c  *Journal of the Commons House of Assembly of South Carolina.* Columbia, The Historical Commission of South Carolina.
   1913    *Journals of the Commons House of Assembly of South Carolina for the two sessions of 1697.* Columbia, The Historical Commission of South Carolina.

1914 *Journals of the Commons House of Assembly of South Carolina for the two sessions of 1698.* Columbia, The Historical Commission of South Carolina.

1924 *Journals of the Commons House of Assembly of South Carolina, October–November, 1700.* Columbia, The Historical Commission of South Carolina.

1925 *Journal of the Commons House of Assembly of South Carolina, February 4, 1701–March 1, 1701.* Columbia, The Historical Commission of South Carolina.

1926 *Journal of the Commons House of Assembly of South Carolina, August 13, 1701–August 28, 1701.* Columbia, The Historical Commission of South Carolina.

[331] 1928 *Records in the British Public Record Office relating to South Carolina, 1663–1684.* Atlanta, Foote and Davis Company.

1929 *Records in the British Public Record Office relating to South Carolina, 1685–1690.* Atlanta, Foote and Davis Company.

1932 *Journals of the Commons House of Assembly of South Carolina for 1702.* Columbia, The Historical Commission of South Carolina.

1934 *Journals of the Commons House of Assembly of South Carolina for 1703.* Columbia, The Historical Commission of South Carolina.

1939 *Journal of the Commons House of Assembly of South Carolina, November 20, 1706–February 8, 1706/7.* Columbia. The Historical Commission of South Carolina.

1940 *Journal of the Commons House of Assembly of South Carolina, June 5, 1707–July 19, 1707.* Columbia, The Historical Commission of South Carolina.

1941 *Journal of the Commons House of Assembly of South Carolina, October 22, 1707–February 12, 1707/8.* Columbia, The Historical Commission of South Carolina.

1947 *Records in the British Public Record Office relating to South Carolina, 1701–1710.* Columbia, The Historical Commission of South Carolina.

[332] 1953 *Narratives of early Carolina 1650–1708.* New York, Barnes and Noble, Inc.

Schoolcraft, Henry Rowe

1847 *Historical and statistical information respecting the history, condition, and prospects of the Indian tribes of the United States.* Vol. 2. Philadelphia, Lippincott, Grambo and Company.

1855 *Historical and statistical information respecting the history, condition, and prospects of the Indian tribes of the United States.* Vol. 5. Philadelphia, Lippencott, Grambo, and Company.

Sears, William H.

1952 Ceramic development in the South Appalachian province. *American Antiquity* 18: 101–109.

1955 Creek and Cherokee culture in the eighteenth century. *American Antiquity* 21: 143–149.

1956 *Excavations at Kolomoki, final report.* University of Georgia Series in Anthropology 5.

1958    The Wilbanks site (9CK-5). Georgia. River Basin Survey Paper 12. *Bureau of American Ethnology Bulletin* 169: 129–194.

Serrano y Sanz, Manuel, ed.
- 1912    *Documentos historicos de la Florida y la Luisiana.* Madrid, Biblioteca de los Americanistas.

Sheppard, Thomas
- 1912    *Early Hull tobacco pipes and their makers.* 2nd edition. Hull, A. Brown and Sons.

Sleight, Frederick W.
- 1949    Notes concerning an historic site of central Florida. *The Florida Anthropologist* 2: 26–30.

Smith, Buckingham, ed.
- 1857    *Colección de various documentos para la historia de la Florida y tierras adyacentes.* London, Trubner and Company.

Smith, Hale G.
- 1948    Two historical archaeological periods in Florida. *American Antiquity* 13: 313–319.
- 1956    *The European and the Indian.* Florida Anthropological Society Publications 4.

Speck, Frank G.
- 1907    *The Creek Indians of Taskigi Town.* American Anthropological Association Memoir 2, pt. 2.

Stirling, Matthew D.
- 1940    The historic method as applied to southeastern archaeology. *Smithsonian Institution Miscellaneous Collections* 100: 117–123.

Strong, William D.
- 1940    From history to prehistory in the Great Plains. *Smithsonian Institution Miscellaneous Collections* 100: 353–394.

Swanton, John R.
- 1922    *The early history of the Creek Indians and their neighbors.* Bureau of American Ethnology Bulletin 73.
- 1928a    Social organization and social uses of the Indians of the Creek Confederacy. *Bureau of American Ethnology Annual Report* 42: 23–472.
- 1928b    Aboriginal culture of the Southeast. *Bureau of American Ethnology Annual Report* 42: 673–726.
- 1939    *Final report of the United States Desoto expedition commission.* 76th Congress, 1st Session, House Document 71. Washington, Government Printing Office.

Thwaites, Ruben Gold, ed.
- 1905    *Early western travels 1748–1846.* Vol. 20. Cleveland, The Arthur H. Clark Company.

Webb, William S.
- 1938    *An archaeological survey of the Norris Basin in eastern Tennessee.* Bureau of American Ethnology Bulletin 118.

Webb, William S., and Charles G. Wilder
- 1951  *An archaeological survey of Guntersville Basin on the Tennessee River in northern Alabama.* Lexington, University of Kentucky Press.

Wenhold, Lucy L.
- 1936  *A 17th century letter of Gabriel Diaz Vara Calderón, Bishop of Cuba, describing the Indians and Indian missions of Florida.* Smithsonian Institution Miscellaneous Collections 95, no. 16.

[335] Willey, Gordon R.
- 1949  *Archaeology of the Florida Gulf Coast.* Smithsonian Institution Miscellaneous Collections 113.

Willey, Gordon R., and William H. Sears
- 1952  The Kasita site. *Southern Indian Studies* 4: 3–18.

Williams, Samuel Cole, ed.
- 1930  *Adair's history of the American Indian.* Johnson City, Tennessee. The Watauga Press.

Woodward, Thomas S.
- 1939  *Reminiscences of the Creek or Muscogee Indians.* Tuscaloosa, Alabama, Weatherford Printing Company,

Wray, Charles F., and Harry L. Schoff
- 1953  A preliminary report on the Seneca sequence in western New York 1550–1687. *The Pennsylvania Archaeologist* 23: 53–63.

Wyler, Semour B.
- 1937  *The book of old silver.* New York, Crown Publishers.

# Index

Abercrombie Mound, 188–190
Achito. *See* Hitchiti
Addasles. *See* Attasi
Apalachee: archaeological complex, 164, 182, 183, 193; area, 10–11, 87, 164, 167, 168, 183, 193; town, 162, 163; ceramics. *See* ceramics (series), Leon-Jefferson
Apalachicola: site, 188, 190; town, 151, 162, 164, 169, 173–174, 188
archaeology, historic, 1, 2
Attasi, 164, 167, 173
axes, iron, 60, 64, 94, 135

Bartram, William, 44, 48, 49, 53, 55, 56, 71, 73, 74, 153, 162, 170
Big Sandy, 188, 189
beads: glass trade, 88–90, 133; barrel shaped, 64, 65; blue, 61, 63, 65; Cornaline D'Allepo, 60, 67, 68, 89, 90; decahedral, 65–67, 89; large black, 66; "porcelain," 64, 65, 68; seed, 61, 62, 64, 65, 67, 68
bells, metal, 62, 64, 66, 96–97, 133
Board of Commissioners of the Indian Trade, 16–19, 32, 33, 39, 155
Bossu, Jean-Bernard, 72
Boyd, Mark, 164–166
bracelets: brass, 65, 98, 137; iron, 64, 65, 68, 98
buckles, 65, 68, 97, 133

burials: ceramic coverings, 51, 62, 68, 75, 79–80, 145; grave goods, 75–76; historic cremations, 51, 63, 69, 70, 75, 84; inhumations, 59–76; "sitting," 61, 64–65, 71–72; treatment of children, 51, 74, 75. *See also* burial locations; burial locations (possible historic); *specific artifact types*
burial locations: burial 3, 61; burial 4, 61; burial 5, 61, 127; burial 6, 61, 127; burial 7, 61–62; burial 10, 62, 128; burial 11, 63; burial 13, 63; burial 16, 63; burial 24, 64; burial 32, 65; burial 38, 65; burial 39, 65–66; burial 41, 66; burial 42, 66; burial 43, 66; burial 45, 67; burial 47, 67; burial 51, 68, 74, 85, 129; burial 61, 68; burial 62, 68; multiple burial 1, 60, 74, 75, 126; multiple burials 19 and 20, 64, 75
burial locations (possible historic): burial 8, 69, 128; burial 12, 69; burial 21, 69; burial 26, 70; burial 34, 70; burial 40, 70; burial 44, 70; burial 54, 70; burial 58, 70; burial 64, 70
Burrill, Robert, 91
Bushnell, David, 155
buttons, 64–66, 68, 133

Calderon, Bishop Gabriel, 153, 164, 166–168, 174–176
Caldwell, Joseph, 190

Carolina, colony: Indian trade, 6, settlement system 7, Spanish competition 6–7
Catlin, George, 97
cazuelas. *See* ceramics (series), Ocmulgee Fields
ceramics
—brushed wares: *Chattachoochee Brushed,* 114, 179, 184, 188, 189, 190; distribution, 179, 180; relation to complicated stamping, 179, 180, 183; *McIntosh Brushed,* 114; *Plaquemine Brushed,* 180; Seminole brushed types, 181
—European: Dutch, 101; English, 101–102, 132, 103, Spanish, 57, 87, 103, 104, 132. *See also* majolica
—European-influenced, 119, 121, 183, 196
—Lamar and Ocmulgee Fields compared, 179–195
—Lower Creek: compared to Upper Creeks, 192–193; evolution in place, 178–182, 184–185; Lamar origins, 181–182; migration of, 178, 182, 185–186; non-Lamar roots, 181–182, 187; origins, 178–193, 194
—rimstrips, 115, 123, 192
ceramics (series)
—Childersburg: *Childersburg Incised,* 192; *Childersburg Plain,* 192
—Lamar: Lamar Bold Incised, 179; Lamar Complicated Stamped, 179
—Leon-Jefferson: *Aucilla Incised,* 182–183; Jefferson ware, 182–183; *Leon Check Stamped,* 182–183; *Miller Plain,* 182–183; *Mission Red Filmed,* 182
—McKee Island: McKee Island Brushed, 191; McKee Island Cord-marked, 192; McKee Island Incised, 191; McKee Island Plain, 192

—Ocmulgee Fields: *Kasita Red Filmed,* 107, 114, 118–120, 122, 182, 188, 192, 194, 201; *Ocmulgee Fields Check-Stamped,* 62, 107, 121–122, 192; *Ocmulgee Fields Incised,* 68, 78, 107–113, 120, 122, 139, 140–143, 146–147, 179, 183, 188–191, 200–201; *Ocmulgee Fields Plain,* 107, 120–122, 143, 183, 189, 190; *Walnut Roughened,* 69, 79, 107, 113–118, 120–122, 144, 148, 179, 181, 184, 187, 188, 190, 191, 195, 199–200
Charles Town: Barbadoes planters, 6; Indian relations, 6; economics, 6, 12; problems with agriculture, 6; resources, 6; setting, 5, 6. *See also* trade, English; trade, Indian
Chattachoochee River, 3, 10, 22, 152, 173
Cherokees, 9, 13–14, 32, 42, 160, 170, 185–187
Chiaha, 151
Chickasaws, 32, 71, 75
Chicken, Colonel, 43, 42
Childersburg, 72, 73, 75, 191, 192
Choctaws, 11
Chufytachqj, 169, 170, 171, 176, 186; emperor of, 169, 170–173
clay layers, 39
Cofitachiqui. *See* Chufytachqj
coils, copper, 68
clothing, European, 99, 68
coins, Spanish, 92–94
Commissioners of the Indian Trade. *See* Board of Commissioners of the Indian Trade
Confederate trench, 26, 39, 50, 51, 61
Congarees, 32
Coosa: Desoto site, 191; old fields, 191, 192; Upper Creek town, 163, 164, 191, 192
corn, evidence for, 39, 80–81; possible ceremonial use, 80–81
Coweta, 10, 11, 63, 155, 159, 162–164, 167, 169–171, 175, 185, 187, 189

Coxe, Daniel, 186
Crane, Verner, 9, 32, 34, 152–154, 186
cups, ceramic, 121. *See also* ceramics, European-influenced
Cuscowilla, 49

deerskins, numbers in trade, 12
DeJarnette, David, 192
designs: incised cazuela, 108–111, 146, 147; *Walnut Roughened,* 148
Desoto, 154, 163, 169, 173, 176, 177, 186, 191, 196
Dodsworth, Anthony, 166, 159

Elliptio hopetonesis lea, 40
Ennis site, 189
Etowah River, 185, 186

Fairbanks, Charles, 30, 88, 122, 160–162, 178–179, 180, 182, 184–185, 189, 190
Fort Hawkins, 26, 153

Gatschet, Albert, 151, 153
glass, bottle, 63–65, 102; mirror, 98–99, 60, 62
Glen, Governor, 13–14
Goggin, John, 179–180
Green Corn Ceremonies, 80–81
Guale, 7, 9, 168, 184, 187
gun parts: dating, 84–86; description, 83–87; dog-catch flintlock, 85; gunflints, 60, 62–65, 67, 130, 134; illustrations, 130, 131, 138; lock plates, 63, 67, 68, 84, 85, 129, 131; matchlock pan cover, 86, 138; musket balls, 60–66, 87, 130; ramrod worm, 87, 130; side plate, 86, 138; silver butt ornament, 68, 85, 129
guns, 13, 83–84, 85–86
Gunterlands V, 192
Guntersville Basin, 192

Haas, Mary, 176
Halsted's Old Fields, 26
Handles on pots, 181, 191, 200

Hansen, Asael, 192
harness equipment, 100–101
Hastier, John, 85
Hawkins, Benjamin, 152, 153, 165, 168, 189, 196
head deformation, 62, 67, 68, 73–74
Heimlich, Marion, 192, 193
Hillabees, 32
historic period, 1–3
Hitchiti: language, 26, 176–177, 151; town, 151, 162–167, 187
hoes, iron, 94, 136
horses, 15, 20, 22, 36, 76, 170
houses, Lower Creek: construction, 47; dating, 50, 51; descriptions, 47–49; dimensions, 47–48, 58; entranceways, 52–55; implications for social organization, 49, 58; locations, 50; specific structures: Houses I and II combined, 51–53, 79, 80; House V, 54–55, 70, 73, 79; House VIII, 55 – 56; House IX, 57–58
houses, "pit," 56–57, 58, 68, 78, 79, 101
Hull, John, 85

Indian agents, 17, 19, 155

Jalpasle, 164
Jennings, Jesse, 30

Kasita: site, 188–189; town, 10, 154, 158, 162–164, 167, 169, 171–173, 175, 176, 185, 187–189
Kealedji, 167
Kelly, A. R. 27, 157
knives, iron, 60, 64, 67, 95–96, 136
Kolomi, 10, 164, 167, 168

Lamar, 160, 161, 164, 178, 184–187, 195. *See also* Lamar and Ocmulgee Fields compared; ceramics (series), Lamar
Lamhatty, 155, 165
lithics, 104–106
Lewis, Jackson, 71, 72

Lords Proprietors, 5, 6, 15, 16, 88, 169, 170
Louisiana, 11
Lower Creeks: battle with Spanish forces, 11; Chattachoochee towns, 10, 12, 22, 166, 174, 194; contact with English, 10; culture, 161, chronological periods, 3; compared to neighbors, 161–162; emergence, 161; Ochese Creek towns, 10; lists, 164, 165, 175; Moore's raid, 11, movement to Ocmulgee, 10, 152; towns (see Attasi, Coweta, Hitchiti, Kasita, Kolomi, Oconee, Sawokli)
Lower Creek town site, 47–81. See also Ocmulgee
Lower Creek Trading Path, 21, 27, 43–44, 57, 69, 128, 152, 153, 155, 156

Macon Plateau, 25, 27, 44, 50, 59, 71
majolica, 87–88
maps: Barnwell, 152; Crisp, 155, 185, 186; DeBrahm, 156; De Lisle, 155, 165; Le Maire 155; Melish, 186, 191; Mitchell, 31, 151, 152, 155, 165, 185; Moll, 155, 165, 166, 185, 186; Nairne, 154, 155, 186; Popple, 156, 165, 186; Purcell, 156, 185, 186; Wright, 156
Matheos, Commander, 10, 153, 164, 166–168, 174–176
Middle Plateau, 26–27, 29–30
mirrors, glass, 60, 62, 98–99
missions, Spanish: Santa Cruz de Sabacola el menor, 175; San Francisco de Ocón, 167, 168, 184
Moore, Colonel James, 11, 154, 156–157, 165
Morse, Dan, 80–81
Morton, Samuel, 62
Mound C, 27, 49, 51, 59, 71, 99
Muskhogean, 163–164, 176–177
Muskogee. See Muskhogean
mussels, river. See Elliptio hopetonensis lea

Nairne, Thomas, 17, 42, 154, 155
National Monument. See Ocmulgee National Monument

Ochese Creek. See Ocmulgee River
Ochese Creek settlements, 10, 11, 15, 27, 151, 154
Ocmulgee: Old Fields, 3, 10, 26, 17, 31, 43, 153; town, 3, 10, 12, 40, 151–159, 162–164, 167, 168, 185, 187–188, 194; River, 10, 12, 21, 27, 43, 151, 154–156; trading house (see trading house, Ocmulgee)
Ocmulgee National Monument, 3, 22, 25, 26, 28, 31, 59, 67, 70, 154, 189, 194
Oconee, 151, 152, 155, 156, 162–164, 167–168, 173, 184, 185, 187, 188
Oconi. See Oconee
Ocute, 164, 168–169, 174
ollas, 112–113, 141, 143
ornaments: brass, 167; conch, 61, 64–66, 74, 75, 123, 124, 138; copper 66, 97, 98. See also bells; buttons; buckles
Osuchi, 164

paint, red, 99
Pardo, Juan, 168, 185–186
pendants, blue glass, 71, 99–100
pipes: green stone, 124, 134; kaolin, 39, 67, 90–92, 134; terra cotta, 92
pits, refuse: Early Woodland, 77; historic, 76–81; Macon Plateau, 76–77
points, metal projectile, 100; stone projectile. See lithics

Romans, Bernard 71

Sabacola. See Sawokli
St. Augustine, 7
Santee, 33, 39
Sawokli, 151, 164, 167, 173
Savano Town, 21, 33, 34
Sears, William, 160, 161, 162, 167, 180, 185–187
scissors, iron, 96

scrap, brass and copper, 67, 137
scrapers, bottle glass, 65, 124, 134
seals, bale, 60, 95, 138
Shaftesbury Papers, 171, 172, 173
shot, lead, 60–66, 68, 130
silver mines, 170, 172
slaves. See trade, English
Smith, Hale, 2, 92, 182
Spain: claims, 5, 6; competition with England, 6, 7, 11, missions, 7, 15; settlements, 5, 7, 170; trade, 13, 100
Spalding's Lower Store, 34
stamp, metal, 138
surface finishes: brushing, 116–117, 191; check-stamping, 107, 121–122; cob-marking 117, 188, 189, 190; cord-marking, 192; roughening, 117–118; stippling, 117, 188
Swan, Caleb 49, 50, 53, 55, 71, 72, 73
Swanton, John, 37, 64, 71–75, 151, 162, 165–168, 174, 176, 177, 186
sword, 60, 96

Tallapoosa, 167
Tasakigi, 10, 164, 167, 168
Tatikequias. See Chufytachqj
tools, metal, 94–95. See also axes, iron; knives, iron; hoes, iron
trade, English: attraction for Indians, 13; controlling Indians by means of, 12, 13, 194; economic impact, 12; illegal, 18; interior vs. exterior, 83, licensing 17, 18, mechanics of, 21, 22; monopolies, 16; products traded, 15; planter dominance, 16; proprietory monopoly 15, 33; regulation, 16, 17, relation to warfare, 7; slaves 9, 14–16, 18
trade, French, 13
trade, Indian. See trade, English
traders: abuses by, 11, 18, 19, 20; character, 18, 19, 20, 21; companies, 21; debts 19, 20; independents; 21; labor corvees, 20, 22, 32; treatment of wives, 19; unlicensed 18; use of liquor, 19

traders (by name): Child, James, 158–159; Dodsworth, Anthony, 159, 166; Hastings, Theophilus, 32; Lucas, William, 157–158, 159; Mackoone, Robert, 159; Musgrove, John, 157–159; Pight, John, 158, 159; Probat, Anthony, 158, 159; Steen, William, 159; Walsh, Thomas, 159; Williams, Francis, 159; Veals, Samuel, 159
trading house, Ocmulgee: archaeological remains, 31–46; dating, 194; dimensions, 34; discovery, 34; ditch, 41–43, 125; footing trench, 34; gates, 34–36; identification, 31; location, 26, 194, 125; map, 35; other interpretations, 40–41; pits, 39, 125; possible interior structures, 38, 39, 44, 45; possible log removal, 37; postmold patterns, 37, 38; stockade, 34, 38, 45, 46; type of construction, 36–37
Taitt, David, 19, 53, 192
Tallapoosa, 167
Tippet, Robert, 91
Tuckabatchie, 53, 167, 164

Upper Creeks, 47–48, 72, 168, 192, 193

vase, ceramic, 121
vermillion, 62

Westo, 9, 10, 14, 164, 166, 170, 172, 173
Wilbanks, 180
Willey, Gordon, 189
Wineau Bay, 33
Woodward, Henry, 7, 9, 10, 14, 34, 153, 169, 170, 172, 173, 175, 186
Woodward, Thomas, 170
Woolfolk, 112, 113

Yamassee: town, 158, 162, 166, 187; War, 11, 12, 17, 18, 20, 21, 22, 32–33, 40, 151–152
Yuchi, 166